The New Yo
in Popular

MW00487904

The New York Mets in Popular Culture

Critical Essays

Edited by DAVID KRELL

McFarland & Company, Inc., Publishers
Jefferson, North Carolina

LIBRARY OF CONGRESS CATALOGUING-IN-PUBLICATION DATA

Names: Krell, David, 1967– editor.
Title: The New York Mets in popular culture : critical essays / Edited by
David Krell.
Description: Jefferson, North Carolina : McFarland & Company, Inc.,
   Publishers, 2020 | Includes bibliographical references and index.
Identifiers: LCCN 2020036766 | ISBN 9781476680101 (paperback : acid free paper ∞)
   ISBN 9781476640792 (ebook)
Subjects: LCSH: New York Mets (Baseball team)—History. | Mass media and sports—
   New York (State)—New York—History. | Sports—Marketing.
Classification: LCC GV875.N45 N49 2020 | DDC 796.357/64097471—dc23
LC record available at https://lccn.loc.gov/2020036766

BRITISH LIBRARY CATALOGUING DATA ARE AVAILABLE

ISBN (print) 978-1-4766-8010-1
ISBN (ebook) 978-1-4766-4079-2

On the cover: Tom Seaver pitching in the 1973 world series
(National Baseball Hall of Fame Library, Cooperstown, N.Y.)

Printed in the United States of America

McFarland & Company, Inc., Publishers
   Box 611, Jefferson, North Carolina 28640
      www.mcfarlandpub.com

For anyone who's ever won.
For anyone who's ever lost.
And for everyone who's still in there trying.
—Movie poster caption
for *Working Girl* (1988)

Acknowledgments

The strength of an essay collection relies not only on the talent of the contributors, but also their passion. I'm privileged to have the experience of working with Debra Schmidt Bach, Scott Doughtie, Rob Edelman, Donna L. Halper, Leslie Heaphy, Paul Hensler, Elizabeth Jardine, Douglas Jordan, Jemayne Lavar King, Bill Lamb, Martin Lessner, David M. Pegram, Richard Pioreck, Alexandra Rojas, Matt Rothenberg, William J. Ryczek, Derek Stadler, and Charlie Vascellaro. Their research provokes new questions and covers uncharted territory for the loyal, proud lot known as Mets fans.

It is the editor's responsibility for providing guidance, checking facts, and confirming that endnotes are formatted according to the rules and guidelines in *Chicago Manual of Style*.

Oversights or errors fall on my shoulders.

The National Baseball Hall of Fame and Museum in Cooperstown, New York, is the starting point for research on the National Pastime. Jim Gates and Cassidy Lent at the Giamatti Research Center deserve praise and appreciation for helping scholars navigate baseball's rich and complex history. John Horne helped me in identifying pictures to accompany the essays.

Jay Horwitz, the veteran public-relations chief of the Mets, supplied answers to my queries with the speed of a Tom Seaver fastball.

The New York Public Library's main branch located at 42nd Street and Fifth Avenue—otherwise known as the Stephen A. Schwarzman Building—is a world-renowned treasure for researchers. In addition to housing one of the largest collection of books in the world, it has a microfilm collection including existing and long-defunct New York City newspapers. The library was a well-traveled location during the fact-checking process. The New York Public Library for the Performing Arts (Dorothy and Lewis B. Cullman Center) and the Springfield (New Jersey, and the hometown of the editor) Public Library were also instrumental. Contributors used microfilm and various databases for access to newspapers in their research.

Debra Schmidt Bach thanks former Miss Rheingold Anne Newman

Bacal and University of Utah professor Derek Hoff for sharing their invaluable insights regarding the Liebmann brewery and its Miss Rheingold beauty contest.

Jemayne Lavar King credits the research of hip-hop's early days conducted by Joseph Ewoodzie, Jr., Davidson College's Malcolm O. Partin Assistant Professor of Sociology.

Because of Rob Edelman's passing during the production of this book, I did not get the opportunity to work with him as much as I would have liked. Rob's presence was a given at Baseball Hall of Fame and Society for American Baseball Research conferences. Whether at the podium or in the audience, his voice brought passion for baseball and popular culture into any room that he entered, and his intrepid research uncovered new information and fresh approaches concerning baseball's connection to Broadway, vaudeville, burlesque, music, television, literature, and movies. So, I'm grateful to his widow, Audrey Kupferberg, for taking the mantle of shepherding Rob's essay through the editorial process.

We also lost Richard Pioreck, who encouraged scholarship regarding the intersection between baseball and popular culture. It was a privilege to appear on a panel with Rich at the annual Cooperstown Symposium on Baseball and American Culture; his passing leaves another void for baseball historians. We shall continue on the path that Rich and Rob pioneered in the still novel area of popular-culture research regarding the National Pastime. But we have huge footprints to fill, indeed.

The editor highlights Mark Goldman and Fred Weiner, who were top executives at Sports Phone. Mark and Fred shared memories and stories that were invaluable for researching the background of the popular pay-per-call service.

Of course, thankfulness must be noted for Layla Milholen and Gary Mitchem at McFarland. While *The New York Yankees in Popular Culture* was in the editorial phase, they championed the idea of a companion book about the Mets. While I deeply appreciate the opportunity to lead the project, I also greatly admire their unyielding dedication to publishing baseball scholarship.

Table of Contents

Introduction

"Let's go, Mets!"

The chant is as common to the parlance of Mets fans as comedic insights about everyday minutiae to celebrity rooter Jerry Seinfeld. But it is not limited to crucial moments at Citi Field. The battle cry is heard as fans of New York's National League team take their initial steps off the 7 train at Willets Point, resplendent in their jerseys with the thick, cursive "Mets" looking like a template for elementary schoolchildren to practice the lost art of handwriting. Mets caps of different colors adorn their heads, but the blue model prevails, paying respect to the team's NL predecessors—Brooklyn Dodgers for the color and New York Giants for the intertwined, orange NY.

Mets fans know, perhaps more than any other cluster of connoisseurs, the extremes of a squad's existence. Bottom to Brigadoon, they have experienced the nascent years marked by the 40–120 inaugural season; Jerry Koosman's two World Series victories in the "miracle" of 1969; Jon Matlack's Rookie of the Year award in 1972; the optimistic chant "Ya Gotta Believe" propelling the Mets to a World Series contest against the dynastic A's and ending in a seventh-game loss; Tom Seaver's three Cy Young Awards; "Midnight Massacre" trades of Seaver and Dave Kingman; "K Corner" honoring Dwight Gooden's mastery on the mound; Darryl Strawberry's Rookie of the Year award; the 1986 World Series championship; Mike Piazza going into the Hall of Fame as a Met; Citi Field honoring Ebbets Field in design; World Series appearances in 2000 and 2015; and Jacob deGrom's two Cy Young Awards.

Conversations about the Mets, whether at the bar or the ballpark, will inevitably turn from power hitters to popular culture. From Rheingold to rap music, the Mets have a popular-culture pedigree that has been both culturally significant and joyously compelling.

Debra Schmidt Bach examines the rich history of the beer industry in New York City with a focus on Rheingold, the first beer sponsor of the Mets. The Liebmann family brewed this brand, which had prominent advertising space on the center field scoreboard at the Polo Grounds. In addition to the

1

Mets sponsorship, one animated television commercial underlined Rhein-gold's connection to New York by mentioning different parts of the city and its environs in the lyrics. While the association with the Mets appealed to men's fascination with sports, Rheingold connected to carnality using the time-honored marketing strategy of sexualizing women with the Miss Rhein-gold contest.

The essay by the late Rob Edelman, a University at Albany lecturer and a fixture in scholarship about baseball and popular culture, examines the lin-eage of the Mets on the silver screen. Examples are abundant. The roster of credits includes *The Odd Couple* featuring a fictional triple play that was staged and shot before a 1967 Mets-Pirates game at Shea Stadium; *Frequency* using a memorable moment from the 1969 World Series as a critical story point; and *City Slickers* showing famed Yankees fan Billy Crystal wearing a Mets cap rather than one for his beloved team. Rob died during the produc-tion of this book. His widow, University at Albany lecturer emeritus Audrey Kupferberg, another well-respected film scholar and Rob's co-author for sev-eral books, graciously okayed the inclusion of the essay.

Donna L. Halper discusses the glorious career of Mets broadcaster Bob Murphy, which began before the team's inaugural season of 1962—Boston and Baltimore are part of the happy recapper's pre–Mets résumé—and lasted more than 40 years. In 1994, the National Baseball Hall of Fame and Museum awarded Murphy the Ford C. Frick Award for broadcasters.

Leslie Heaphy highlights the somewhat unsung Joan Payson, the well-known owner of the Mets from their early 1960s inception to her death in 1975 and a familiar sight at Shea Stadium. She preferred to see games from her box in the stands, kibitzing with players, coaches, and managers before the game. But her interests went beyond the ballpark. Well beyond. Payson, born into New York City society as Joan Whitney, was an esteemed art col-lector known throughout the community for a keen eye and a generous heart. Her benefaction for museums and other philanthropic endeavors was in the Whitney ethos, earning her gratitude from recipients and setting a standard for her peers in wealth, status, and power.

Paul Hensler looks at the Mets of the mid- to late 1980s as a part of the decade's overall popular-culture aura of brashness. While tens of millions of television viewers marveled at manipulation in the decade's nighttime soap operas and elevated J.R. Ewing on *Dallas* and Alexis Carrington on *Dynasty* as the antagonists you love to hate, fans of other NL squads had the same emotional paradigm regarding the team that Mets fans idolized and everyone else loathed. Or seemed to. But the team delivered with a World Series title and a second NL East pennant by the end of the decade.

Scott Doughtie and Douglas Jordan analyze the understudied pitching performance of the Mets from 1969 to 1973 against the backdrop of events that changed America. Their research gives credence to the thesis that the hurlers were not merely good or effective, but exemplary. Notice is scant in either baseball scholarship or good-old-days discussions because the '69 World Series championship was so stunning in the team's annals that it over-shadowed what came immediately after and faded as the years and decades passed.

Jemayne Lavar King brings rap, otherwise known as hip-hop, to the forefront of popular-culture studies. Although the Yankees have a well-known connection to the genre because Jay-Z has incorporated a Yankees cap as part of his wardrobe, the fellas from Flushing have a substantial place in hip-hop. Jemayne not only evaluates the impact of hip-hop on Mets culture, but also offers a primer on the genesis, evolution, and controversies involving the music, artists, and lore.

Bill Lamb, winner of the 2019 Bob Davids Award from the Society for American Baseball Research, explores the history of the Mets' 19th century namesake, a ball club that existed for five seasons. It might have been a longer-lasting enterprise, but Bill points out that the owners also controlled the New York Giants and tended to that organization with more concern and money.

Martin Lessner highlights the influence of Mr. Met on the development, growth, and appeal of mascots. Once a curiosity, mascots have become an integral part to the ballpark experience, but they don't need a logical con-nection to the team. While the Padres have the Swinging Friar, for example, they also have the San Diego Chicken. And the presence of a vegetable for a minor-league team in Delaware has a backstory that some might dismiss as humorous myth rather than historical record.

David M. Pegram recounts the ruckus caused by Ben Affleck's refusal to wear a Yankees hat during a scene in *Gone Girl* and Billy Crystal's donning the Mets head gear for *City Slickers*. The former triggered, or perhaps enhanced, animus between Affleck, a Boston-area native and well-known Red Sox fan, and director David Fincher. The two settled on a Mets cap. Crys-tal, a charitable sort who uses his fame for fundraising, wore a Mets cap because of the team's generosity for one of his favorite causes. The comedian's renowned devotion to the Yankees took a back seat because his beloved team dismissed requests for a donation.

Richard Pioreck is another good friend and baseball historian that we lost. *Everybody Loves Raymond* is one of the examples in his consideration. Though the Barone brothers were mentioned as Mets fans throughout the show's nine-year run, an episode with cameos from the 1969 World Series championship team underscores the fraternal bond between Ray and Robert while also emphasizing that childhood heroes never fade in memory or affec-tion.

Matt Rothenberg treks through the history of the Mayor's Trophy Game, an annual, crosstown event that was special and fun, but lost its uniqueness when interleague play became a reality in the late 1990s. The game precedes the Mets' existence, though. During New York's tenure as a three-team city, an exhibition, not yet dubbed the Mayor's Trophy Game, showcased the novelty of teams from different leagues facing each other outside of the World Series.

William J. Ryczek critiques the persona and performance of Casey Stengel as the Mets' first manager. Stengel's managerial stretch with the Yankees from 1947 to 1960 yielded seven World Series titles. But the Mets never won more than 53 games during his helmsmanship. Stengel lasted three full seasons and left the team in late August 1965, after an injury sustained in a fall in Toots Shor's restaurant; his 1965 record was 31–64.

Derek Stadler, Elizabeth Jardine and Alexandra Rojas highlight the importance of Shea Stadium as a venue for concerts. With terrific detail, the trio shows why the Mets' longtime home was a destination for rock-and-roll icons beginning with The Beatles' 1965 show and ending with Billy Joel's 2008 performances that closed the chapter on its musical legacy.

Charlie Vascellaro recalls the moon shots launched by Dave Kingman, a Goliath at the plate who brought excitement to Mets fans during his two stints in the mid–1970s and early 1980s. Kingman banged 442 round trippers, though his treatment of a female sportswriter late in his career gained him a chauvinistic notoriety that dominated headlines as much as he did pitchers.

I have the privilege of contributing two essays, one about an iconic prime-time television show and the other about a famous telephone service for sports fans. *The West Wing* features the personal and professional lives of fictional White House staffers, but the topic of baseball appears now and then in dialogue and, in one episode, a ceremonial first pitch at Camden Yards. An assessment of Josh Lyman and Toby Ziegler as avatars of Mets fans and Yankees fans, respectively, gives new insights regarding the characters' psyches.

Sports Phone relied on the thirst of fans wanting updated information. During the pay-per-call service's heyday in the 1970s and 1980s, they were not hostages to newscasts and newspapers to learn about trades, games, and quotes. Sports Phone's advertising campaign is an emblem of the era's commercial culture, appealing to the increasingly information-conscious sports fan. Through historical research, plus interviews with two announcers—including Mets broadcaster Howie Rose—the essay reveals the challenges, strategies, and reasons that transformed Sports Phone from a telephonic novelty into an information icon.

And so, it's time to meet the Mets!

"Of Great Renown"

A Brief History of an Early Mets Sponsor

Debra Schmidt Bach

> On Lexington and Madison, and both sides of Park, they ask for Rheingold Extra Dry before and after dark. From Coney to Connecticut, on Flatbush Avenue, from Jersey, scenes way out to Queens, they sing as millions do. My Beer is Rheingold the Dry Beer....[1]

Rheingold Extra Dry beer became an official sponsor of the New York Mets in 1962 for the team's inaugural season. Sponsorship of the new baseball team by the city's favorite hometown beer was a natural coupling. Perhaps less obvious to many observers, the sponsorship also symbolized the brewery's 110-year heritage as well as its significance to the fascinating 400-year history of beer in the city of New York. In the words of one of the brand's newspaper advertisements, "When you buy Rheingold, you buy New York."[2]

Rheingold had been brewed for about 30 years before its association with the Mets; its parent company, Liebmann Breweries, began fortifying New Yorkers in 1854. Beer, in fact, was a vital part of New York life far earlier than the 19th century. Beginning in the 1630s, after the Dutch West India Company settled on the shores of the port they named New Amsterdam, a brewery and tavern were constructed near the corporation's fort. As colonial New York City grew, its inhabitants endured dangerously limited access to potable water. Consequently, brewed ale and beer were safer to drink. During the 1700s, New Yorkers largely brewed beer at home or purchased it at the town's many taverns. Over time, a handful of commercial brewers emerged and dominated the city's brewing trade with small batches of common beers, ales, and porters. This changed drastically by the 1840s, when immigrants from German beer-producing regions sought asylum in the United States.

Those trained as brewers brought age-old brewing traditions with them, including recipes for crisp lagers. With this storied past, it is no surprise that Rheingold Extra Dry, a German-style lager, became symbolic of New York and the fitting sponsor of the city's up-and-coming ball team.

Basic Ingredient

Clean, fresh water was a precious commodity in Old New York until the mid–19th century. With only limited access to drinkable water sources, most early New Yorkers relied on rainwater collected from the city's cisterns or from over-used sources, such as lower Manhattan's polluted Collect Pond (located, at the time, near today's Foley Square). By 1800, the filthy pond was an exhausted dumpsite for the tanneries and other manufactories that had grown up around it. Those who lived closer to Manhattan's eastern and western shores relied on the Hudson and East Rivers for sources of brackish water.

After the opening of the Erie Canal in 1825, New York City became the main port of exchange for the United States. As the nation's primary clearinghouse for imported and exported goods, including agricultural products shipped along the Erie Canal to and from the nation's hinterlands, the city grew into an economic powerhouse. Emergence as an international shipping and finance center, however, brought increasing exposure to deadly epidemics and incidences of catastrophic disasters. The need for fresh water became tragically evident after the cholera epidemic of 1832. Although unknown at the time, the deadly virus is a water-borne disease. Three years later, lower Manhattan was devastated by the Great Fire of 1835, a two-day-long conflagration fanned by gale-force winds, below-freezing temperatures, and iced-over rivers.

In the wake of these events, and after years of debate, New York State legislators approved the construction of a central reservoir for Manhattan fed by the Croton River in Westchester County.[3] When the system, along with the reservoir's main distribution pool located at 42nd Street and Fifth Avenue—today, the site of the main branch of the New York Public Library—opened in 1842, New Yorkers celebrated the availability of ample supplies of fresh upstate water that was also ideal for brewing beer. Conversely, the city of Brooklyn benefited from its location on Long Island and ready accessibility to fresh water available from local aquifers. When the Ridgewood Reservoir, bordering Brooklyn and Queens, opened in 1859, it gave Williamsburg and Bushwick a fresh water supply that was equally ideal for its burgeoning beer trade.[4]

Hundreds of thousands of German immigrants settled in the United States between 1830 and 1860. The 1850 federal census recorded over 580,000

German-born inhabitants living in the United States. By 1860, the German-born population exceeded 1.2 million.[5] A majority of these new arrivals landed in New York, Philadelphia, and Baltimore. Beer was an important part of their social customs. As in many Northern European countries, such as England, Belgium, and Germany, where cool weather prevailed, beer became both a nutritional staple as well as a time-honored tradition. Brewing flourished where barley and hops—two of the four basic ingredients in beer, along with yeast and water—grew or were easily available. German immigrants honored these traditions by introducing Americans to German-style breweries, beer halls, and beer gardens in their new home cities, where they drank and served German-style lagers.

Lager Here

Lager is a low-alcoholic, effervescent beer created with bottom-curing yeasts that ferment under cool temperatures. Lighter in body and taste than ales, it is generally served cold. Fresh upstate and Long Island water, and large populations of Germans accustomed to making and consuming lager-style beer, transformed New York's age-old brewing trade and stimulated its exponential growth. The introduction of lager to the United States is often attributed to Frederick and Maximillian Schaefer, German-immigrant brothers who arrived in New York City in the 1830s and established the F & M Schaefer Brewing Company in Brooklyn.

Following the Civil War, German-style breweries proliferated in Manhattan and Brooklyn. Manhattan was home to 57 breweries by 1880, located primarily in Yorkville (Upper East Side) and on the Lower East Side. Brooklyn numbered 38 breweries around that time, located principally in Williamsburg and Bushwick. Among these breweries, lager was the dominant brew manufactured.[6]

Samuel Liebmann (1799–1872) was a German brewer who settled in New York during the mid–19th century. Born into a Jewish family from Aufhausen (located in Bavaria), Liebmann opened the Zum Stern brewery near Stuttgart in 1840. A prominent merchant, Liebmann was outspoken and known for opposing the state's dictatorial monarch. In the wake of political upheavals in Germany in 1848, Liebmann feared for his family's safety; his son, Joseph, emigrated to the United States "to determine the best site for a brewery."[7] He immediately opened the family's first American brewery, S. Liebmann, in Williamsburg. Four years later, Samuel Liebmann arrived with the rest of his family. Within that first year, the S. Liebmann Brewery relocated to Brooklyn's Bushwick neighborhood and joined the area's growing German brewing community.

Liebmann Breweries

Liebmann and his sons became prominent members of New York's brewing trade. Sons Joseph, Heinrich (Henry), and Charles partnered with their father, assuming the positions of finance manager, brew master, and engineer, respectively. After the elder Liebmann retired, his sons assumed full control of the brewery's operations.[8] One of the city's largest beer manufacturers by 1879, it produced over 57,000 barrels of beer that year. S. Liebmann's Sons, as it was known at the time, continued to grow into the 1880s and 1890s. By the early 1900s, it produced more than 200,000 barrels, or more than five times its 1877 amount.[9]

Liebmann's sons ran the brewery until they retired in 1905. Each brother then installed two sons to run the business. Unfortunately, continued success was short-lived. The United States' entry into World War I in 1917 was accompanied by pervasive anti–German sentiment. In response, Americans shunned businesses owned by Germans or with German-sounding names, including S. Liebmann & Sons. One year after the war ended, prohibition was enacted. Like many other breweries, the Liebmann firm further declined. Brooklyn was home to 23 breweries before prohibition. Two years before prohibition was repealed in 1933, only 10 remained.[10] S. Liebmann & Sons was one of New York's few lucky breweries; the firm survived prohibition by manufacturing lemonade, soft drinks, and low alcoholic "Near Beer."[11]

Das Rheingold

Liebmann Breweries first introduced Rheingold beer in 1883.[12] A sparkling, bottom-fermented, German-style lager, the beer's crisp gold color inspired its Teutonic name. Liebmann sold the brand through at least the 1910s. Rheingold Extra Dry beer was reintroduced in 1937 as part of the firm's celebration of the centennial of Samuel Liebmann's first German brewery. As the *New York Times* announced: "The new brew was described as meeting the steadily increasing demand for a 'dry' beer."[13] The launch was feted by a major advertising campaign presented in newspapers, magazines, on billboards, and in store window displays.[14] Rheingold's popularity was immediate. Like many major American companies, Liebmann Breweries fortified the brand's popularity through sponsorship of the 1939 World's Fair in New York.

The reintroduction of Rheingold corresponded with the arrival of the firm's new brewery manager, Hermann Schülein (1884–1970). Like Samuel Liebmann three generations earlier, Schülein was a German-Jewish immigrant. When he arrived in New York from Munich in 1936, he transplanted his own long family history in the beer trade and over two decades of personal experience as a renowned German brewer. Schülein's family owned numerous breweries in Bavaria, including the distinguished Löwenbräu (est. 1872).[15] After earning a Ph.D. in law, politics, and economics, Schülein worked his way up in the family trade and, by 1924 was Löwenbräu's managing director.[16]

Despite the rise of Nazism in Germany during the 1920s and 1930s, Schülein's Jewish background did not prevent him from expanding Löwenbräu. In addition, he became internationally recognized as a brewing expert. During his tenure, Schülein reinvigorated Löwenbräu, once one of Germany's largest breweries, by increasing its export trade, including to the United States, paying his employees well, and instituting safe working conditions. Schülein and his family, long regarded as eminent Munich business leaders, adeptly navigated Nazi anti–Semitism until 1933, when Adolf Hitler was elected Chancellor of Germany. Löwenbräu was immediately boycotted, and Schülein and the other family members serving as the brewery's officers were forced to relinquish their positions. Still, Schülein remained involved in Löwenbräu's operations through 1935, when he and his family were forced to withdraw all stakes in the brewery and pay a "Flight Tax" to leave the country. Schülein escaped to Switzerland and then arrived in New York in 1936. Among those he quickly connected with was Samuel Steiner, another immigrant from a preeminent German hops-growing family and a Liebmann son-in-law who likely assisted his countryman in securing a management position with the Brooklyn brewery.[17]

Schülein brought extensive German brewing experience to the Liebmann operation, serving as the firm's managing director and general manager until 1950 when he became the company's board chairman and chief executive officer.[18] A powerful figurehead, he was featured in advertisements highlighting his academic and Bavarian credentials. One 1956 newspaper ad introducing a new Rheingold bock beer pictured a professorial, bow-tied "Dr. Schuelein [*sic*]" holding a beer mug while explaining:

> Of all the "bocks" brewed in New York, only Rheingold *Genuine* Bock measures up to strict old-world requirements. Integrity in brewing is more than a tradition. It's a promise we make to you and to ourselves. It's Rheingold's *exclusive* ingredient.[19]

When Schülein arrived at the company, Liebmann Breweries manufactured approximately 375,000 barrels of beer annually. Although still a regional brand, by 1949 Liebmann's was considered the sixth largest brewery in the United States. Efforts were also underway for the brewery to gain a national presence. The brewery set its sights on the expansive West Coast market by purchasing Acme Breweries of San Francisco and Los Angeles in 1954. Production ceased in those cities within three years.[20] Schülein retired two years before Rheingold's Mets sponsorship.

"My Beer Is Rheingold, the Dry Beer"

Schülein's tenure coincided with the entry of Samuel Liebmann's great-grandson, Philip Liebmann (1916–1972), into the family business. A graduate of the University of Pennsylvania's Wharton School of Business, the younger Liebmann was the force behind the "My Beer Is Rheingold, the Dry Beer" campaign and creation of the annual Miss Rheingold contest. According to Derek Hoff, a University of Utah professor and business historian, Philip immediately became the firm's de facto head of marketing.[21] Advertisements from the 1940s defined Rheingold as a new, modern, dry beer, "not sweet," but thirst quenching, with a "cleaner, brisker, more satisfying … flavor."[22]

The Miss Rheingold contest, which ran from 1941 to 1964, reflected the company's ambitions to gain broad national exposure. With its bevy of attractive young female spokespersons, Rheingold advertised the annual beauty contest extensively in newspapers, on radio, and even on television as early as 1948.[23] More prominent than Liebmann's roster of celebrity spokesmen, the sexy, angelic-looking Rheingold Girls traveled through the United States promoting the brand.[24]

A national sensation, the Miss Rheingold campaign vividly reinforced American, Cold War–era, middle-class mores. Although sponsored by an urban brewery owned by a Jewish family descended from German immigrants, the contest idealized women who embodied a mid–20th century suburban ideal. The contestants were young, attractive, thin, white, seemingly Protestant, and often depicted as athletic. As recalled by Anne Newman Bacal, a 1960 Miss Rheingold finalist and producer of the 2016 documentary, *Beauty and the Beer*, the multi-million dollar contest awarded each of the six finalists with a $25,000 prize (the winner was awarded $50,000), identical, figure-hugging, designer wardrobes, comfortable New York City accommodations, chaperoned travel, and the opportunity to make valuable social connections.[25] Once selected, the finalists assembled in New York for six weeks of nonstop vetting. Closely overseen by Philip Liebmann, the vetting process included multiple public appearances across the tri-state area each day, and also regular clothing fittings, photo shoots, and luncheon meetings with the contest's principals and a roster of celebrities that included Rosalind Russell and Bob Cummings. Fondly remembered by Bacal as an exhilarating, life-changing experience, the contestants "belonged to the company," and spent all of their time in New York promoting Rheingold.[26]

Fueled by the public's participation in voting for each year's Miss Rheingold, the annual contest became a much-anticipated event affording the brewery with unprecedented media coverage. Millions of Americans voted for their favorite Miss Rheingold finalists. The contest also tripled the firm's sales.[27] In 1962, the year of the Mets' inaugural season, more than 20,000,000 ballots were cast. As Hoff notes, the scope of the contest was "second only to a presidential election."[28]

Under Philip Liebmann, Rheingold also jumped into "new media" advertising. As televisions became readily available to the American public during the 1950s, commercials, many of which were animated, emerged as significant marketing tools. One mid–1950s commercial, solidified the connection between Rheingold and its city by featuring animated Rheingold bottles and cans jauntily parading along busy mid-town streets and across a bridge resembling the Triborough with a soundtrack of new lyrics set to the tune of *The Sidewalks of New York*. As the commercial's lyrics explained, New York and the tri-state area was, first and foremost, Rheingold country:

> East Side, West Side, and Uptown and Down, Rheingold Extra Dry Beer is the Beer of Great Renown. On Lexington and Madison, and both sides of Park, they ask for Rheingold Extra Dry before and after dark. From Coney to Connecticut, on Flatbush Avenue, from Jersey, scenes way out to Queens, they sing as millions do. My Beer is Rheingold the Dry Beer....[29]

And, what better way to solidify that association than through the endorsement of a new hometown ball team?

Batter Up!

Beer and baseball were proven, lucrative partners by 1962. Jacob Ruppert, the proprietor of another major New York beer maker, the Manhattan-based Ruppert Brewery, owned the Yankees from 1915 to 1945. Under Ruppert, the team lured Babe Ruth from the Boston Red Sox and settled into their new home at Yankee Stadium[30]; New Jersey's P. Ballantine & Sons brewery took over sponsorship of the Yankees from 1945 to 1966[31]; and F & M Schaefer Brewing Company became a sponsor of the Brooklyn Dodgers in 1950.

The growth of broadcast television further compelled partnerships between beer companies and baseball teams. When Anheuser-Busch purchased the St. Louis Cardinals in 1953, the deal resulted in fat profits and national recognition for both the firm and the team.[32] Similar sponsorships followed in Milwaukee between the Miller Brewing Company and their hometown baseball team, the Milwaukee Brewers. In 1961 alone, Rhode Island's Narragansett Beer sponsored the Boston Red Sox; Milwaukee's Stroh Brewery sponsored the Detroit Tigers; and Pennsylvania's Iron City Brewing Company took on the Pittsburgh Pirates.[33]

Competition for sponsorship of the Mets was stiff in New York. F & M Schaefer was first in line for the radio and television sponsorship. But late in 1961, Liebmann Breweries secured a five-year, $6 million deal for Rheingold through its advertising firm, Foote, Cone & Belding.[34] Leading up to the Mets' Opening Day, the brewery ran welcoming, full-page newspaper advertisements featuring smiling pictures of team manager Casey Stengel, club president, George Weiss, Miss Rheingold 1962 (Kathy Kersh), and the team's mascot, a beagle appropriately named Homer, inviting viewers to beer and baseball.

> We're saving a seat for you! The big day is April 13. National League baseball comes back to our town with a bang in the uniform of the New York Mets. There's a seat for you at the Polo Grounds ready and waiting. Come fill it and root Casey and the boys home.... Incidentally, if you can't make it out to the park, you've always got a grandstand seat for the game right in your own living room. Follow the Mets all season on radio and TV—courtesy of Rheingold Extra Dry.[35]

A powerful duo, Stengel and Kersh occupied a series of upbeat advertisements that urged fans to join them. One ad invited viewers to enjoy watching "Kathy and Casey at the bat."

> His business is baseball—the New York Mets. Hers is New York's largest selling beer—Rheingold Extra Dry. Rheingold is proud to welcome National League baseball back to town—and to bring you the games on both television and radio. If you can't get out to the Polo Grounds, be sure to tune in and root for the home team![36]

Rheingold's sponsorship during the early days of the New York Mets gave the brewer a competitive toehold in the lucrative market of beer-drinking sports fans (National Baseball Hall of Fame and Museum, Cooperstown, N.Y.).

Liebmann's highly visible Mets sponsorship masked the reality that the brewery was entering its twilight years. Sadly, this was part of a larger industry-wide trend that began during the 1930s. Prohibition weeded out breweries that could not parlay their manufactories into the production of non-alcoholic goods. With the number of active American brewers already declining steadily, the playing field changed further after World War II when large or successful regional breweries such as Anheuser-Busch set out to overtake markets outside of their jurisdictions. As the large breweries pushed to become national by moving into new regional markets, smaller breweries were forced to compete against the well-funded enterprises. In New York, declining beer sales were exacerbated in 1949 by an 82-day industry-wide strike. To replace unavailable regional beer during the strike, national brewers quickly shipped their products to the city's beer drinkers. After the strike ended, New Yorkers persisted to drink national brands. This struggle continued into the 1950s. As regional beer sales declined into the 1960s, five breweries remained in New York.[37]

Many other factors were blamed for the demise of New York's beer trade. Technological innovations, such as faster transportation systems and wide-reaching broadcast television, intensified completion between smaller, regional and larger, national breweries. Hard liquor and soft drink companies also entered into this competitive market. Other explanations included increases in white-collar jobs and decreases in arduous, thirst-inducing labor, the growing use of air conditioning, which eliminated the need for beer to be enjoyed as refreshment, and the demise of the Miss Rheingold contest. By 1965, the nation's largest brewers—Anheuser-Busch, Schlitz, and Pabst, among them—served 40 percent of American beer drinkers.

To make matters worse, the federal government also monitored national brewery activities. Among the Justice Department's investigations during the early 1960s were consolidation or anti-trust complaints against several national breweries, including Schlitz and Pabst, as well as regional brands such as Rheingold in the wake of its acquisition of New York's Ruppert Brewery.[38]

With diminishing sales, the smaller, independent, regional brewers either closed or were absorbed by larger national breweries. Although Liebmann had been acquiring smaller New York breweries for years, the firm itself was purchased by the Pub United Corporation, a subsidiary of Pepsi United Bottlers, in 1964 for $26 million.[39] When the new owners terminated the Miss Rheingold contest, they replaced it with a $9 million advertising campaign and a new, lukewarm slogan: "As good to your taste as it is to your thirst."[40] A flurry of novel promotions followed, including a "25 Greatest Mets Fans" contest. The brewery was also renamed for its most famous brand—Rheingold.

It was around this time that the brewery started marketing its products to non-white consumers. Probably motivated by tightening competition,

Rheingold launched seemingly more diverse radio and television commercials during New York Mets games. One 1965 commercial zealously depicted "a Chinese dinner, an Italian wedding, a Puerto Rican feast, an Irish farewell party, a Greek gathering and a negro blues singer." The spots were accompanied by haphazard slogans, "Why do Puerto Ricans [or Italians…] like Rheingold? We don't know. But we must be doing something right."[41] Or, not. Pub United continued to brew Rheingold until 1974, when the brand was sold to Chock full o'Nuts. Two years later, the brewery permanently closed. New York's other remaining breweries endured similar fates. Piels shuttered in 1973, followed by F & M Schaefer in 1974. A few years beforehand, a prescient 1966 *New York Times* article lamented that "beer does not have as wide an appeal to the public as it did 345 years ago." Eleven years later, beer was no longer brewed in New York City.[42]

Rheingold has been resurrected several times since 1976. Using an original recipe and funded, in part, by Liebmann descendants, the Rheingold Brewing Company began operations in 1998. Three former Miss Rheingolds ushered in the new incarnation, along with retired Mets players Tommie Agee and Ed Kranepool, and renewed sponsorship of the team's radio broadcasts.[43] Fortunately, beer brewing has returned to the city with gusto. All five boroughs of New York are home to microbreweries, beer halls, or beer gardens, and Brooklyn and Manhattan are again the seats of the city's most active breweries. Brewing supply shops dot the city, providing varieties of barleys, yeasts, and hops to homebrewers. With nearly 400 years of brewing history, New York hasn't lost its taste for beer and it is always ready for another Rheingold.

NOTES

1. Lyrics from Rheingold Extra Dry commercial, ca. 1950s, available at "Rheingold Beer Commercial (1950s)," You Tube, accessed December 6, 2019, https://www.youtube.com/watch?v=FVvKJq_RmH0. The jingle was sung to the tune of *The Sidewalks of New York*.

2. Rheingold advertisement, *Staten Island Advance*, July 2, 1975: 47.

3. The Croton system supplies about 10 percent of the city's present water supply. New York State Department of Environmental Conservation, "Lower Hudson River Basin," https://www.dec.ny.gov/docs/water_pdf/wilhudscroton.pdf.
See National Research Council's Consensus Study Report, *Watershed Management for Potable Water Supply: Assessing the New York City Strategy* (Washington, D.C.: National Academy Press, 2000), 45–48, 59, accessed November 1, 2019, https://www.nap.edu/read/9677/chapter/4#47.

4. Jeffrey Kroesler, "Brooklyn's Thirst, Long Island's Water: Consolidation, Local Control, and the Aquifer," *Long Island History Journal* 22, no. 1 (2011): 2–4. Also available at City University of New York Academic Works, accessed December 6, 2019, https://academicworks.cuny.edu/jj_pubs/44/. New York City consolidated Brooklyn, Queens, the Bronx, and Staten Island with Manhattan in 1898.

5. See "Region and Country or Area of Birth of the Foreign-Born Population, with Geographic Detail Shown in Decennial Census Publications of 1930 or Earlier: 1850 to 1930 and 1960 to 1990," United States Census Bureau, accessed December 6, 2019, https://www.census.gov/population/www/documentation/twps0029/tab04.html.

6. Joy Santlofer, *Food City: Four Centuries of Food-Making in New York* (New York: W.W. Norton & Company, 2017), 249.

7. Will Anderson, *The Breweries of Brooklyn: An Informal History of a Great Industry in a Great City* (New York: self-published, 1976), 100, 102. Germany was not the only European country facing political unrest. There were revolutions throughout Europe.

8. Will and Testament of Samuel Liebmann, proven December 2, 1872. New York, *Kings County Probate Records*, New York: Surrogate's Court, Kings County, New York; "New York, Wills and Probate Records, 1659–1999 for Samuel Liebmann," Ancestry.com, accessed November 11, 2019, https://www.ancestry.com/interactive/8800/004154129_00382?pid=11786296&backurl=https://search.ancestry.com/cgi-bin/sse.dll?indiv%3D1%26dbid%3D88 00%26h%3D11786296%26tid%3D%26pid%3D%26usePUB%3Dtrue%26_phsrc%3DkxE3% 26_phstart%3DsuccessSource&treeid=&personid=&hintid=&usePUB=true&_phsrc=kxE3 &_phstart=successSource&usePUBJs=true&_ga=2.217703958.1667308572.1572665744–940 940484.1572665744#?imageId=004154129_00384.

9. Anderson, *The Breweries of Brooklyn*, 102, 104.

10. Frank J. Trial, "A Look at Why City Brewery Industry Went Flat," *New York Times*, February 9, 1974: 31; Santlofer, 256, 266.

11. Anderson, *The Breweries of Brooklyn*, 104–106. Near Beer consists of 3.2 percent alcohol.

12. Phillip Karlsson, Gigi Lau, Matthew Novoselsky, Natasha Requña, Poupak Sepehri, and Regina Young, "Rheingold Beer" unpublished case study, 2, New York University, Stern School of Business, May 2003, accessed November 1, 2019, http://people.stern.nyu.edu/rwiner/Rheingold_case.pdf.

13. "News and Notes of the Advertising World: To Launch Drive on New Beer," *New York Times*, November 15, 1937: 28.

14. "Advertising News and Notes," *New York Times*, April 9, 1936: 43; "Beer Campaign Increased," *New York Times*, March 17, 1937: 46; and "News and Notes of the Advertising World," *New York Times*, November 15, 1937: 28.

15. "Biographical Notes on Dr. Hermann Schuelein [*sic*], Chairman of the Board and Managing Director of Liebmann Breweries, Inc.," Leo Baeck Institute, Herman Schülein Collection, New York.

16. Martin Munzel and Beate Schreiber, "Hermann Schülein." In *Immigrant Entrepreneurship: German-American Business Biographies, 1720 to the Present*, 4:4, edited by Jeffrey Fear, German Historical Institute, accessed November 2, 2019, https://www.immigrantentrepreneurship.org/entry.php?rec=200.

17. Although Liebmann Breweries was a male-dominated venture, Liebmann daughters played important supporting roles in securing the firm's success through notable marriages. Rosa Liebmann, the founder's daughter, helped to cement the dynasty by marrying a Brooklyn brewer, David Obermeier. Liebmann's great-granddaughter, Sadie, married Samuel Steiner in 1895. See Münzel and Schreiber, "Hermann Schülein," *Immigrant Entrepreneurship*; Rolf Hofmann, "The Originators of Rheingold Beer: From Ludwigsburg to Brooklyn—A Dynasty of German Jewish Brewers," originally published in *Aufbau*, June 21, 2001. Hops are essential ingredients that lend beer and ale their distinctive bitter taste and antimicrobial properties.

18. "Julius Liebmann Retires," *New York Times*, February 27, 1950: 29; "Dr. Schuelein Dies; Ex-Rheingold Chief," *New York Times*, December 18, 1970: 36. Philip Liebmann became president of the company in 1950.

19. Rheingold Advertisement, "Chairman of the Board Makes a Promise," *New York Times*, March 14, 1956: 68

20. "Biographical Notes on Dr. Hermann Schuelein [*sic*], Chairman of the Board and Managing Director of Liebmann Breweries, Inc."; Anderson, *Breweries of Brooklyn*, 105–106.

21. Derek S. Hoff, "Dry Beer, Lively Contest: Crowning Miss Rheingold at the Crest of the Consensus," (lecture, Business History Conference, Baltimore Embassy Suites Inner Harbor, Baltimore, Maryland, April 6, 2018). My thanks to Derek Hoff for sharing this paper as well as his insights about the brewery.

22. Rheingold advertisement in *New York Times*, July 16, 1941: 38.

23. "Radio and Television: Gen. Eisenhower to Speak on United Nations Appeal for

Children Program Aug. 17," *New York Times*, August 6, 1948: 34. Liebmann broadcast "a series of five-minute programs" featuring interviews between six Miss Rheingold finalists and announcer Tom Shirley. They aired on the New York stations belonging to CBS, ABC, and the Dumont Network, in addition to independent station WPIX.

24. Münzel and Schreiber, "Hermann Schülein," *Immigrant Entrepreneurship*.

25. Interview with Sheryl McCarthy on *One to One* (CUNY-TV, 2016), accessed December 6, 2019, available at missrheingold.com.

26. Anne Newman Bacal, telephone interview with Debra Schmidt Bach, August 15, 2019. My deepest gratitude to Anne Newman Bacal for her time and for discussing her personal experiences of the contest with me.

27. "History," Miss Rheingold web site, accessed November 1, 2019, http://missrheingold.com/history/missrheingold.com. According to the website, created by Bacal, during its peak years, the contest cost the brewery $8 million annually.

28. Hoff, "Dry Beer, Lively Contest." When the contest began in the early 1940s, "all Rheingold dealers within fifty miles of New York" voted for Miss Rheingold. "Advertising News and Notes," *New York Times*, October 9, 1940: 38.

29. Lyrics from Rheingold commercial, ca. 1950s, accessed December 6, 2019, https://www.youtube.com/watch?v=FVvKJq_RmH0.

30. Ruppert died in 1939, but his estate owned the team until 1945. "Yankees Timeline: 1940s," accessed November 1, 2019, http://newyork.yankees.mlb.com/nyy/history/timeline.jsp; "Babe Ruth Accepts Terms of Yankees," *New York Times*, January 7, 1920: 22.

31. Val Adams, "Ballantine Beer Drops the Yanks," *New York Times*, September 28, 1966: 75.

32. Kevin Richard, "The Glory Days of Baseball and Beer Marketing," *Ballpark Digest*, February 2, 2017, accessed November 1, 2019, https://ballparkdigest.com/2017/02/02/the-glory-days-of-baseball-and-beer-marketing/.

33. Ibid.

34. Philip B. Shabecoff, "Advertising: Home Run for Rheingold Beer?," *New York Times*, November 13, 1961: 48; "TV Agreement Near on the Met Games," *New York Times*, December 20, 1961: 67; "Advertising: One Forecast Bright for 1984," *New York Times*, February 26, 1962: 43. The dollar amount varies in the reporting. It is listed as $5 million in the November 13, 1961, article. The February 26, 1962, article breaks the deal down as $5 million, but then states it as $1 million–$1.2 million per year, which totals between $5 million and $6 million. In addition, the article also states that Liebmann Breweries shared the opening-season sponsorship with the Brown & Williamson Tobacco Corporation, makers of top cigarette brands Viceroy and Kool, and Sir Walter Raleigh tobacco. Brown & Williamson also sponsored radio and TV broadcasts of games for the Cincinnati Reds and Los Angeles Angels.

35. Rheingold advertisement, "We're saving a seat for you!," *New York Times*, April 9, 1962: 36.

36. Rheingold advertisement, "Kathy and Casey at the Bat," *New York Times*, April 16, 1962: 36.

37. Santlofer, *Food City*, 291.

38. Leonard Sloane, "Problems Are Brewing in Beer Industry," *New York Times*, December 4, 1966: F1.

39. "Control of Liebmann Breweries Purchased by Pub United Corp.," *New York Times*, June 2, 1964: 46.

40. Peter Bart, "Advertising: Cult of Personality Is Fading," *New York Times*, March 30, 1964: 46.

41. Walter Carlson, "Advertising: Selling to the Ethnic Groups," *New York Times*, April 25, 1965: F18.

42. Leonard Sloane, "Problems Are Brewing in the Beer Industry," *New York Times*, December 4, 1966: F1; and Santlofer, 292.

43. Douglas Martin, "Bringing Back a Taste of Brooklyn: Rheingold," *New York Times*, March 31, 1998: B3; Roberta Hershenson, "Rheingold Returns with a Family Link," *New York Times*, May 3, 1998: WE1.

Mets in the Movies

ROB EDELMAN

Of the real-life New York baseball nines that have been featured (or referenced) onscreen, The Bronx Bombers and their stars have been the most represented. Such a list begins with *Headin' Home*,[1] *Babe Comes Home*,[2] and *Speedy*,[3] all featuring Babe Ruth. To a lesser extent, the late lamented Brooklyn Dodgers often were depicted or referenced. In the 1940s, Dodger blue was cited in *It Happened in Flatbush*,[4] *Whistling in Brooklyn*,[5] *Guadalcanal Diary* and *Arsenic and Old Lace*.[6]

In the 1950s, prior to the Bums' abandoning the Borough of Churches, Brooklyn was represented in everything from biopics (*The Jackie Robinson Story*[7]) and kiddie movies (*Roogie's Bump*[8]) to portrayals of life in a baseball tryout camp (*Big Leaguer*[9]). Actually, New York Giants wannabes (as well as Edward G. Robinson's performance as Hans Lobert and Carl Hubbell playing … Carl Hubbell) are the star attractions in *Big Leaguer*. Almost four decades earlier, the Jints were represented in *One Touch of Nature*,[10] featuring John McGraw, and *Right Off the Bat*,[11] starring Mike Donlin and McGraw.

But what of the New York Mets? When it comes to Big Apple baseball teams and the movies, the Metsies come in a distant fourth place. Across the decades, baseball films (as opposed to films with baseball-related sequences) spotlight the other New York nines—but *never* the Mets. There have been biopics of Babe Ruth and Lou Gehrig, Jackie Robinson and Roy Campanella, but *never* Tom Seaver or Mike Piazza, Darryl Strawberry or Doc Gooden. Meanwhile, quite a few New York ballplayers have graced the big screen. Babe Ruth acted in those 1920s silent features; played himself in *The Pride of the Yankees*,[12] the Lou Gehrig biopic; and appeared in various short subjects. Gehrig starred in *Rawhide*,[13] a B-Western. Jackie Robinson played himself in *The Jackie Robinson Story* (1950); his life and times were depicted in *42*.[14] And so on.… However, if you want to find a Met in the movies, the first name that pops into mind is Greg Goossen, the 1960s' catcher–first sacker: he of the

.202 batting average in his four Mets seasons. Starting in the late 1980s, Goossen worked as Gene Hackman's stand-in and also appeared onscreen. In films as diverse as *The Package*,[15] *Loose Cannons*,[16] *Class Action*,[17] *Unforgiven*,[18] *The Firm*,[19] *Wyatt Earp*,[20] *Midnight in the Garden of Good and Evil*,[21] *The Replacements*,[22] *Heist*,[23] *The Royal Tenenbaums*,[24] and *Behind Enemy Lines*,[25] all released between 1989 and 2001, his characters respectively were: "Soldier in Provost Marshal's Office"; "Marsh Policeman"; "Bartender at Rosatti's"; "Fighter"; "Vietnam Veteran"; "Friend of Bullwacker"; "Prison Cell Lunatic"; "Drunk #2"; "Officer #1"; "Gypsy Cab Driver"; and "CIA Spook."

There *is* good news, however: When it comes to baseball on celluloid, the Mets have not been completely shut out. Far from it—and one New York Mets/Shea Stadium celluloid reference is a bona-fide classic. It is found in *The Odd Couple*,[26] a screen adaptation of Neil Simon's smash-hit play. One of the two central characters is, of course, New York sportswriter/slob extraordinaire Oscar Madison (Walter Matthau). Madison is forever garbed in a Mets cap, and his apartment is decorated with photos of Stan Musial, Yogi Berra, and various long-forgotten Mets of the pre–Tom Seaver era. At one point, he covers a game at Shea Stadium. The Mets are a run up on the Pittsburgh Pirates, who have loaded the bases with Bill Mazeroski coming to bat.

"That's the ballgame," predicts a fellow scribe (Heywood Hale Broun, in a cameo), not expecting the Mets to hold such a slim lead. "What's the matter, you never heard of a triple play?" is Madison's response. Just then, the writer's new roommate and nemesis, neurotic Felix Ungar (Jack Lemmon), phones with an "emergency": He tells Madison not to eat any frankfurters because he's making franks and beans for dinner. At that moment, Maz smacks into a game-ending triple play. "Greatest fielding play I ever saw ... [and] you missed it," yells Broun, to Madison's consternation. (Reportedly,

Pittsburgh Pirates second baseman Bill Mazeroski volunteered to hit into a triple play for a scene staged at Shea Stadium in the 1968 film *The Odd Couple*. Roberto Clemente refused the role (National Baseball Hall of Fame and Museum, Cooperstown, N.Y.).

Hall of Famer Roberto Clemente was scheduled to be at bat during the gag but declined the indignity.)

The sequence was filmed on location right before a Mets-Pirates game on June 27, 1967. The following day, the *New York Times* reported, "Scoring a dramatic, ninth inning triple play, the Mets toppled the Pittsburgh Pirates for the second time in a row before 33,610 fans at Shea Stadium." However, the following one-line paragraph noted, "It was a scriptwriter's dream." Simon created the scene for the movie. "It took two takes and four and a half minutes [and] cost approximately $10,000" to film. The author of the piece was not Leonard Koppett, Deane McGowen, or another *Times* sportswriter. It was Vincent Canby, who then was covering show business stories for the paper.[27]

The Odd Couple is far from the lone film to feature a clever New York Mets reference. Billy Crystal, that diehard New York Yankees fan, stars in *City Slickers*[28] (1991) as Mitch Robbins, a vacationing New York radio ad salesman and average American male who runs with the bulls in Pamplona garbed in a Mets jersey and cap. On their next vacation, Mitch and his buddies head off to a western ranch where they will participate in a cattle drive. Mitch tries on different cowboy hats, which he will wear on the drive. None looks right. None feels right. But then he dons his Mets cap. Finally, he smiles. It also is amusing to see Mitch astride a horse and herding cattle while garbed in the cap. (I asked Crystal why he chose the Mets over the Yankees as the character's favorite team while interviewing him in Cooperstown, where he was presenting to the Hall of Fame memorabilia related to *61**,[29] his 2001 HBO movie about the Mantle-Maris 1961 home run chase. Crystal explained that he did so because the Mets organization was a big contributor to his Comic Relief charity.)

The Mets are the centerpiece of a comedy sequence in *Two Weeks Notice*.[30] Lucy Kelson (Sandra Bullock) and George Wade (Hugh Grant) have first-row seats at Shea as the New York nine takes on the San Francisco Giants; Pedro Astacio is on the mound for New York. Tsuyoshi Shinjo is at bat for the San Franciscans and the fans, as they've done for ages, are chanting, "Let's Go Mets!" Shinjo smacks an Astacio pitch, but the movie audience does not see if it's a hit or an out. The next batter (who wears #17 and has the name "DeVault" on his jersey) then hits a foul popup right where Lucy and George are seated. Mike Piazza, the Mets backstop, rushes toward the spot and crashes into Lucy, who also is trying to nab the horsehide. Piazza of course fails to make the catch and tumbles into the stands. After acknowledging George, a super-rich land developer who is as celebrated as Donald Trump, Piazza looks at Lucy with disdain and tells her, "Hey, next time go to a Yankee game."

But this is not the punchline. Even though Lucy is garbed in a Mets jacket and cap, she is booed by the fans around her. Then her face is shown on the ballpark's Diamond Vision screen and all those in attendance jeer her.

They even are encouraged by Mr. Met himself—and one might surmise that she may as well move to Chicago and change her name to Steve Bartman. (Piazza also is referenced in *Kate & Leopold*,[31] which features a poster of the 1969 World Champions and a character who proves that he can copy any accent by impersonating a "Victorian dude who's never seen a Mets game [and is] watching [one on] TV.")

If Brooklynites by nature are supposed to be Mets (as opposed to Yankee) fans, then it is not surprising that Spike Lee more than occasionally references the Mets. In *Do the Right Thing*,[32] it is appropriate that Mookie the pizza delivery guy (who is played by Lee) shows up at work garbed in a Brooklyn Dodgers jersey. Is it because the setting is Bedford-Stuyvesant, a Brooklyn neighborhood, and Mookie is a Dodgers fan? Not necessarily. What is key here is that Mookie wears a #42 Jackie Robinson jersey. (Once upon a time, Lee attempted to direct a Jackie Robinson biopic, but the project fell through.) But Lee does not ignore the Mets. For one thing, Mookie's son wears Mets pajamas. For another, Mookie tells Vito (Richard Edson), his boss' son, "See that game last night? Best pitcher in the game. Dwight Gooden." Vito protests, claiming that Roger Clemens is superior. "Clemens sucks, man," Mookie declares. "He can't carry Dwight's jock."

The black-versus-Italian tension also is found in Lee's *Jungle Fever*.[33] Here, Mike Tucci (Frank Vincent) and his sons (David Dundara, Michael Imperioli) watch the Mets on TV. "I'm glad they got rid of Strawberry," one of them declares in voiceover. "He was too much fucking trouble. If he wants his ass kissed, let him go to L.A. and let Lasorda kiss it. Now he says he's a born-again Christian. Fuck born-again. Play the fuckin' game." All the while, another voice is heard sarcastically chanting "Daaaaryl, Daaaaryl...." Mike and his boys wear their racism on their sleeves, and so a question arises: Is their anti–Strawberry rant meant to be racially tinged? Would the Italians disrespect Gary Carter or Ray Knight—or John Franco or Lee Mazzilli? And regarding *Do the Right Thing*, would Mookie claim that Clemens was the superior hurler if he was black and Gooden was white? These are questions you'd have to pose to Spike Lee.

However, later in *Jungle Fever*, Gator Purify (Samuel L. Jackson), a black crack addict, "borrows" his parents' color TV set because, he says, he wants to "watch the Mets." When confronted by his brother, Gator grumbles that the Mets lost yet again, referring to them as "sorry mother-fuckers." Of course, Gator's true intention is to sell the TV for drug money. So in the world of Spike Lee, as portrayed in *Jungle Fever*, no one is perfect. Whites from Brooklyn's Bensonhurst community may be bigots. Blacks from Manhattan's Harlem may be crackheads. One thing they do share is that they grouse about the Mets.

The Mets also are cited by Lee in *Mo' Better Blues*.[34] The first reference

is in the film's first scene. It is 1969, and four boys with baseball gear are outside a Brooklyn brownstone imploring their pal Bleek to join them. At the
insistence of his mother, Bleek declines as he is busy practicing the trumpet.
His father, meanwhile, is watching the Mets on TV. Rod Gaspar, #17, is at the
plate for the New Yorkers, who are battling the Pittsburgh Pirates at Shea.
Bob Moose is on the mound for the Bucs. The date is September 20, and
Moose is in the process of tossing a no-hitter. Lee then cuts to the present,
and Bleek (now played by Denzel Washington) has grown up to be a jazz
trumpeter. Giant, his manager (played by Lee), has a gambling issue and is
placing bets on games. The Mets and Pirates are meeting in a double header.
"Gimme the Pirates in both games," Giant says. "The Mets need some more
black ballplayers." Giant is no less cynical about the Yankees. "In the American
League," he adds, "gimme the Yankees over the Tigers—even though Steinbrenner needs to go."

As in *Jungle Fever*, other Mets celluloid references are connected to key
dates or events in the club's history. The 1969 World Series triumph is one of
the central elements in *Frequency*.[35] Frank Sullivan (Dennis Quaid), a New
York firefighter, lives in Queens, loves his wife and son, and passionately roots
for the Amazins. Frank and his boy both wear Mets caps. In one scene, parents
and kids are at a picnic and a Series game is airing on TV. Frank snaps a
photo of the group. To get them to collectively smile, he tells them: "Everybody say 'Amazin' Mets.'"

At the outset, we are told that Frank perished in a warehouse fire several
days into the Series. Cut to 30 years later. Sullivan's now-grown son John (Jim
Caviezel) is a New York cop whose life is at its nadir. He is drinking way too
much, and his wife has just left him. Of his father, he observes, "I wish I
could remember him better." But then he stumbles upon his dad's old ham
radio and, miraculously, he uses it to speak across time with his father in
1969, despite the three decades that have passed. In their first conversation,
John observes that he will "love Ron Swoboda until the day I die."

The core of the story involves the nabbing of a serial killer, the key role
of the '69 Series, and father-son connections through baseball. At the finale,
we see John's son—and Frank's grandson—playing ball while garbed in a
Mike Piazza jersey.

One of the momentous dates in Mets history is October 25, 1986: Game
Six of the '86 Fall Classic, which is famous (or infamous, as the case may be)
for Mookie Wilson's groundball trickling through Bill Buckner's legs. This
date and game are the subjects of *Game 6*,[36] the tale of Nicky Rogan (Michael
Keaton), a Bosox-obsessed playwright who, on the day of the game, sees a
"tragedy in the making" given the Sox's sorry history. Throughout the film,
radio pundits and fans discuss the game and Nicky adds his perspective by
observing, "I hate the Mets. I can't respect them. 'Cause when the Mets lose,

they just lose…. But the Red Sox … we have a rich history of really fascinating ways to lose crucial games … defeats that just keep you awake at night."

When Dave Henderson homers in the top of the 10th inning, giving the Sox a 4–3 lead, Nicky's companion observes that "life is good"—and Nicky adds, "Baseball is life." But we all know what happened in the bottom of the 10th and, for Red Sox fans, baseball also is a reflection of life's heartbreak. When Mookie grounds to Buckner, Nicky visualizes Buckner making the play. That, of course, is an illusion. As a reality test, the actual footage is seen and re-seen onscreen. Even though the Mets won Game 6—and Game 7—the film is a Boston Red Sox movie. Within the framework of the story, the Mets are the secondary players.

A *fictional* Mets-Dodgers playoff series plays a central role in *Bad Lieutenant*.[37] Over the opening credits, the distinctive voice of Chris "Mad Dog" Russo is heard on the soundtrack. Russo, hosting a talk radio sports show, sets up the scene when he declares, "Hey folks, I know the Mets are down three-zip in a best-of-seven. I don't know a [playoff] team [that] has ever come back from three-oh down to win four straight." (This, of course, is prior to the 2004 American League Championship series between the Red Sox and Yankees.) Russo continues, "I know they haven't played well. I know the pitching's been bad. I know no clutch hitting…. '86 and '69 seem a long time ago. And … goodness gracious, there's no Donn Clendenon. But you are not out of it until you lose four games in a best-of-seven. That is all there is to it." Then, in some back-and-forth repartee that captures the zeal of opinionated fans, Russo gets into a passionate argument with "Bruce from Bayside," a caller who trashes the Mets and their comeback chances.

The Mets remain present in the first post-credits scene—the title character (played by Harvey Keitel), a nameless drug-abusing New York cop, drives his sons to school while the kids continue the "debate" between "Mad Dog" and "Bruce from Bayside." The lieutenant's contribution is that "Strawberry's killing 'em," but it must be noted that ex–Met Darryl is now a Dodger. In *Bad Lieutenant*, New York is depicted as being Mets-obsessed. In several sequences set at grisly murder scenes, the lieutenant and his fellow cops casually place bets on the series while discussing crime-related issues. Meanwhile, the lieutenant has bet heavily on the ex–Brooklynites. "The Dodgers are a lock," he says. But of course, they aren't. In the next game, Strawberry stands in against the Mets' David Cone and hits one of his "moonshots." The lieutenant's elation dissipates upon learning that Darryl's dinger has made the score 11–3, Mets. And so it goes, during this and the following three games, the Mets roar back to win them all and prevail in the series.

The lieutenant becomes increasingly desperate. After another contest, which ends on a double-play ball thrown by John Franco to Kal Daniels, he grabs his gun and shoots his car radio. While Mets fans are thrilled by the heroics, the victories are catastrophic for the doomed lieutenant. Throughout *Bad Lieutenant*, the voices of play-by-play announcers Warner Fusselle and Bob Murphy reference plenty of real-life ballplayers, from the Dodgers' Eric Davis, Lenny Harris, Orel Hershiser, Ramón Martínez, and Mike Scioscia to the Mets' Bobby Bonilla, Vince Coleman, Sid Fernandez, and Dwight Gooden—and it is a special treat to hear Murphy yet again describe a Mets game.

On occasion, a Mets movie reference is slight—but at least it is undeniable. In *Friends with Benefits*,[38] Mila Kunis and Justin Timberlake play the title characters; the "benefits" of their friendship are the sexual trysts they enjoy without the complications of an emotional attachment. In one sequence, they are going at it in bed while the Mets are on TV and there is a close-up of #7, Jose Reyes, who runs the bases after smashing a homer. Then, there is a Mets logo on the screen. Several trysts later, a Mets cap is spied atop a drawer.

Shea Stadium has played a part in a number of films, most significantly, perhaps, in *Bang the Drum Slowly*[39] if only because the story told is set in the baseball world. In the opening credits, it is noted that the "baseball sequences [were] filmed at Yankee and Shea stadiums," and the New York Mammoths—the fictional team depicted in the story—play their home games at a very recognizable Shea Stadium. Shea also has a cameo in *Kiss of Death*.[40] The opening shot begins with a subway on elevated tracks and the camera pans an auto graveyard filled with cars in various states of disrepair. At one point, there is a name: F&F Used Auto Parts. Eventually, the camera catches a glimpse of Shea, with the presence of the ballyard helping to establish the film's setting. During the opening credits of *3 Men and a Little Lady*,[41] two of the trio and the "little lady," who is six, are cheering the Mets at Shea. Because of her gender, the child is comically blindfolded while accompanying the guys into a Shea men's room.

The Wiz,[42] a musical version of *The Wizard of Oz*,[43] features a chase scene up and down the ballpark's pedestrian ramps featuring Dorothy (Diana Ross), her cohorts, and some motorcycle-riding meanies. Baseball references abound in Woody Allen films; in a sequence from *Small Time Crooks*[44] that might be dubbed "Ray and May at Shea," characters named Ray (played by Woody) and May (Elaine May) attend a game at Shea and look on as a Met belts a dinger. Then-Met Bernard Gilkey has a cameo in *Men in Black*.[45] As he roams the Shea outfield, he is distracted by a spacecraft overhead and is hit on the noggin by a fly ball. In *Old Dogs*,[46] "sports marketing kings" Dan (Robin Williams) and Charlie (John Travolta) have on-field access at Shea, where they take pre-game batting practice. (Thirty-one years earlier, Travolta briefly swung a bat in *Grease*.[47]) They and Dan's kids get player autographs and Mets caps, and then sit in the stands when, in a blink-and-you'll-miss-it moment, David Wright crushes the ball. Later, Dan's son excitedly declares that they got to "hang out with the New York Mets."

One of the more telling Shea Stadium references is found in *Alice in the Cities*,[48] a West German film directed by Wim Wenders. The following analysis of the sequence, written by Scott Jordan Harris and published in 2011 in *World Film Locations: New York*, grabbed my attention:

> We hear it before we see it. "Sounds like an organ," says our protagonist, a travelling German journalist whose name is not yet known to us…. "That's … Shea Stadium," he is told. We cut to the famous sports ground. A baseball game is in progress. The players, tiny and bright in their white uniforms against the grey grass are part of a team, but their smallness and their regimented distance from each other emphasizes each man's isolation.[49]

The final film worth citing here actually was released in 1956: six years before the birth of the Mets. Its title is *The Man in the Gray Flannel Suit*.[50] Gregory Peck stars as Tom Rath, a harried suburbanite and World War II veteran who commutes into Manhattan every workday. One day, while passing time on the train, Tom's mind wanders and he recalls an incident from a decade earlier—and a world away from the peacetime America of the 1950s—where he killed a young German soldier. Then, in an instant, he is thrust back into the reality of 1956 when the man sitting next to him grimly declares, "There's no use trying. I just can't get used to it." "Used to what?" Tom asks. His fellow commuter responds, "The idea of the Brooklyn Dodgers as world champions."

I would bet my Topps Tom Seaver rookie card that, if *The Man in the Gray Flannel Suit* had instead been made in 1970, that line would have been: "The idea of the New York Mets as world champions." And it would have been just as credible.

NOTES

1. *Headin' Home*, directed by Lawrence C. Windom (1920; Kessel & Baumann, Yankee Photo Corporation).
2. *Babe Comes Home*, directed by Ted Wilde (1927; First National Pictures).
3. *Speedy*, directed by Ted Wilde (1928; The Harold Lloyd Corporation).
4. *It Happened in Flatbush*, directed by Ray McCarey (1942; Twentieth Century Fox).
5. *Whistling in Brooklyn*, directed by S. Sylvan Simon (1943; Metro-Goldwyn-Mayer).
6. *Arsenic and Old Lace*, directed by Frank Capra (1944; Warner Brothers—First National).
7. *The Jackie Robinson Story*, directed by Alfred E. Green (1950; Jewel Pictures).
8. *Roogie's Bump*, directed by Harold Young (1954; John Bash Productions, Republic Pictures).
9. *Big Leaguer*, directed by Robert Aldrich (1953; Metro-Goldwyn-Mayer).
10. *One Touch of Nature*, directed by Edward H. Griffith (1917; Thomas A. Edison).
11. *Right Off the Bat*, directed by Hugh Reticker (1915; Arrow Film Corporation).
12. *The Pride of the Yankees*, directed by Sam Wood (1942; The Samuel Goldwyn Company).

13. *Rawhide*, directed by Ray Taylor (1938; Sol Lesser Productions as Principal Productions).

14. *42*, directed by Brian Helgeland (2013; Warner Brothers, Legendary Entertainment).

15. *The Package*, directed by Andrew Davis (1989; Orion Pictures).

16. *Loose Cannons*, directed by Bob Clark (1990; TriStar Pictures).

17. *Class Action*, directed by Michael Apted (1991; Interscope Communications, Twentieth Century Fox).

18. *Unforgiven*, directed by Clint Eastwood (1992; Warner Brothers, Malpaso Productions).

19. *The Firm*, directed by Sydney Pollack (1993; Davis Entertainment, Mirage Enterprises, Paramount Pictures, Scott Rudin Productions).

20. *Wyatt Earp*, directed by Lawrence Kasdan (1994; Warner Brothers, Tig Productions, Kasdan Pictures, Eaves Movie Ranch, Paragon Entertainment Corporation).

21. *Midnight in the Garden of Good and Evil*, directed by Clint Eastwood (1997; Warner Brothers, Malpaso Productions, Silver Pictures).

22. *The Replacements*, directed by Howard Deutch (2000; Bel Air Entertainment, Dylan Sellers Productions, Warner Brothers).

23. *Heist*, directed by David Mamet (2001; Morgan Creek Entertainment, Franchise Pictures, Indelible Pictures, Art Linson Productions, Epsilon Motion Pictures, Heightened Productions, Linson Entertainment, Mel's Cite du Cinema, Stolen Film Productions).

24. *The Royal Tenenbaums*, directed by Wes Anderson (2001; Touchstone Pictures, American Empirical Pictures).

25. *Behind Enemy Lines*, directed by John Moore (2001; Twentieth Century Fox, Davis Entertainment).

26. *The Odd Couple*, directed by Gene Saks (1968; Paramount Pictures).

27. Vincent Canby, "Mazeroski Hits into Triple Play in 'Odd Couple' Filming at Shea," *New York Times*, June 28, 1967: 39.

28. *City Slickers*, directed by Ron Underwood (1991; Castle Rock Entertainment, Nelson Entertainment, Face Productions, Sultan Entertainment).

29. *61**, directed by Billy Crystal (2001; HBO Films, Face Productions).

30. *Two Weeks Notice*, directed by Marc Lawrence (2002; Castle Rock Entertainment, Village Roadshow Pictures, NPV Entertainment, Fortis Films).

31. *Kate & Leopold*, directed by James Mangold (2001; Konrad Pictures, Miramax).

32. *Do the Right Thing*, directed by Spike Lee (1989; 40 Acres & a Mule Filmworks).

33. *Jungle Fever*, directed by Spike Lee (1991; Universal Pictures, 40 Acres & a Mule Filmworks).

34. *Mo' Better Blues*, directed by Spike Lee (1990; Universal Pictures, 40 Acres and a Mule Filmworks).

35. *Frequency*, directed by Gregory Hoblit (2000; New Line Cinema).

36. *Game 6*, directed by Michael Hoffman (2005; Serenade Films, Double Play, Vox3 Films, ShadowCatcher Entertainment).

37. *Bad Lieutenant*, directed by Abel Ferrara (1992; Bad Lt. Productions).

38. *Friends with Benefits*, directed by Will Gluck (2011; Screen Gems, Castle Rock Entertainment, Zucker Productions, Olive Bridge Entertainment).

39. *Bang the Drum Slowly*, directed by John Hancock (1973: ANJS, Dibs Partnership, Paramount Pictures).

40. *Kiss of Death*, directed by Barbet Schroeder (1995; Twentieth Century Fox).

41. *3 Men and a Little Lady*, directed by Emile Ardolino (1990; Touchstone Pictures, Interscope Communications, Silver Screen Partners IV).

42. *The Wiz*, directed by Sidney Lumet (1978; Universal Pictures, Motown Productions).

43. *The Wizard of Oz*, directed by Victor Fleming (1939; Metro-Goldwyn-Mayer).

44. *Small Time Crooks*, directed by Woody Allen (2000; DreamWorks, Sweetland Films).

45. *Men in Black*, directed by Barry Sonnenfeld (1997; Columbia Pictures, Amblin Entertainment, Parkes+MacDonald Image Nation).

46. *Old Dogs*, directed by Walt Becker (2009; Walt Disney Pictures, Tapestry Films).

47. *Grease*, directed by Randal Kleiser (1978; Paramount Pictures, Robert Stigwood Organization, Allan Carr Production).

48. *Alice in the Cities*, directed by Wim Wenders (1974; Westdeutscher Rundfunk, Filmverlag der Autoren).

49. Scott Jordan Harris, "Alice in the Cities," in *World Film Locations: New York*, ed. Scott Jordan Harris (Fishponds, Bristol, United Kingdom: Intellect Books, 2011; Chicago: The University of Chicago Press, 2011), 52. Citation refers to the University of Chicago Press edition.

50. *The Man in the Gray Flannel Suit*, directed by Nunnally Johnson (1956; Twentieth Century Fox).

Murphy Before the Mets

Donna L. Halper

Bob Murphy was best known as the voice of the New York Mets, a job
he held for more than four decades. But when I was growing up in Boston
in the 1950s, I knew a different Bob Murphy—the sidekick to popular Red
Sox announcer Curt Gowdy on WHDH radio, 850 on the AM dial. During
the '50s, AM radio was still king; when you wanted to hear the game, chances
an AM station was broadcasting it. I had no idea that these two Red Sox
broadcasters had been on the air in Oklahoma City, nor that Murphy originally came from Tulsa. All I knew was that he and Curt made a great team
and even though the Sox never won the pennant in those days (and sometimes didn't finish above .500), they could make any game more interesting.

Bob Murphy arrived in Boston in early 1954, and almost immediately,
he became a fan favorite. Of course, nobody back then could have predicted
that both broadcasters would go on to become nationally known; I doubt
that many fans were even thinking about that. If you had asked what the fans
were thinking about, they would undoubtedly have told you they wondered
why the Red Sox weren't winning more games; on paper, the team had some
talented players, yet the Sox kept finishing third or fourth in the standings.
And some of us also wondered when the Sox management would finally add
a black player—all the other teams had done so long before the Red Sox
finally did in 1959.

As a young female fan of the Red Sox, in an era when it was widely
believed that women and girls didn't care about sports, what I was thinking
about was how much I appreciated these two sportscasters. They made even
the most complex plays understandable. And that was important to me
because I was still learning the ins and outs of the game, and I really had
nobody I could ask. I don't recall how I was first introduced to Major League
Baseball. I was a big fan of listening to the radio, so I may have found the
Sox games entirely by accident. Nobody in my family was a fan—my father

27

took me to a couple of games, but he mostly did it because I asked him to. So, when I wanted to become more knowledgeable about baseball, I found myself relying on Gowdy and Murphy. Unfortunately, there was no Internet back then, and no way for me to find other young female fans, which meant I had nobody with whom I could talk baseball. Sometimes, I tried to talk baseball with some of the boys at school; they were always surprised that a girl knew anything about the Red Sox, but they didn't seem especially happy to encounter a girl who knew as much about sports as they did. So, I ended up just listening to the games on WHDH by myself. And when I wasn't listening to baseball, my other favorite activity was listening to a top 40 station that played the latest hits. I knew from a young age that I wanted to be on the air—I thought about becoming a deejay, or perhaps a sportscaster, but it was the 1950s, and I was told girls couldn't be either one. I remember how the Red Sox began having an annual contest to choose a "Junior Broadcaster," who would work with Curt and Bob and maybe even call a few of the plays during a Red Sox game. I wanted to apply, but the contest was only open to boys.[1]

Meanwhile, in 1954, Bob Murphy's first season in Boston, the Sox had an especially disappointing year, winning 69 and losing 85; they did better the following year, winning 84 and losing 70. But whether the Sox won or lost, the fans were grateful that a consistently excellent broadcasting team was calling the games. Boston had a long tradition of hiring talented sportscasters, and Gowdy and Murphy were no exception. They received lots of praise from local baseball writers for their accuracy and eloquence. Gowdy, as chief announcer, tended to get more attention—after all, he was "the voice of the Red Sox," while Murphy was his "capable assistant"[2]; but Murphy soon began receiving critical praise too, including from national publications like *Sports Illustrated*, where one writer said he "…reports the game simply and has one of the better deliveries in the business."[3]

Although the Sox weren't contenders during the years that Murphy called the games, there were still some exciting moments for the broadcasting team to report. Fenway Park was a wonderful place to see a game, and there were plenty of times when Sox players sent the fans home happy: for example, there was Mel Parnell's no-hitter at Fenway on July 14, 1956. And then, several days later, on July 17, Ted Williams hit career home run #400. Williams kept achieving milestones throughout the late 1950s. In 1958, when he was 40 years old, he won another batting title—his sixth. Third baseman Frank Malzone, was a defensive wizard, winning a well-deserved Gold Glove for three straight years, from 1957 to 1959. And another fan favorite, right fielder and 1958 American League MVP Jackie Jensen, made the All Star team in 1955, and led the American League in runs batted in with 116; in 1958, he did it again, with 122 RBI, and he returned to the All Star team.

I can still recall the chemistry that Gowdy and Murphy had on the air, whether they were chatting with each other during a pitching change, or relating an anecdote about someone on the team, or doing the play-by-play. And I recall being disappointed when the newspapers reported in early 1960 that Bob was leaving Boston to join the Baltimore Orioles' broadcasting team; but I was glad I could still hear him, because WBAL's signal got into Boston late at night. Evidently, I was not the only one who was aware of this; *Boston Daily Record* radio–TV columnist Bill Buchanan also listened to Bob calling Orioles night games on WBAL and he found it amusing that the guy who so faithfully represented the Red Sox for six seasons had now become "pro–Baltimore."[4]

I also recall having mixed emotions when I heard that Bob had gotten a job with the new expansion team in New York, the Mets, several years later; on the one hand, I was happy for him, but on the other, I still wished he could come back to Boston to broadcast the Red Sox games again. Of course, he never did; he went on to become the voice of the New York Mets for more than 40 years; he was inducted into the New York Mets Hall of Fame in 1984, and he earned a Ford C. Frick Award at the Baseball Hall of Fame in 1994. But even now, after all this time, I'm glad I was able to hear him doing play-by-play in Boston and Baltimore, early in his major-league career. And I was not surprised that he went on to have such a long and illustrious career.

Bob Murphy never planned to become a sports broadcaster; his dream was to become a professional athlete. He was born in Tulsa, Oklahoma, on September 19, 1924. While his World War II draft card later stated that his birth name was Robert Allen Murphy, other sources, including federal census documents,[5] said it was actually Robert Alan Murphy. His dad, James Raymond (Ray) Murphy was an oil lease broker, and his mother Eula was a homemaker; he also had an older brother named Jack. Bob attended Tulsa's Will Rogers High School, where he participated in wrestling and track, and he also played American Legion baseball. Then, like many young men who came of age during the early 1940s, he joined the military. During World War II, he served in the Marine Corps. Stationed in the South Pacific, he worked as a Weather Observer and a Navigator.

When Murphy returned to Tulsa, he was uncertain about a career. But still hoped that he could become a professional athlete and briefly thought about boxing. But baseball was his final choice. However, as much as he loved the game, he had to admit he didn't hit well enough to play professionally.[6] So, he enrolled at the University of Tulsa, to study petroleum engineering[7]; but that, too, didn't seem like the right fit for him. He sometimes wished he were more like his brother—Jack had known from the time he was a kid that he wanted a career as a writer, and he was now working at a local newspaper, the *Tulsa World*. It was Jack who encouraged Bob to try sportscasting—after all, if he couldn't play sports professionally, at least he could report on them and keep the fans informed.

What gave Jack this idea was seeing how involved his brother Bob had become with college radio. In early March 1947, the University of Tulsa had gotten a new radio station, KWGS. Its call letters were derived from the initials of William Grove Skelly, who was one of the station's most generous donors; Skelly was a successful oil executive and then-owner of Tulsa radio station KVOO.[8] The new college station was an educational FM outlet, and while its early schedule was still a work in progress—KWGS expanded its broadcast day in May,[9] but was not formally dedicated until October—the station carried some college sports almost immediately. Despite having little experience and not yet sounding smooth in his broadcasting skills,[10] Bob was soon getting on-the-job training by broadcasting the university's football and basketball games, plus track competitions. He also became the station's sports director.[11]

However, it is not certain that he ever graduated from the University of Tulsa. While there are some sources that say he did,[12] others disagree. To cite one important example, there is the University of Tulsa's 1948 yearbook. It contains several mentions of his work as a sportscaster at KWGS; he is referred to as a senior.[13] But Bob Murphy's name and biographical sketch are not included in the alphabetical listing of that year's graduates. Further, his 2004 *New York Times* obituary also says he left the university without graduating.[14] One possible explanation for why he didn't finish his degree was offered by Rik Espinosa, a reporter from the newspaper where his brother Jack had worked: Espinosa wrote in 1998 that Bob abandoned his studies in his senior year because he had decided he loved sportscasting, and when an opportunity to do it fulltime arose, Bob took it, rather than waiting to graduate.[15]

After college, he started at KAKC, owned by local entrepreneur Sam Avey, who also owned the Tulsa Coliseum. Bob broadcast Tulsa Oilers minor-league hockey games, his first professional job as a sportscaster.[16] Then in July 1948, a new station went on the air in Muskogee, about an hour from Tulsa. KMUS, 1380 AM, needed an announcer to do play-by-play of the Class C Muskogee Reds of the Western Association, at that time a farm team of the St. Louis Browns, and Bob gained valuable experience calling their games. In 1947, the Reds, under manager Ray Baker, had won 75 and lost 64 and finished third; but the fans who came out to Muskogee's Athletic Park in 1948 saw the Reds win only 61 and lose 70, finishing 5th in the league. And that same year, Bob also broadcast some games of the Double-A Tulsa Oilers baseball team on KAKC; the Oilers, managed by Al Vincent and affiliated with the Cincinnati Reds, had a winning season in 1948, finishing second with a record of 93–63. But whether the hometown team was winning or losing,

Bob's brother Jack had given him useful advice and he followed it faithfully—sports broadcasting was much like print journalism. The radio reporter used a microphone, the print reporter used a typewriter, but the job was to tell the story of the game.[17]

In September of 1948, Bob was hired as a sports reporter at KOMA in Oklahoma City, where the station's sports director was a young man from Wyoming named Curt Gowdy. Curt had been with the station since 1945,[18] broadcasting University of Oklahoma Sooners college football and Oklahoma A&M Aggies basketball games; among Bob's duties was helping him to call the games, the first time the two men worked together. In addition to doing college football and basketball, Curt was also on the air at another local station, KOCY, broadcasting minor-league baseball—for several years, he was the play-by-play announcer for the Oklahoma City Indians, a Double-A team in the Texas League, and a farm team of the Cleveland Indians at that time. Then, in early 1949, Curt suddenly announced he was leaving Oklahoma to take a major-league job in New York, working with Mel Allen on the Yankees games. The general manager of KOCY, Matthew H. (Matt) Bonebrake, decided that Bob would make an excellent replacement for Curt. So, Bob left KOMA, and beginning in April 1949, he began broadcasting the Oklahoma City Indians games for KOCY[19] and became the station's sports director. In addition, his duties included hosting a daily sports show, *Sports by Murphy*, and he took over Curt's role as play-by-play announcer for University of Oklahoma football and Oklahoma A&M basketball.

Nineteen forty-nine was a good year to debut as the Indians' play-by-play announcer. In 1948, local oil executive Harold O. Pope had sold the team to Cleveland Indians owner Bill Veeck, along with his two partners, Veeck's Cleveland business manager Rudie Schaffer and E.J. "Jimmie" Humphries, who had held numerous front office positions with the Oklahoma City club for three decades.[20] The new owners got new uniforms for the Oklahoma City franchise and added more than 700 seats to Holland Field, now renamed Texas League Park. Veeck was a master showman, who enjoyed creating interesting promotions; plus, the team had some exciting players, including first baseman Herb Conyers, who was the Texas League's Most Valuable Player. That year, attendance soared.[21] And while Veeck sold his shares of the team several years later, the commitment to ballpark promotions and events, many of which Bob emceed,[22] remained. It did not take long for Bob to become popular with the fans, who enjoyed both his play-by-play and the opportunity to meet him at these events. Local newspapers soon referred to him in ads as the station's "ace sportscaster" and sell-out crowds came out to see him each year as he hosted "Radio Appreciation Night." He also called the Texas League All-Star game for KOCY from 1950 through 1953, sometimes live and sometimes by recreating the game from wire reports; and he became a popular emcee for sports banquets and charitable fundraisers. Bob got married in 1951; but his devotion to sports seems to take precedence over his devotion to his new wife Jean—during their honeymoon, he took time to cover the NCAA basketball playoffs.[23]

Bob's years in Oklahoma were central to his development as a broadcaster, and for those who know the state, that should come as no surprise: Oklahoma has a history of giving soon-to-be-famous broadcasters their start. Curt Gowdy and Bob Murphy were among a long list that even included legendary news anchor Walter Cronkite, who announced college football at WKY Radio in Oklahoma City back in 1937.[24] But more important than the work Bob did in Oklahoma City announcing college football and basketball, and sometimes calling schoolboy sports, it was the experience he got as a baseball announcer that set the stage for what was to come in his career. Curt agreed with this assessment. Long after leaving Oklahoma for an impressive career covering pro sports of all kinds, Curt often told interviewers that his years doing minor-league baseball were crucial to his own development; he said that even covering the teams of legendary University of Oklahoma head football coach Bud Wilkinson did not compare to what he learned covering the Oklahoma City Indians. As he explained to a reporter, "Someone once asked me if I had to take a young broadcaster and mold him from scratch, what would I do…. I said I'd make him handle minor league baseball. It's the greatest teacher there is."[25]

Meanwhile, Curt spent 1949 and 1950 assisting Mel Allen in New York, calling the Yankees games. But in November 1950, the Boston Red Sox announced Curt would become their new play-by-play announcer for the 1951 season.[26] The reason why a new Red Sox announcer was needed involved a decision made by the previous announcer, Jim Britt. While today, we expect to hear (and see) every game of our favorite team, prior to the early 1950s, that rarely happened in most cities. Rather, it was usually just the home games that were broadcast on radio; and after TV came along, a small number of home games were also televised. Away games might be summarized, or sometimes, they might be re-created,[27] often using sound effects, to simulate being there. National networks broadcast a game of the week live, on radio, and later, TV; but the game they were broadcasting might not involve your favorite team. In Boston, prior to the 1951 season, neither the Red Sox nor the Braves broadcast their entire schedule. It was mainly the home games of each team, along with a few exhibition games. And during much of the 1940s, the broadcasters who did the play-by-play were Jim Britt and his sidekick, veteran local sports announcer Tom Hussey: when the Sox were at home, they'd call those games, and when the Braves were in town, that's what the fans would hear.

In the early to mid–1940s, the games were broadcast by radio station WNAC, but then, in 1947, all the games moved over to WHDH, and so did

Britt and Hussey.[28] At that time, WHDH Radio was affiliated with the same company that owned the *Boston Herald-Traveler* newspapers, giving their sportswriters new and better access to the players. By the late 1940s, there were also a few televised Sox and Braves home games: they alternated between the two TV stations on the air in Boston at that time—WBZ-TV (channel 4) and WNAC-TV (channel 7); the same broadcasters who handled the play-by-play on radio also handled it on TV. But then, in 1951, Boston Red Sox fans got some good news: for the first time, *all* the Red Sox games, home and away, would be broadcast on WHDH radio. And there was one other change that occurred that same year. The Braves management decided to move their games back to WNAC; Jim Britt, who had done all the Sox and Braves home games, now agreed to broadcast the Braves games exclusively,[29] which opened a position for a Red Sox chief announcer—and that was the slot filled by Curt Gowdy.

In addition to hiring Curt, the Sox chose a new assistant for him—Bob Delaney, a WHDH sports announcer who had previously broadcast Boston Bruins hockey and college sports (as well as an occasional major-league baseball game). By 1952, they were sometimes joined by veteran local sports announcer Tom Hussey, who had come back over from WNAC Radio; also in the booth was ace statistician Joe Costanza; Curt had worked with Joe previously and was impressed with his encyclopedic knowledge of baseball trivia.[30] Then, at the end of 1953, Bob Delaney decided to leave Boston to broadcast the New York Giants games, along with Russ Hodges, over station WMCA.[31] Suddenly, there was an opening on the Boston Red Sox play-by-play team for the 1954 season. Many sportswriters, who got along well with him and were sorry to see him leave,[32] began to speculate about who might replace him—some hoped a local announcer would be promoted to the position: WHDH sportscaster Don Gillis was one suggestion.[33] Meanwhile, as many as 50 broadcasters from all over the country applied for the vacancy; Tom Hussey was one of them, and another was former Quincy resident Ken Coleman, currently the radio voice of pro football's Cleveland Browns.[34] But nobody expected that the new guy would be someone from Oklahoma City, a much smaller market than Boston. To put this in perspective, according to 1950 U.S. census data, Oklahoma City had a population of about 244,000 people, while Boston's population was more than three times as big—about 801,000 people, which made it the 10th largest city in the United States at that time.

As the sports reporters soon found out, the selection of Bob Murphy was not an accident: Curt Gowdy had recommended him. And once the Sox owners and advertisers heard him, they were very impressed with his ability to call the games.[35] Back then, it wasn't just the radio station that decided which sportscaster would get the job. The sponsors of the games—in this case, the Narragansett Brewing Company, Atlantic Refining Company, and Liggett & Myers Tobacco Company—were every bit as influential; in fact, without their approval, a sportscaster could not get hired. Fortunately for Bob, all the decision-makers agreed, and in early January 1954, he officially became part of the Red Sox broadcasting team, soon to be reunited with Curt in the booth. But before Bob, his wife Jean, and their two kids left Oklahoma City— his first scheduled Red Sox broadcast would be in early March, during spring training—the local YMCA honored him at its annual baseball banquet.[36]

While my recollections of Bob Murphy do not include an Oklahoma accent, it turns out that was thanks in large part to Curt's mentorship. When Bob arrived, he sounded like someone who had spent all his life in the Southwest; but Curt practiced with him and helped him to acquire a more neutral-sounding delivery.[37] The two developed an excellent rapport, and it was obvious they both enjoyed working together. In fact, more than three decades later, Bob still had fond memories of calling the Red Sox games with Curt: as he told a reporter, "I loved every minute of my six years [in Boston.]"[38]

Bob made his début as a Red Sox announcer on March 6, 1954, in Sarasota, home of the Red Sox's Grapefruit League facility, Payne Park. (The Sox would eventually move to a new spring training site in 1959, when they began playing in Scottsdale, Arizona.) Bob's first regular season game was in Philadelphia on April 13, when the Red Sox opened their season against the Athletics. Little did he know that in 1954, the Sox would have a losing record; but both he and Curt had called the games for teams that didn't set the world on fire, and they knew how to keep the fans informed. Meanwhile, Bob and his family settled into their new home in Needham, Massachusetts, about 30 minutes from Boston. Working for the Red Sox meant doing the games on both radio and TV; although the entire schedule was not yet televised, an increasing number of games were being seen—in 1954, about 75 of them.[39] But fans still relied on radio to keep up-to-date with what the Sox were doing.

Like many sports announcers, Bob was expected to do more than just the play-by-play. He was soon doing a post-game wrap-up; and when the Red Sox were not playing, he hosted a daily sports roundup show on WHDH Radio. He also became an in-demand guest speaker at local schools, churches, and synagogues. Each year, he tried to generate enthusiasm, even if the Sox were only mediocre—one talk he gave was about the "phenomenal" 1955 Red Sox.[40] They finished fourth that year. When baseball season ended, he could be heard announcing college sports, the same schedule he had in Oklahoma. In Boston, he began announcing Boston University's football games, along with Tom Hussey, beginning in late 1954; in subsequent years, his sidekick was Don Gillis. And at various times in the mid–1950s, he also called the plays for the Holy Cross football team; periodically, he even handled a high school football game or two.

And in addition to serving as Curt Gowdy's sidekick, there were times when Bob had to step into the chief announcer role. One night in late June 1954, Curt came down with a bad cold, and Bob had to call the game by himself—normally, that would not have been such a chore, except this one lasted seventeen innings. And to make matters worse, the Sox lost to the Orioles, 8–7. Veteran sportswriter George C. Carens noted that Bob had to be on the air from about 8:00 p.m. to 1:00 a.m., not only doing play-by-play but reading all the live commercials. Carens was impressed: "It was a tough assignment for the young man," he wrote the next day. "Yet, he gave a clear account of the record-breaking game, and remained enthusiastic throughout the five-hour stretch."[41]

A similar situation recurred in 1957. Curt had suffered from recurring back problems since the early 1940s, and in early April, he was in so much pain that he ended

Bob Murphy began his broadcasting journey with the Mets in the team's first season and stayed for more than 40 years. But his career before 1962 took him to the Boston Red Sox and the Baltimore Orioles, two future World Series opponents for the fellas from Flushing (National Baseball Hall of Fame and Museum, Cooperstown, N.Y.).

up hospitalized. The doctors said he needed prolonged rest; and so, aided by Don Gillis, Bob stepped in and took over the majority of the announcing, as well as taking on some of Curt's other work for WHDH.[42] Recuperation took much longer than expected, however; Curt was able to broadcast one of his regular sports programs from his home, as he rested his sore back; but he was not able to return to doing any play-by-play that season.[43] While fans and sportswriters praised the work that Murphy and Gillis did in his absence, everyone was glad when Curt was once again in the broadcast booth for the next season; that included the sportswriters, whose newspapers had been getting numerous calls every day from fans asking when Curt would be back on the air.[44]

In 1958, Boston sports fans got an additional option for watching the games, as WHDH-TV, channel 5, was now on the air. Where in the past, the games had alternated between channel 4 and channel 7, now all televised Sox games would be on one channel; there was no change to the radio schedule, which remained with WHDH radio. Technology was improving, too: the new TV station would be using four cameras (three had been the previous state-of-the-art), assuring fans a far more intimate look at the game and the players. As for the play-by-play team of Curt Gowdy and Bob Murphy, they both were signed to new contracts. Said one reporter, summing up the general sentiment, "Almost everyone in this area agrees that [they] are the best baseball voices in the announcing profession."[45]

By all accounts, Bob was happy in Boston, and so was his family; he and his wife now had four kids, and although the marriage would later end in divorce, in the late 1950s, things seemed to be going smoothly, both personally and professionally. Along with the other sportscasters at WHDH, he raised funds for charities, hosted sports banquets, and participated in various fan events. He had a good relationship with his bosses, the sponsors liked him (as did the fans), and he enjoyed calling the Red Sox games, even though the team continued to disappoint. But then, in Baltimore, there was an unexpected shake-up on the Orioles play-by-play team after the 1959 season: Ernie Harwell took a new job as chief announcer for the Detroit Tigers. The Orioles management, and the sponsors, were very familiar with Bob's work, and they wanted to hire him as the chief announcer, to work alongside Herb Carneal and Joe Croghan at WBAL Radio. The fact that he was being considered for the job was one of the worst kept secrets at Fenway Park; even his colleagues at WHDH were aware that Bob was in contention for the Baltimore opening.[46] But although it was a good opportunity, Bob was uncertain about leaving a city he loved and a job he enjoyed, with people he cared about. It was Curt Gowdy who encouraged him to make the move, telling him that the chance to become the chief announcer was one he should not pass up.[47]

Bob spent the next two years in Baltimore; he and Herb did the play-by-play on WBAL Radio, which carried the entire Orioles schedule, home and away; and they also did the play-by-play for the 50 games that were televised on WJZ-TV, channel 13. When the games were on TV, Joe Croghan stepped in to help with radio play-by-play. Meanwhile, back in Boston, before Bob had even left, there were rumors that Ted Williams was planning to quit baseball and become an announcer; but veteran sportswriter Hy Hurwitz let everyone know there was no chance of that happening at any time soon.[48] As it turned out, the new addition to the Sox broadcast team was not a ballplayer—he was an experienced sportscaster named Art Gleeson, who had formerly been the sports director for the Mutual radio network.

While Bob couldn't have predicted it, 1960 turned out to be an exciting time for calling Orioles games. During 1959, his last year with the Red Sox, the team ended up fifth in the American League and had a losing record. But the 1960 Orioles surprised everyone. They were a youthful and dynamic group of players, and they kept finding new and interesting ways to win. Sportswriters jokingly referred to the 1960 Orioles as the "Baby Birds,"[49] with good reason. Among the team's star players were pitchers Steve Barber (age 22) and Chuck Estrada (age 22), as well as a 22-year-old shortstop named Ronnie Hanson (who would become the American League Rookie of the Year for 1960). Along with some more experienced players like third-baseman Brooks Robinson (only 23, although he had been with the Orioles off and on for five years), slugging first baseman Jim Gentile, and veteran knuckleball pitcher Hoyt Wilhelm, the Orioles contended well into September; they finished second, with a record of 89–65. And Bob, who had become adept at creating enthusiasm with losing teams, was suddenly with a winner. As he told a local reporter, "Man, why didn't someone tell me it would be this much fun? It's great to be following a team … playing ball like these kids are."[50]

After being the talk of the American League in 1960, Baltimore fans were convinced that the following year, the Orioles would win it all, and I remember hearing about the team's new slogan, "It *can* be done in '61." At Baltimore's Memorial Stadium, fans could get bumper stickers with that slogan. Because I was in Boston, I wasn't able to get one; but when I listened to WBAL late at night, I remember the play-by-play announcers sometimes plugging the promotional items available at the ballpark. The Orioles even had a team song, "We're gonna win, Birds"—I can still remember hearing it on WBAL, and I still remember the lyrics. So, I sent away for a 1961 Orioles yearbook and I was pleased to see that it contained a photo of manager Paul Richards displaying the bumper sticker proudly. It also contained photos of Bob and Herb. Unfortunately, despite all the enthusiasm and team spirit, the Orioles did not win the pennant in 1961; in fact, they finished third. They won more games than the year before, but finished 14 games out of first, much to the disappointment of the fans, and the dismay of whoever thought up that slogan.

Meanwhile, Bob was receiving his own disappointing news. He found out that, through no fault of his own, he was out of a job. When Bob came to Baltimore, it was because the team's major sponsor, the Theo Hamm Brewing Company, approved of his joining the broadcasting team. But in September 1961, a previous sponsor, National Beer, reacquired the rights to the Orioles games and wanted to hire its own announcers. At the end of the Orioles' season, Bob and Herb Carneal were replaced.[51] Herb ended up in Minneapolis–St. Paul, calling the Minnesota Twins games. And Bob was hired in mid–January 1962, to work alongside Lindsey Nelson, calling the games of the expansion New York Mets. Many broadcasters applied, and competition was intense, but once again, Curt Gowdy, who was still broadcasting Red Sox games, gave him a very positive recommendation. So did American League President Joe Cronin.[52] The *Daily Oklahoman* often kept up with where he was and what he was doing, and when the Mets announced that Bob had been selected, sports editor and columnist John Cronley shared the news with readers; Cronley recalled Bob's time on the air calling Oklahoma City Indians games, and commented that the move to New York City proved Bob had definitely "made it big" in radio.[53]

It seems like only yesterday when I was listening to Bob Murphy on the radio, and I can still remember what a talented broadcaster he was and how I looked forward to hearing him calling the games with Curt. The guys who told me back in the 1950s and 1960s that I would never be a sportscaster were right; but they were wrong when they said I'd never get on the air. I spent more than three decades in broadcasting, as a deejay and a music director, and later, as a radio consultant. Those experiences reinforced my admiration for announcers who sound natural and conversational. It really is an art; not everyone can do it. I especially appreciate the radio announcers who can paint a picture with words and make listeners feel like they are there at the event. I don't know why Bob never achieved the national profile that sportscasters like Vin Scully and Mel Allen did. But during his long and impressive career, Bob Murphy's work as a broadcaster touched many lives, and many fans, including me, remember him fondly.

NOTES

1. "Contest Opens for Boys to Broadcast," *Boston Traveler*, June 28, 1957: 22.
2. John Gillooly, "The Voice of the Red Sox a Yawkey Triumph," *Boston Sunday Advertiser*, June 5, 1955: 25.
3. "Analysis of This Year's Red Sox," *Sports Illustrated*, April 14, 1958: 67.
4. Bill Buchanan, "Sullivan Features Jazz," *Boston Daily Record*, August 16, 1960: 26.
5. "Robert Alan Murphy in the U.S., Social Security Applications and Claims Index, 1936–2007," https://search.ancestry.com/cgi-bin/sse.dll?indiv=1&dbid=60901&h=36572367&tid=&pid=&usePUB=true&_phsrc=WRf1&_phstart=successSource (Last accessed November 10, 2019).
6. "Murphy Takes Post to Air Indians Games," (Oklahoma City) *Daily Oklahoman*, February 6, 1949: 4B, 28. Murphy was a shortstop in the Marines.
7. Richard Sandomir, "Bob Murphy, 79, an Original Voice of the Mets," *New York Times*, August 4, 2004: C12.
8. "Tulsa U. FM Outlet," *Broadcasting*, March 3, 1947: 63.
9. "Claim Disputed," *Broadcasting*, November 1, 1948: 12.
10. Richard Sandomir, "Bob Murphy, 79, an Original Voice of the Mets."
11. "T.U. Is on the Air," *The Kendallabrum*, University of Tulsa, 1948, online at http://www.lib.utulsa.edu/yrbks/1940–1949/1948/1948_main.php (Last accessed, November 10, 2019).
12. For example, Curt Smith, *Mercy: A Celebration of Fenway Park's Centennial Told Through Red Sox Radio and TV* (Lincoln, NE, Potomac Books, 2012), 66.
13. "T.U. Is on the Air," *The Kendallabrum*.
14. Richard Sandomir, "Bob Murphy, 79, an Original Voice of the Mets," *New York Times*, August 4, 2004: C12.
15. Rik Espinosa, "The Murph Is His Field of Dreams." *Tulsa World*, January 25, 1998, online at https://www.tulsaworld.com/archive/the-murph-is-his-field-of-dreams/article_3ef74585-3fc6-53b1-9303-7c6f52231869.html.
16. "Murphy Takes Post to Air Indians Games."

17. Rob Parker, "For Murphy, Radio Days Are the Best Days," *Daily News* (New York), August 16, 1987: 66.

18. "News," *Broadcasting*, September 17, 1945: 72.

19. "Murphy Takes Post to Air Indians Games."

20. Laymond Crump, "Veeck and Two Partners Purchase Indians; Humphries Gets Free Hand as New President," *The Daily Oklahoman* (Oklahoma City), December 18, 1948: 30.

21. Bob Burke, *Baseball in Oklahoma City* (Mount Pleasant, SC: Arcadia Press, 2003), 22.

22. For example, "Advertisement for Andy Anderson's Baseball Clinic," *Daily Oklahoman* (Oklahoma City), May 13, 1950: 23.

23. John Cronley, "Once Over Lightly," (Oklahoma City) *Daily Oklahoman*, March 23, 1951: 27.

24. Bus Ham, "All He Wants! Tom Stidham, in First Practice Day at O.U., Says Squad of Four Teams All He Can Handle!," *Daily Oklahoman* (Oklahoma City), September 11, 1937: 8.

25. Bob Hersom, "Talkin' Baseball," *Daily Oklahoman* (Oklahoma City), May 23, 1999: 4B.

26. Joe Looney, "Gowdy in Winning Corner," *Boston Herald*, November 6, 1950: 69.

27. George C. Carens, "Twin Broadcast Tonight of Hose and Tribe Play," *Boston Traveler*, June 26, 1947: 17.

28. "WHDH Brings You Baseball," *Boston Traveler*, April 14, 1947: 30.

29. "Braves Sign to Air 1951 Contests," *Boston Herald*, October 22, 1950: 67.

30. Jack Barry, "How Gowdy's Statistician Figures 'Em," *Boston Globe*, October 24, 1954: 71.

31. "Bob Delaney to Join Hodges on Giants' Radio-Television," *Sporting News*, January 20, 1954: 21.

32. Frank Sargent, "The Lookout," *Lowell Sun* (Massachusetts), January 3, 1954: 22.

33. Bill Buchanan, "Betsy Takes Over for Garry," *Boston Daily Record*, January 28, 1960: 37.

34. Pres Hobson, "Baseball Moves In," *Quincy Patriot-Ledger* (Massachusetts), January 21, 1954: 22.

35. Ed Costello, "Murphy of Tulsa to Assist Gowdy on Radio-TV During Red Sox Games," *Boston Herald*, January 21, 1954: 23.

36. "Knife & Fork League," *Sporting News*, February 24, 1954: 27.

37. Richard Sandomir, "Bob Murphy, 79, an Original Voice of the Mets."

38. Richard Sandomir, "A Happy Recap: Hall-of-Fame Career," *New York Times*, July 29, 1994: B11.

39. Joe Cullinane, "Radio-TV Notes," *Boston Globe*, April 15, 1954: 31.

40. "Temple Israel to Hold Father-Son Breakfast," *Sharon Advocate* (Massachusetts), October 13, 1955: 1.

41. George C. Carens, "Kinder Aids Kid Hurlers," *Boston Traveler*, June 24, 1954: 30.

42. "Voice of Red Sox Listens, but Gowdy to Return Soon," *Boston Traveler*, April 18, 1957: D36.

43. Neil Singelais, "Costanza Has Figures to Prove It," *Boston Globe*, December 21, 1967: 28.

44. John Gillooly, "Gowdy Sees Banner Red Sox Year," *Boston Sunday Advertiser*, February 23, 1958: 26.

45. Ed Costello, "Four Cameras on Sox Games," *Boston Herald*, October 6, 1957: C48.

46. Bill Buchanan, "Betsy Takes Over for Gary," *Boston Daily Record*, January 28, 1980: 37.

47. Curt Smith, *Mercy: A Celebration of Fenway Park's Centennial Told Through Red Sox Radio*, 70.

48. Hy Hurwitz, "Ted Unlikely to Become Broadcaster, Harris says," *Boston Globe* January 5, 1960: 25.

49. "Richards on 'Baby Birds': They Look Like Men to Me," *Salisbury Times* (Maryland), June 20, 1960: 13.

50. Joe Snyder, "Sports Beat," *Hagerstown Morning Herald* (Maryland), June 4, 1960: 14.

51. Stuart Shea, *Calling the Game: Baseball Broadcasting from 1920 to the Present* (Phoenix: Society for American Baseball Research, 2015), 26.

52. Arthur Siegel, "Everything's Rosy Between Holovak, Patriots," *Boston Globe*, January 19, 1962: 16.

53. John Cronley, "Once Over Lightly," *Daily Oklahoman* (Oklahoma), February 4, 1962: E1.

Joan Payson

Beyond Blue and Orange

Leslie Heaphy

In the world of baseball, female owners are a small group, dating back to 1911, when Helene Hathaway Robison Britton took ownership of the St. Louis Cardinals. Britton inherited the ball club after her father and uncle passed away and maintained ownership until 1918.[1] Elsie Lombard Brush and her two daughters held primary ownership of the New York Giants from 1912 to 1918, though they left the day-to-day running to son-in-law Harry Hempstead. Other female owners after Britton include Mrs. James Dunn with the Cleveland Indians in 1922, and Mae Nugent and Laura Baker with the Philadelphia Phillies in 1930. Florence Dreyfuss took over the Pittsburgh Pirates in 1932 after her husband's death; Grace Comiskey held the reins of the Chicago White Sox from 1939 to 1956 and her daughter maintained ownership through the 1959 season.[2] Later owners include Sue Burns with San Francisco, Joan Kroc with San Diego, Louise Nippert and Marge Schott with Cincinnati. The Negro Leagues also had its share of female owners, including Hall of Famer Effa Manley, Olivia Taylor, Hilda Bolden Shorter, Henryene Green, and Minnie Forbes.[3]

Another name to add to this group is Joan Whitney Payson, owner and president of the New York Mets from 1962 to 1975. Payson is unique in this group because she did not inherit her shares of the Mets but bought the team outright with her own money. Payson is remembered as the lovable, grandmotherly owner of the expansion Mets but she was so much more than that. Her life was filled with baseball, boxing, horses, theater, art and charitable causes. On and off the diamond, Payson lived a full and exciting life, but never let anyone forget her love for the New York Mets.

Joan Payson developed her love for baseball and everything else in her life at an early age. Her family, especially her mother, nurtured her interests

41

and gave her the resources to indulge those loves. Payson was born on February 5, 1903, in New York. Her father, Payne Whitney, came from a family of politicians and businessmen. His father, William, worked as Assistant Secretary of the Navy under President Grover Cleveland and made his money owning a streetcar line. Payne inherited his fortune from his uncle, Colonel Oliver Payne, who had no children of his own.

Joan's mother, Helen Hay Whitney, also came from a prominent family of politicians. Helen's father, John Hay, was assistant private secretary to President Abraham Lincoln as well as Secretary of State to Presidents McKinley and Roosevelt. Her mother, Clara, inherited her fortune from her grandfather, Amasa Stone, a Cleveland railroad tycoon. Payne built a new home for his bride at Greentree Estate, one of many places where she spent time growing up. Besides money and social standing, Payson gained a deep love of sports and art from her parents, who were athletically inclined, though she was not. Payne crewed at Yale, as did his father before him, and owned stables and breeding operations that were passed on to Joan and her brother, Jock. Joan went with her father to boxing matches and New York Giants games with her mother, who also loved horses and took over Greentree Stables after Payne died in 1927. The press came to refer to her as "Grand Lady of the Track" with her horses winning the Kentucky Derby and the Belmont Stakes, in addition to the Grand National Steeplechase title four times in the 1920s and 1930s.[4] "Mother used to take me to the ball park all the time," Joan remembered. "We would even go to Brooklyn when the Giants were playing there. She was the greatest fan around. Once she wanted to vote for Joe DiMaggio in a box-top contest. I didn't know about it, but she told the cook to feed our children Wheaties and save the box tops for her."[5] In 1962, Payson also indicated, "I don't remember when I first saw the Giants play. My mother used to take me to the Polo Grounds when I was a little girl, and I almost feel as if I'd grown up there. Mother, of course, adored the game. One of my earliest memories is of watching her playing baseball at Palm Beach in the old days."[6]

Growing up surrounded by wealth, privilege, and status gave Joan the opportunity to see Broadway shows, travel throughout Europe, and sit in on board meetings at art museums and hospitals. At her sixteenth birthday party, Helen gave her daughter a Degas painting called *Children and Ponies in a Park*, painted in 1868. It was the first painting for the future Mets owner and art philanthropist, beginning a life-long passion for collecting. There was also a bit of sibling rivalry because Jock also became a collector.[7]

The Whitneys' wealth gave their daughter a high-level education—an all-girls school Miss Chapin's followed by a year at Barnard and business classes at Brown.

She also traveled to The Breakers in Rhode Island during the summer, visiting her aunt Gertrude Vanderbilt Whitney. Given the family's social position, it is no surprise that two events around her nineteenth birthday—a costume ball and a debutante ball—took place at The Plaza. Two years later, the Whitneys were announcing their daughter's engagement to Charles Shipman Payson, who came from a long line of politicians and clergymen, dating all the way back to a signer of the Constitution.

Charles graduated from Yale where he boxed and crewed. After their society wedding at Christ Episcopal Church, the couple continued to attend boxing matches, horse races, baseball games and began their family—five children, two boys and three girls. They were given 110-acres of land at Greentree after their 1924 wedding; Charles contracted with architect William Delano to build his new bride a home that was completed in 1928. It served as both a showpiece and a home.[8] Boxing continued to be a huge part of Joan's life: "I remember I was pregnant at the first Dempsey-Tunney fight in Philadelphia," Mrs. Payson explained in a 1962 interview for *Sports Illustrated*. "In fact, I always seemed to be pregnant at championship fights. But I particularly remember it at the Philadelphia fight, because this man pushed me as we were leaving in the rain, and I yelled, 'Don't you dare push me, I'm pregnant.'"[9]

Payson took her love of baseball to a new level in 1950, when she bought a single share of stock in the New York Giants. During the next 10 years, M. Donald Grant, her stockbroker, bought up 10 percent of the team in her name. She tried to buy the Giants from Horace Stoneham when he decided to move the club to the West Coast in 1957, but he refused and so she had to fly out to San Francisco to watch her beloved Giants. The void was filled when she got involved in the efforts to bring baseball back to New York by agreeing to fund a New York club in the new Continental League (CL) led by William Shea and Branch Rickey. Major League Baseball prevented the CL from being a reality, but acknowledged they needed a National League team in New York. So, the Mets were formed; the other three expansion teams were the Los Angeles Angels, Houston Colt .45s (later Astros), and a second Washington Senators club because the first one had moved to Minnesota after the 1960 season and became the Twins.

Payson was awarded the New York franchise along with her fellow investors M. Donald Grant, G. Herbert Walker, Jr., Pete Davis, and Franklin Trask. She had to sell her stock in the Giants to be the Mets owner and pay a $1,000,000 franchise fee. She said that she always wanted to own a baseball team and hated having no National League club in New York. Many names were suggested. Payson wanted to call them the Meadowlarks, but the Metropolitans name won out.[10]

On May 8, 1961, the announcement for New York's new team was made. Payson served as primary owner until her death on October 4, 1975, but she was not a silent partner. Though she did not interfere with the games, Payson attended meetings and made the day-to-day business decisions involved in running an MLB team, including bringing her favorite player, Willie Mays, back to New York in 1972. Mays had been with the Giants for more than 20 years when Payson finally got her wish. She had reportedly tried to buy Mays' contract years before but Stoneham would not sell. The Mets gave the Giants $50,000 and minor-league pitcher Charlie Williams.

Mays was 41 when the trade took place and while he had a good début with the Mets, hitting his 647th career home run, his career was winding down. Payson brought Mays to New York as part of her nostalgia for the past as the Giants had been her childhood team. Mays retired in 1973 in the city where he started, thanks to Payson's efforts. She also worked hard to bring in Casey Stengel as the team's original manager because of his success with the Yankees. Another player she wanted on the 1962 team had ties to the Giants, pitcher Johnny Antonelli. She pushed for Cincinnati's Elio Chacón to be added to the roster after seeing him play the year before.[11]

From day one the press wanted to interview the new woman owner, but Payson was not fond of interviews and tried to stay out of the limelight as much as she could. The press caught many pictures of her sitting behind the dugout watching her beloved Mets, interacting with the children in the stands and always wearing her Met colors, blue and orange. When she had to miss a game because of traveling, she sent her chauffeur to watch and report to her on the progress, so she never missed a result. She carried a portable radio on her trips to the racetrack and even had one in her purse at social gatherings so she could stay on top of what her Mets were doing. During the first season, Payson spent the summer in Greece but kept abreast of the team by telegram. She celebrated when the club did well and suffered with the players when they struggled.[12]

To her players, Mrs. Payson was the friendly mom/grandmother so many of them missed having around. She took care of them, watching out for them all the time. Gifts came on special occasions. After Ron Hunt's wife, Tracy, gave birth to a baby girl, the Mets owner sent a sterling silver Tiffany set. She also gave players gifts for their achievements on the field—flowers, tickets, and other presents for a game winning hit, a home run, or a win. She hosted parties and trips for the ball club, wearing her affiliation for the Mets proudly. Her allegiance could be seen on her hats, her car license plate, and even in the way she decorated her homes. She gave autographed memorabilia to friends and staff. Chris Hobbs, who worked at Greentree like his father before him, remembered receiving a special gift from Mrs. Payson when he was a boy—a ball signed by the team.[13]

Mets fans loved that she would sit in the stands with them and even sign autographs. For the new expansion team, she was a breath of fresh air and what was needed to help everyone love the Mets, even when they were in the basement. No one was more excited when the Mets became World Series champions in 1969; though she also remembered the 1962 players and how hard that season had been for those young men. Her joy was rewarded with another run at the ultimate title in 1973, though they came up short of winning the World Series, losing to the Oakland A's in seven games.

Just as passionate about art, Payson built a collection known among her peers as eclectic and wide-ranging in its scope. For example, she bought Van Gogh's *Irises* in 1947 for $84,000 from a private dealer—Sotheby's sold it in 1987 for $53.9 million. In 1951, she bought *Woman in the Garden of Monsieur Forest* by Henri Toulouse-Lautrec for $42,000, with no intention of selling it. She bought *Au Lapin Agile* in 1952 simply because it reminded her of her son, Daniel, who was killed during the Battle of the Bulge in World War II. She hung the painting outside the library so she would have a daily reminder of her son. Her collection included paintings by Cézanne, Manet, and Gauguin, but she did not buy paintings to resell and make a profit. "She had her own marvellous [sic] taste," described a 2007 profile. "Dealers would call her up and say they had something interesting. She would see it, and if she liked it she bought it, if she didn't, she didn't. There was nobody around telling her she had to have a well-rounded collection."[14]

Payson's massive collection prompted a question familiar to collectors: What will happen to it after her death? She bequeathed parts of her collection to each of her children and her husband. Her paintings found several other homes, beginning with 23 paintings given to the Metropolitan Museum of Art.[15]

Maine institutions have benefited from the Payson family's generosity. It was a place of fondness due to her many visits while she was growing up.[16] She wanted others to enjoy what she had enjoyed for so long and John continued her legacy. Beneficiaries of Payson's art collection have included Maine institutions Westbrook College (where a gallery bears her name), Colby College, and the Portland Museum. The collection includes paintings by Marc Chagall, Gustave Courbet, Joshua Reynolds and Edgar Degas. Payson also donated an American Chippendale table to the Map Room at the White House after being asked to serve on a committee to help redo the decorating.

The beauty of her collection was also revealed in the interest shown when pieces of her collection were sold. For example, a piece by Paul Gauguin, *Te Poipoi* (*The Morning*), sold for nearly $40 million.[17]

Art and baseball were true loves for Payson, but so was Greentree Stables (Manhasset, Long Island) and a stud farm (1,000 acres in Lexington, Kentucky), which she and her brother, Jock, inherited from her parents. She became a passionate racing fan just as her mother had been. After her mother took over running Greentree, Jolly Roger won the Grand National Steeplechase and their filly Glade won two races. The Kentucky Derby title was claimed in 1931 and 1942 with winners Twenty Grand and Shut Out. Joan liked to name her horses after baseball terms such as Hall of Fame, One-Hitter, and the Gashouse Gang referred to their retired horses. Devil Diver was the real star, however, with 47 races and 22 wins, and a record-setting three consecutive runnings of the Metropolitan Handicap in the 1940s. He earned over $200,000 for Greentree and was inducted into the National Horseracing Hall of Fame in 1980.[18]

While not a rider herself, Payson loved to go to the racetrack and appreciated the beauty of the horses and the talent of those who rode. At a horse auction in 1938, Payson paid $7,000 for a colt sired by Stimulus, paying the third highest price for any colt behind her brother and one other buyer.[19] Along with her friend Mrs. Thomas I. Laughlin, Payson bought two colts for a total cost of $8,000. With that investment, they opened Manhasset Stables so they could race their own horses. Their most successful horse, Thingumabob, won his only race in 1938 before he had an accident and broke his leg. Later, Payson and her brother combined their interests with their mother's stable to expand the Greentree breeding program and enterprise.[20]

Her horses earned more than $6 million between 1946 and 1960, led by Tom Foolery who went undefeated in 1953 and Devil Diver. Capot won the Preakness and Belmont Stakes in 1949. Their horses led all money winners in 1951 and in 1968, the winning continued when Stage Door Johnny won the Belmont Stakes. All told, Greentree claimed 91 stakes winners under the Payson name.[21]

"In partnership with her brother, Joan Whitney operated the highly successful Greentree stable, winning numerous important Graded stakes races including the Kentucky Derby twice, the Preakness Stakes once, and the Belmont Stakes four times. The Paysons displayed some of their legendary art collection in the 50-room mansion as well as the Whitney family estate in Manhasset, New York." She also saw her love of boxing and horseracing mix a bit when heavyweight boxer Abe Simon trained at Greentree because Joan's brother was part owner of Simon's contract, along with boxer Gene Tunney.

After art, boxing, and horse racing, Payson also had an interest in theater and philanthropic causes. Some of her causes she inherited from her mother and others were her own interests or those she shared with her brother. Jock loved a good investment and movies proved to be lucrative. Their most famous movies include *A Streetcar Named Desire* and *Gone with the Wind*. Jock was Chairman of the Board for Selznick International Pictures and they purchased the film rights for *Gone with the Wind* for $50,000. When Selznick International liquidated its assets in 1942, Jock and Joan sold their rights to *Gone with the Wind* to MGM; their profit was more than 400 percent. They also invested in *Kind Lady*, *Rebecca*, and *A Star Is Born*. Ties to the country's

Joan Payson was an owner of the Mets, but her devotion to the team went beyond the bottom line. She adored her team, often talking with players, coaches, and managers from her front-row seat at Shea Stadium. A member of New York's society set, Payson (née Whitney) had a well-earned reputation in the city's art circles as a keen-eyed collector and generous donor (National Baseball Hall of Fame and Museum, Cooperstown, N.Y.).

cultural power base were on display when Payson hosted a dinner party for her brother before he left for London as ambassador. CBS President William Paley, Senator Jacob Javits, and publisher Samuel I. Newhouse were on the guest list, a "Who's Who" of the racing world, theater, and New York City hospital personnel.[22]

Mrs. Payson's interest in helping others was always a part of her life. In 1928, she opened Young Books, a children's bookstore, with her friend, Mrs. Richard Kimball. It was a success in providing books to neighborhood children on the Upper East Side. The store survived the Great Depression by adding detective novels to encourage male patrons to come to the store. After World War II began, the store merged with the Wakefield Store but Payson remained the owner, providing a resource for their New York neighborhood. Her bookstore and movie ventures added to her already substantial wealth, which made it possible for her to donate $50,000 to the Emergency Unemployment Relief Committee during the Great Depression. To honor her mother in 1943, she endowed the Helen Hay Whitney Foundation created for medical research. Today, the foundation awards 20 fellowships each year. Payson later donated land to North Shore University Hospital, where she became a director, to improve the services it was able to offer the local community. The hospital's Payson Wharton Legacy Society is named after Payson and Irving Wharton. Anyone who gives a legacy gift to the hospital becomes a member of the society. She served as a director of the New York Hospital, and St. Mary's Hospital in West Palm Beach, Florida. She was also a trustee for the United Hospital Fund and the Lighthouse for the Blind.

Hofstra College awarded her an honorary degree for her support of charities. Continuing the tradition of using her fortune to help others, Payson financed the Children's World Center at the New York World's Fair and supported the Country Art Gallery (Long Island) to help new, up-and-coming painters. Martha and Ralph Cahoon were examples of such artists. Payson convinced them to let her show a couple of their paintings at the Country Art Gallery and when they sold right away, the Cahoons agreed to hold a show there in 1954. This success led them to show their folk art all over the country.[23]

Payson and her husband created a charitable foundation, have their names on the library at Pepperdine University where their son attended school; a donation to Yale resulted in the gymnasium being named after Payne Whitney. There is a two-year art fellowship at Yale called the Cullman-Payson Fellowship. Eligible museum educators work at Yale and the Museum of Modern Art in New York, where Payson had served on the Board of Directors.

She was also a founding partner in the investment firm Payson and Trask. In 1976, a year after her death, New York Presbyterian Hospital opened The Joan Whitney Payson Rehabilitation Pavilion.[24] These honors and recognitions represent only a few ventures and causes supported by the Paysons.

Her son, John, indicated that part of the proceeds from the sale of Vincent Van Gogh's 1889 *Irises* would be donated to the Joan Whitney and Charles Shipman Payson Charitable Foundation in honor of his parents "to support the arts in Maine." It sold at auction for nearly $54 million in 1987.[25] John used the money to fund a $6 million endowment for Westbrook College, home to the Joan Whitney Payson Gallery, which got an additional $2 million.[26]

Payson's daughter, Lorinda de Roulet, followed her brother's lead, putting *Au Lapin Agile* up for sale in 1989. The expected sale price of over $40 million would be used to create the Patrina Foundation, which focuses on education for girls and young women. The Payson estate at Greentree was divided after Payson's death and today is run by the Greentree Foundation, used for international justice and human rights conferences associated with the United Nations.[27]

People's interest in Payson extended to every part of her life. Her fame as the owner of the lovable Mets, her charity work, and her art collections made people want to know more about her. Numerous stories were written about her homes, her private collections, her European travels, and which players were her favorites. Her homes were objects of curiosity, too. For example, one reporter entitled his article about the family homes "White House Is Nice, but It's No Greentree." It was a family favorite while they also spent time on their plantation in Georgia and their summer home on Fisher's Island. Their home in Manhasset had 50 rooms sitting on just over 100 acres.

For her foreign travel, Payson liked to stay at their family home in Surrey, England, but where she felt most at home was their apartment in Manhattan, near where she grew up. They also owned their own Pullman car which led to having seven Pullman uniforms in their collection as well. In her various homes, alongside all her Mets memorabilia, were a variety of miniatures, figurines, and snuff boxes. She also collected lots of historical pieces highlighted by a handwritten copy of Lincoln's final public speech delivered on April 11, 1865. Lincoln asked for clemency for the south as the war was ending.[28]

Payson's popularity and the high esteem people held her in showed in the many awards she received. In 1963, the People to People Sports Commission in New York City honored her for her work in horse racing and baseball. The monetary award she received was given to help international sports growth and to provide equipment to less developed parts of the world. The honor made her the first woman to be so recognized.

In the same year, Payson was named "Sportswoman of the Year" by the Nassau Chapter of the Association for the Help of Retarded Children. The New York Mets' new minor league facility in St. Petersburg was dedicated as the "Joan Payson Baseball and Recreation Center," honoring her commitment to the Mets, making it the only stadium named for a woman at the time.[29] The New York chapter of the B.B.W.A.A. gives an annual award in her honor to a player recognized for their community service work.

Joan Whitney Payson owned a baseball team which made her unique in the baseball world, but that was only a small part of who she was. Payson found meaning in life through art, working with charitable causes, collecting and investing, raising her children, and shepherding her fortune. She gave back to the community every chance she had and while she was a private person, Payson also recognized that her status gave her opportunities many others did not have. Payson's life was full and exciting, and her ownership of the New York Mets added to her everyday joys and made her a darling of the press. Upon her death, a Met staff member called her the "ultimate fan." A version of "Take Me Out to the Ballgame" was played at her funeral. Her legacy lives on with the Mets as a member of their Hall of Fame; Payson was elected in 1981 along with manager Casey Stengel. As another researcher stated, "yet no owner was quite as beloved as Mrs. Payson, who was the old grande dame of the organization and of baseball."[30]

NOTES

1. Joan M. Thomas, "Helene Britton," Society for American Baseball Research, Baseball Biography Project, accessed November 14, 2019, https://sabr.org/bioproj/person/ecd910f9. "The will left by Stanley Robison revealed that he had bequeathed controlling interest in the St. Louis Cardinals to his niece, Helene Robison Britton. The remaining shares went to Helene's mother, the widow of former club co-owner Frank DeHaas Robison."

2. For background on the family conflict regarding the Comiskey family's ownership, see Robert Creamer, "The Comiskey Affair," Sports Illustrated, February 24, 1958, 44–46.

3. "Female Baseball Owners," Baseball Reference, accessed November 14, 2019, https://www.baseball-reference.com/bullpen/Category:Female_Owners.

4. Becky Johnston, "The Whitney Handicap: A Look at a Treasured American Family," BloodHorse, accessed November 13, 2019, http://cs.bloodhorse.com/blogs/racinghub/archive/2008/07/25/the-whitney-handicap-a-look-at-a-treasured-american-family.aspx, July 25, 2008; "Mrs. Payne Whitney Dies in Hospital, 68," New York Times, September 25, 1944: 17; Greentree Stud and Stable Records, Yale University Archives, Finding Aid, accessed November 13, 2019, https://archives.yale.edu/repositories/12/resources/4887.

5. Joseph Durso, "Joan Whitney Payson, 72, Mets Owner, Dies," New York Times, October 5, 1975: 63. See David Dempsey, "Says Mrs. Payson of the Mets, 'You can't lose them all,'" New York Times Magazine, June 23, 1968: 28–33.

6. Alfred Wright, "Happy Blend of Sport and Cash," Sports Illustrated, May 14, 1962, 84.

7. Colin W. Sargent, "Good Eye," Portland Monthly, accessed November 14, 2019, https://www.portlandmonthly.com/portmag/2010/04/good-eye/, May 2010.

8. Joan M. Thomas, "Joan Payson," Society for American Baseball Research, Baseball Biography Project, accessed November 14, 2019, https://sabr.org/bioproj/person/88dc3fa9; Rita Reif, "Auctions: The Paysons' Home on View," New York Times, April 27, 1984: C18.

9. Wright, "Happy Blend of Sport and Cash," 85.

10. Red Smith, "Saga of the Lady and the Star," New York Times, 10 May 1972: 57; Matthew Silverman, New York Mets: The Complete Illustrated History (Minneapolis: MVP Books, 2001), 13; Press reports vary on Payson's investment. A 1969 Associated Press article reported the figure as $5 million. "Publicity Shy Joan Payson in a Tizzy," Associated Press, Hutchinson News (Kansas), October 10, 1969: 9. Dempsey's New York Times Magazine profile mentioned a "$3 million stake."

11. Wright, "Happy Blend of Sport and Cash," 92; Larry Granillo, "Wezen-Ball: The Willie Mays Trade," Baseball Prospectus, accessed November 14, 2019, https://www.baseballprospectus.com/news/article/17787/wezen-ball-the-willie-mays-trade/.

12. Joe King, "Clouting 'Em … with Joe King: A Sentimental Journey—Back to the Polo Grounds," Sporting News, April 18, 1962, 33.

13. Jennifer Fauci, "Manhasset's Historical Gem," Manhasset Press, accessed November 13, 2019, https://manhassetpress.com/manhassets-historical-gem/, May 1, 2019.

14. Peter Aspden, "Fortune from a Family's Wall," Financial Times, accessed November 14, 2019, https://www.ft.com/content/8d47e124–88fa-11dc-84c9–0000779fd2ac, November 2, 2007.

15. Sargent, "Good Eye," Portland Monthly.

16. Ibid.

17. Carol Vogel, "A Disappointing Night for Painting Sales at Sotheby's," New York Times, November 8, 2007: B4.

18. Becky Johnston, "The Whitney Handicap: a look at a treasured American family"; Thoroughbred Champions: Top 100 Racehorses of the 20th Century (Lexington, KY: Blood Horse Publications, 1999), 158–159.

19. "Whitney Pays $14,000," August 5, 1938, New York Times: 14.

20. Wright, "Happy Blend of Sport and Cash," *Sports Illustrated*, May 14, 1962, 84, 86, 88.

21. "John Hay Whitney dies; one of nation's wealthiest," Associated Press, *New York Times*, February 9, 1982: D7; Natalie Voss, "Kentucky Farm Time Capsule: Greentree Stud," Paulick Report, accessed November 14, 2019, https://www.paulickreport.com/news/ray-s-paddock/kentucky-farm-time-capsule-greentree-stud/, January 29, 2018, https://www.paulick report.com/news; "Belmont Stakes Winner from Mrs. Payson's Stable," *Sporting News*, June 15, 1968, 21.

22. "Whitney Is Guest at Dinner on L.I.," *New York Times*, January 12, 1957: 12.

23. Ralph and Martha Cahoon—Cape Cod Folk Artists, Cahoon Museum of American Art, accessed November 14, 2019, https://cahoonmuseum.org/ralph-and-martha-cahoon/.

24. "Our History: New York–Presbyterian/Weill Cornell," New York–Presbyterian Hospital, accessed November 14, 2019, https://www.nyp.org/rehabmed/services/our-history-newyork-presbyterian-weill-cornell.

25. "Dealer Selling Van Gogh to Support Arts in Maine," *South Florida Sun-Sentinel*, accessed November 14, 2019, https://www.sun-sentinel.com/news/fl-xpm-1987-09-05-8703 110967-story.html#, September 5, 1987; Paula Span and Judd Tully, "$53.9 Million for Van Gogh," *Washington Post*, November 12, 1987: B1.

26. Chris O'Malley, "Bloomsday," *Chicago Tribune*, December 16, 1987: A26.

27. Suzanne Muchnic, "Rose-Period Picasso Heads for Auction Block," *Los Angeles Times*, September 8, 1989: E22.

28. Reif, "Auctions: The Paysons' Home on View"; Fauci, "Manhasset's Historical Gem."

29. Fred Lieb, "Mets Name St. Petersburg Complex for Mrs. Payson," *Sporting News*, February 24, 1968, 37; Jack Lang, "St. Pete Unveils Mets' Complex," *Sporting News*, March 23, 1968, 23.

30. Taryn Cooper, "The Thrill of Victory, the Agony of the Mets: Joan Whitney Payson," Studious Metsimus, accessed November 13, 2019, www.studiousmetsimus.blogspot.com/2017/02/, February 20, 2017. A note at the end of Cooper's piece explains that "The Thrill of Victory, the Agony of the Mets" is a 13-part series on "Mets players and personnel who experienced the best of times and the worst of times with the team."

Swagger Comes to Town

The Evolution of Attitude
at Shea Stadium in the 1980s

PAUL HENSLER

In 1977, the difference between the New York Mets and the New York Yankees could not have been starker. Rebounding from the Cincinnati Reds sweeping them in the 1976 World Series, the Yankees—thanks to the open checkbook of owner George Steinbrenner and the shrewd personnel moves of general managers Gabe Paul, Cedric Tallis, and Gene Michael—headed to the World Series, where they beat the Los Angeles Dodgers. A rematch in 1978 resulted in another championship for the Yankees.

The Mets began a dreadful run, finishing in the basement five seasons between 1977 and 1983; they rose to fifth place twice in this period. Shea Stadium had a saving grace for those brave enough to withstand the mediocre play—it had real grass rather than artificial turf, which was the playing surface dominating the new breed of circular, multipurpose stadiums.

Life as New York's second-class baseball citizens was difficult for the Mets in the wake of the infamous "Midnight Massacre," which saw slugger Dave Kingman and ace hurler Tom Seaver traded on June 15, 1977, in the wake of contract disputes. But the hiring of former Baltimore Orioles executive Frank Cashen in the early 1980 began a new era. Cashen approached the tedious process of assembling the pieces of a respectable club that would ignite the same championship spirit of the late 1960s, when the Mets emerged from the depths of the National League standings to become World Series champions in 1969. When Cashen handed the managerial reins in 1984 to Davey Johnson, then a rookie skipper, the reversal of fortune for the Mets was unmistakable. Seasons of 87 or more wins led to first- and second-place finishes for the remainder of the decade. Consequently, attendance surged.

Cashen's trades for players from other teams combined with development of talent at the minor-league level, resulting in a success model studied by prospective and present general managers. To a degree, the success excused the players' conduct, which, at times, was less than role-model quality off the field, though reflective of the evolution of America's societal attitudes in the 1980s. This evolution came, as it often does, at the hands of tastemakers in popular culture.

The Post-Massacre Nadir

When Jimmy Carter won the presidency in 1976, America was wracked by the fallout from the recently ended conflict in Vietnam and bordered on recession. Inflation and interest rates were high; oil and gasoline prices continued to rise. Carter, the former governor of Georgia when he won the Democratic nomination, benefited from the backlash against Richard Nixon's resignation and the Watergate scandal. But the narrow win against Gerald Ford hardly provided him with a mandate. Plus, the nation endured 444 days of the Iran hostage crisis, which began with an attack on the U.S. embassy in Tehran and more than 50 Americans taken hostage.

The unsettled mood in the country born of these trying times impressed many citizens that Carter, though possessed of a pleasant personality and firmly held religious convictions, was nonetheless politically ill-equipped to effectively handle problems of broad foreign and domestic scope. When Ronald Reagan swept into office in 1981, he used his first term to "reviv[e] national confidence at a time when there was a great need for inspiration."[1]

The New York Mets in this span from the late 1970s to the early 1980s reflected the Carter administration in their own way: trying hard, yet ineffectual. The faltering Mets front office and woes on the field drew the attention of longtime super-fan Karl Ehrhardt, who took a swipe at the club's besieged ownership when he hoisted aloft from his third-base box seat one of his famous placards: WELCOME TO GRANT'S TOMB. The Mets Chairman of the Board, M. Donald Grant, became demonized for his handling of the Seaver imbroglio; in 1978, he was replaced by Lorinda de Roulet, daughter of former Mets owner Joan Payson.

Despite the infusion of players received in the Kingman and Seaver trades—including 1976 National League Rookie of the Year co-winner Pat Zachry—the Mets produced results just below the 100-loss mark, or in the case of the strike-shortened 1981 season, a record of 41–62. The club, now under the ownership of Doubleday & Company and led by new president Fred Wilpon, pinned its hopes on a local kid made good, Lee Mazzilli, once heralded by the *New York Times* to be "emerging as a symbol of [the] Mets' new winning mood"[2] and who also drew comparisons to Reggie Jackson as the Shea Stadium version of "the straw that stirs the drink."[3]

Brooklyn-born and cutting a handsome figure, Mazzilli apprenticed for three seasons in the minor leagues after being selected by the Mets in the first round of the June 1973 amateur draft. He made the big club for keeps with a late-season call-up in 1976. Patrolling center field and earning selection to the 1979 National League All-Star squad, Mazzilli's star power and box-office appeal dimmed greatly when he batted .228 in 1981. The Mets traded him to the Texas Rangers on the brink of Opening Day in 1982. Phil Pepe labeled the ex–Met "the innocent victim of the Great Met Hype, the creation of the Madison Avenue think tank."[4]

Luring fans back to Shea Stadium was a priority, just as it was when the Doubleday/Wilpon consortium bought the Mets. An advertising company, Della Famina, Travisano, and Partners, recast the Mets' image in 1980, with the slogan "The Magic Is Back!" But exactly what that magic was remained a mystery. Reinvention was apparent in the 1980 Mets Media Guide and Year-book—"The New NEW YORK Mets ... the People's Team." These efforts did little to persuade fans.

The Mets roster was at a crossroads. Dave Kingman, Mike Jorgensen, and Rusty Staub were back at Shea for their second tours of duty, plus slugger George Foster came in a trade from Cincinnati. But Foster's lackluster 1982 offensive production (.247, 13 home runs, 70 RBI) did little to raise the team's fortunes. The former Red was further burdened by the contract lavished on him by the Mets to prevent him from exercising his free-agent privileges—his five-year, $10 million deal became an extravagance that yielded a very poor return on investment. Cashen had installed former Baltimore Orioles pitching coach George Bamberger as the new manager, replacing Joe Torre, but the player and managerial adjustments did nothing to improve the Mets' lot.

The 1983 season would prove to be the endpoint for the decade-long doldrums at Shea Stadium. Bamberger resigned for health reasons in early June and was replaced by third-base coach Frank Howard, the former manager of the San Diego Padres, whose single season out west produced a pathetic winning percentage of .373 in 1981. Now at the helm of the Mets, Howard improved only to .448 as they compiled a 52–64 record under him. Cashen was nothing if not a survivor—with nearly four years of service to the Mets and a blot of mostly sixth-place finishes on his Met résumé, Cashen had weathered the change of team ownership but experienced no good luck in attempting to reverse the club's fortune. Not yet, anyway.

Though the patience of Mets fans was tested in the decade since the team's last World Series appearance in 1973—a seven-game contest against the Oakland Athletics—Cashen's seeds of talent in the farm system promised a bountiful, future harvest. When Davey Johnson came to the Mets, he had valuable experience on a dominant ball club helping to anchor the Baltimore infield during its heyday of the late 1960s and early 1970s. He also had a connection to Mets lore—Johnson was the last batter in the 1969 World Series, flying out to Cleon Jones. It ended the miraculous season for the ball club seven seasons removed from its birth.

But Johnson was untested as a big-league skipper. He had stints managing a team in the short-lived Triple-A Inter-American League (1979) and a pair of Mets minor-league clubs—Double-A Jackson Mets (1981) and Triple-A Tidewater Tides (1983), barely breaking the .500 mark with both squads. With the parent Mets struggling and their field leadership now in the hands of a manager with barely a winning record on the farm, there was little reason for a heightened anticipation of any kind of breakthrough.

Beset by a lack of stability in many corners of the organization, the Mets' brass, and Cashen in particular, had little to lose by entrusting Johnson with the team's reins. But the arrival of new players whom Johnson had coached in Jackson and Tidewater as well as the dichotomous approach Johnson employed when handling his players—tough on the playing field but lax away from it—soon proved to be a winning formula that contributed to the club's new status as contenders in the National League East.

Evolving Attitude and Trends of Society

The Mets' poor track record of late entitled them to no degree of braggadocio whatsoever, but as the contagion of winning spread among the players beginning in 1984, a change in attitude among the uniformed personnel became evident. That spirit would turn heads and make people take notice, but not necessarily in the positive sense. In the 1980s, a popular-culture shift was taking place, and heroes no longer wore white hats nor did they pretend to. J.R. Ewing on *Dallas* was the oil baron everybody loved to hate but secretly envied for his ruthless attention to his family's oil business. Gordon Gekko embodied the movers and shakers of the financial system in *Wall Street* when he exclaimed, with pride, "Greed is good."

Being created at this time was a new culture of young adults whose wealth and confidence in their ability to improve their lot led to a craving for consumer goods previously unattainable or products connoting status and privilege. As the word *upscale* assumed its place in the American lexicon, Izod shirts, Perrier bottled water, big-screen televisions, VCRs, and BMW sports cars were among the treasures that fitted well with the lifestyle now sought by young, urban professionals, who were termed *yuppies*. The year 1984 was even proclaimed to be the "Year of the Yuppie" by *Newsweek*. Yuppies dealing with personal and professional crises found prime-time avatars dealing with angst on *thirtysomething* and *L.A. Law*.

Débuting in 1981, the new cable channel Music Television, more popularly known as MTV, showcased music videos that accompanied the release of many new pop and rock songs and further allowed musicians, previously confined to the recording studio and concert venues, to become quasi-actors and facilitate their self-promotional aims, whether through the creation of more interest in their music or the outrageous behavior that was exhibited by some musician-actors. Madonna, through the platform of MTV, celebrated the unabashed lust for the better things in life with the release of her 1985 pop standard "Material Girl" and the music video, which paid homage to Marilyn Monroe's rendition of "Diamonds Are a Girl's Best Friend" in *Gentlemen Prefer Blondes*. Indeed, the culture of this era seemed to inspire a competition among other likeminded twenty-somethings for acquiring more and more luxury goods regardless of their need for such items.

Also present from the late 1970s and through the 1980s were programs on major television networks "that portrayed the often tortured lives of the rich and powerful," with *Dallas*, *Dynasty*, and *Knots Landing* receiving the most notoriety.[5] People of wealth and means were not exempt from the travails of life, even if their troubles could be known by few among the *hoi polloi*. Meanwhile, in 1984, the London-born entertainment reporter Robin Leach launched the syndicated series, *Lifestyles of the Rich and Famous*, that profiled the extreme luxury and comforts enjoyed by celebrities.

Boastfulness was in vogue.

And so it was with the Mets. Known across baseball for their swagger, which seemed to be an indicator of the zeitgeist, they mirrored the popular culture. But the Mets were not alone in the world of sports. The Oakland (and Los Angeles) Raiders of the National Football League had the mantra "Just win, baby!"—it reflected the philosophy of owner Al Davis, who winked and nodded at poor manners displayed by some team members after hours. Delinquency could be tolerated as long as wins were racked up.

By the close of 1986, when the New York Mets prevailed in a stunning World Series over the Boston Red Sox, the newly crowned champions had earned the right not only to brandish their swagger, but also, because of the youth and depth of its roster, to feel that they would be displaying that bravado for years to come. By simple trophy count, this was only the Mets' second Fall Classic title, a far cry from the total of their Bronx rivals, who counted 22 world titles to that point in time.

But there's a difference between attitude and action. One can have swagger but not disregard decorum in public places. Johnson endorsed the former while ignoring, or not acting on, the latter. In a social context, an argument can be made that the manner in which the Mets conducted themselves was a reflection of the times—the 1980s was a decade of success, vigor, and wealth. Materialism, increased income, and the prestige of higher social status took the American dream to a new level, and from the economic swoon of the late 1970s emerged a decade imbued with a class superiority complex. The success of the Mets by 1986 was also infected by that same complex.

The Coalescing of a Championship Team That Came to Be Hated

During this revival of excellence came two budding superstars courtesy of Cashen's sage drafting—outfielder Darryl Strawberry, the 1983 National League Rookie of the Year, and pitcher Dwight Gooden, who would capture that same honor in 1984. Additionally, Cashen's acquisitions became touchstones—pitchers Ron Darling and Walt Terrell from the Texas Rangers joined the staff, at the cost of Lee Mazzilli; Keith Hernandez came via a swap with the St. Louis Cardinals in June 1983; and third baseman Ray Knight was hurried to Shea in late August 1984 for three players-to-be-named when the club was surprisingly in the race for the NL East title.

Johnson led the blend of youth and veteran players to win 90 games in his début season. In 1985, perennial All-Star catcher Gary Carter came to Shea Stadium in a trade with the Expos, and he rounded out the nucleus that would later carry the Mets to the World Series. As if to place his personal stamp on his new team, Carter hit the game-winning home run in his first game as a Met. However, he was widely criticized by teammates and foes for his annoying penchant for love of the mirror and camera, his talents with his bat and glove notwithstanding. According to outfielder Mookie Wilson, "Gary had a reputation as a fraud, a great self-

Dwight Gooden set a rookie record with 276 strikeouts in 1984. He was 19 years old. Gooden's exploits inspired the creation of the "K Corner"—a section of Shea Stadium where fans unveiled a placard with the letter "K" every time Gooden notched a strikeout (National Baseball Hall of Fame and Museum, Cooperstown, N.Y.).

promoter who had a strong awareness of what the public deemed appropriate and inappropriate."[6] Carter's moral conviction, noted by Wilson and other teammates, was rooted in his Christian beliefs, and the former Expo would unabashedly proclaim that "[w]ith God, I felt I was the best ballplayer I could be."[7] As disdainful as Carter's uprightness may have been to some, it served as a counterweight to other corrosive behavior that wended through the Mets' clubhouse.

Soaring to 98 wins, the Mets fell short of surpassing their division foes from St. Louis, but as more quality players found their way to Flushing—either from the farm system or imported by trade—Johnson found himself with a manager's dream of a deep roster. The gold rush included Lenny Dykstra, Howard Johnson, Wally Backman, Sid Fernandez, Roger McDowell, and Jesse Orosco.

This collective juggernaut reached a first-place tie after 10 games of the 1986 campaign and never looked back. The Mets won 108 games to swamp the rest of the NL East; the closest competitor was 21½ games behind. A thrilling championship series against the Houston Astros followed, the Mets finally being tested after spending months not having to play a meaningful game. It took the Mets six games to defeat Houston for the NL flag. The ensuing World Series against the Boston Red Sox, themselves participants in a most memorable playoff against the California Angels, has become a classic in its own right because of the Mets' astounding—no other word can describe it—comeback in Game Six. Davey Johnson's charges took Game Seven, an event almost anticlimactic, yet one completing his club's journey with a flourish and putting behind it those dismal days since the departure of Tom Seaver in 1977.

But the jubilation surrounding this capstone achievement was short-lived—only one more divisional pennant would be in the Mets' near future, that coming in 1988. The cocksure attitude that manifested itself during the early years of Johnson's reign evolved into a bull's eye that made him and his players marked men, because although winning breeds confidence, their impudence rankled many outside the franchise and, to a degree, was the source of internal strife as well.

Attending the haughtiness but coursing below the surface away from the public eye was the self-destructive behavior that became the true unraveling of this potential dynasty. Favored to beat the Los Angeles Dodgers in the 1988 NLCS, the Mets fell in seven games and rode into the 1990s on a tide of mediocrity. After peaking at just over three million in 1988, attendance began a swift decline before finally rising again in the late 1990s.

Though the late 1980s Mets had celebrity status because of their swagger, or vice versa, they also featured a pair of scrappers at the top of the order. Wally Backman was a young veteran who gained a reputation as a down-in-the-dirt infielder willing to do whatever it took to win both at second base and from the number-two slot in the batting order. But it was the leadoff man who stood out among the antagonists vexing the opposition.

Centerfielder Lenny Dykstra, according to Hernandez, found favor with his teammates because he "makes no pretense of playing the game in [a] genteel fashion" and "just takes it to the other team with his cockiness and sheer exuberance."[8] His appearance spoiled by the tobacco juice stains on his uniform, Dykstra would have been a perfect fit for the Cardinals' "Gashouse Gang" lineup of yesteryear, but his combative style half a century later did not temper the bile that other teams were actively developing towards the Mets.

Even the team publicity department, led by Jay Horwitz, got into the act by devising an innovation that got under the skin of visiting teams, as if they needed further goading: distribution of cardboard placards, bearing a large letter *K*, to fans showing up at Shea Stadium when Dwight Gooden was scheduled to pitch, thus capitalizing on Doc's reputation as a strikeout artist. "I thought the whole idea was bush," complained Johnson, but the multitude of spectators cheering and waving *K*-cards when Gooden rang up another batter was an opportunity to display team spirit.[9]

As the wins piled up and the Mets put increasing distance between themselves and their divisional rivals, their journey to the NL East pennant in 1986 was tainted by several brawls. "I shouldn't forget Ray Knight as a contributor to our unpopularity," Hernandez recalled, citing the third baseman's central role in an ugly dust-up with Cincinnati's Eric Davis at Riverfront Stadium.[10] Normally mild-mannered, Knight, a former boxer, was unafraid to step up when the occasion demanded attention.

A melee during a game versus the Braves was prompted by yet another action that soured visiting clubs at Shea. The custom of home fans cheering for a curtain call, notably after a dramatic home run, became tiresome for road teams, some taking umbrage at being shown up by the batter who had just sent the crowd into a state of bliss. In this case, Carter was the offending party who "hit a grand slam and then spiced up his curtain call" in a contest against Atlanta, whose pitcher then retaliated by throwing at the next batter, Strawberry, thereby igniting a charge to the mound. Two other fracases against the Dodgers and the Pirates failed to dispel the ill will that rivals had for the New Yorkers. Hernandez noted that "a lot of the [opposition] wanted to see us lose" the NLCS as a comeuppance for the audacity they displayed throughout the season.[11]

Those rooting against New York in the playoff were hopeful that the Mets would stumble, which was possible since they had not played a meaningful game in months and faced virtually no pressure of a pennant race. Houston would not go quietly into the night—four of the six contests were decided by a single run. Not least of these nail-biters was the finale at the Astrodome, a wild, sixteen-inning marathon; the Mets prevailed 7–6.

The freshly crowned National League champions enjoyed the post-game spoils of champagne in the clubhouse—an "idiotic tradition," wrote Frank Cashen later—but the party did not stop there. On the return charter flight to New York, the revelry continued in a manner that reminded one of the fraternity depicted in the film *Animal House*. In his memoir, Cashen evasively stated, "I was sitting in the front of the plane and can't vouch for everything that happened farther back," but the damage caused by overly happy—and intoxicated—players included the mess from a food fight, torn seats, and others that had their backs broken off to be repurposed as card tables.[12]

The tab for this juvenile outburst ran to $7,500, which United Airlines forwarded to the Mets front office. The bill was passed to Johnson, who "was ripping mad—not at us, but at the brass," wrote Gary Carter. "He didn't like them reprimanding us without consulting him. He didn't like them reprimanding us, period."[13] When Johnson brought the issue of the expected payment before a team meeting two days later, he defended his players' actions, claiming that his men "had a right to celebrate" regardless of the consequences.[14]

No record exists as to the final disposition of the payment: Mookie Wilson wrote that Johnson told the gathering, "[I]f we took care of the Red Sox [in the upcoming World Series], all would be forgiven, then [he] turned to his right, tore up the bill and tossed it in the trash. Everyone in the clubhouse cheered with approval."[15] With this abject display of arrogance in the face of wanton destruction by players for whom he was ultimately responsible, there can be no doubt that Johnson himself added staying power to the poor reputation earned by his players. As Wilson further observed, "[I]f Davey hadn't earned every player's trust before, he definitely did at that very moment. It showed us that Davey was in our corner and not management's."[16]

If sex, drugs, and rock 'n' roll were the staples of a rock musician's lifestyle of partying, so, too, can parallel essentials be seen to sustain a good portion of the Mets' players; the insouciance of the 1986 Mets was reflected in the tobacco juice stains on the front of Lenny Dykstra's jersey. The team did not care who made the mess, and as it was the duty of the clubhouse attendant to launder the uniforms, they also believed it was someone else's duty to clean up a mess that the team made.

Although the handsome and well-tailored Ron Darling exhibited yuppie polish, the mindset was decorum be damned for many of Johnson's charges—the ends *did* justify the means. Chutzpah be thy name.

Schadenfreude

For those who had little taste for the Mets and even less stomach for the curtain calls, bombast, and reports of damaged aircraft, the swift unraveling

of this championship coterie likely came as good news. Taking the full cele-
bratory measure of the World Series triumph, several "Hungover Heroes"
never made it to the victory parade in Manhattan, and those who did were
apt to be clad in the same clothes they had been wearing the day before as
they reveled from dusk to dawn. Kevin Mitchell and Dwight Gooden attended
only in spirit, and Darryl Strawberry confessed later, "The deafening roar of
the crowd thundered in our splitting heads, the morning light was like needles
in our eyes, our nerves jangled from speed and coke."[17]

While it can be surmised that not *all* the parade-riders were under the
influence of said substances, there is no doubt that those who dubbed themselves the "Scum Bunch"—whose tendencies toward bacchanalia earned its
members a dubious reputation—were affected the most. "We thought all the
wild behavior was our just tribute for being the best team in baseball" became
Strawberry's attempt to reconcile what evolved into the team's undoing.[18] Yet,
before the Mets had even captured the NL East pennant, the habits of some
were already spiraling out of control.

Strawberry, in his fourth year with the club and only 24 years old, had
already accumulated glowing All-Star credentials, but the demon of drug and
alcohol abuse was wreaking havoc on his marriage. Following in his wake
was Gooden, who, in his memoir, details his limited success in resisting the
allure of drugs. Finally succumbing to the temptation, Gooden became a user
long before Game Seven and admitted that as the World Series celebration
commenced in the Mets clubhouse, "I wanted a sniff of cocaine."[19] Gooden
cited the source of funding for his drug-fueled escapades as the cash that was
readily attainable from payments made to him at baseball card shows or quick
spot endorsements and favors for businessmen who were willing and able to
hand over a tidy sum of money.

As Gooden's life deteriorated, lying to cover up his abuse failed to convince the people who mattered most to him: his family, friends, and, not
least, the Mets front office. By the spring of 1987, "I had the bravado and
delusion of a real coke addict," and after failing a urine test, the young ace
was bundled off to the Smithers Center for Alcoholism and Drug Treatment
in Manhattan.[20] That their star pitcher had to be pulled out of line was not
a complete surprise to the club's upper management, whose suspicions were
confirmed by the urinalysis.

Rather than resting on his World Series laurels, Cashen remained active
to address the ebb and flow of the team roster in 1987. Departing as a free
agent was Knight, a solid veteran with a penchant for equanimity, and then
Cashen executed a trade with San Diego in which the headliners were Kevin
Mitchell (heading west) and Kevin McReynolds (heading to Shea). But the
team fell 16 games short of their 1986 win total and dropped to second place
in the NL East. In 1988, they reached the century mark in victories and were

favored to beat the Los Angeles Dodgers in the NLCS, but they dropped the seventh game and would not return to the postseason for over a decade.

The self-destructive tendencies may have delighted the Met haters, and they certainly detracted from the dynasty in Flushing that appeared to be a foregone conclusion in 1986. Trying to draw a gold nugget from the rubble, Cashen noted that "the 1980s was the decade of the Mets" by virtue of accumulating 816 wins, which ranked first among all major-league teams, but he candidly stated the obvious: "In short, we were let down by ballplayers who chose to use illegal substances."[21] Though Cashen didn't reveal the names of those abusers, it was very clear who they were.

An attempt was made to stabilize the club in 1989 through the employment of a team psychiatrist, an endeavor that invited its own controversy and did nothing to allow the Mets to regain first place in their division. Cashen traded Dykstra to Philadelphia for Juan Samuel, a decent second baseman who was then installed in the outfield with the expectation of filling the hole created by Dykstra's departure but pulled up short. The acquisition of pitcher Frank Viola, a front-rank starter for the Twins, brought some short-term help, but the addition of Gregg Jefferies, a youthful can't-miss prospect who was hyped and indulged by management, never lived up to the billing. Mookie Wilson noted that the budding star was resented by some teammates who believed that he had been doted over far too much by the front office.[22]

The Mets had unwittingly positioned themselves for a tumble: the roster was a chaotic olio, Davey Johnson was fired after 42 games in 1990, and although it appeared that new manager Bud Harrelson was capable of righting Johnson's listing ship, the former Met shortstop and longtime fan favorite also came to ruin. The doldrums that plagued the Mets a decade earlier had an unwelcome reprise for all concerned in the organization.

Analyzing the Demise

Years after his brief tenure with the Mets in 1989, the psychiatrist who once counseled team members offered some opinions on what happened to the fledgling powerhouse at Shea. In his supporting role, Dr. Allan Lans had a unique view of the team, which he described as "a carefully constructed organization that is not distinguished by what they achieved but by how little they achieved."[23]

Lans believes that despite the attempts of the Mets to prudently craft their roster, the disparate personalities involved invariably generated issues that made cohesion and team chemistry a difficult aim to realize. Complicating matters further were drug and alcohol abuse as well as racial friction that roiled the sanctity of the clubhouse.

Using the Yankees as a comparison, Lans observed that the success of their franchise could be attributed to owner George Steinbrenner's complete control—"he saw to it that things did not deteriorate from within"—but in the case of the Mets, no such overarching figure existed.[24] Although Cashen was responsible for the operation of the team, he was nonetheless at a step removed from ownership. Cashen's acquisition of Gary Carter, which filled a crucial void in the Mets' lineup, also brought its own consequences. Long reputed for his penchant for the camera, Carter grated both teammates and rivals with his ego, but his arrival at Shea "also set up something that you didn't want, a competition between Keith [Hernandez] and Gary because now they both wanted to be the team leader."[25] While the captaincy of the Mets would become Hernandez's responsibility, the path to that role also "set up a kind of internal dispute."[26]

While personality clashes are inevitable whenever any group of people are brought together, Carter and Hernandez—as well as Rusty Staub—led by example. This clutch of veterans was "able to put everything out of their minds and prepare for the game, even the way they dressed, the way they put their uniforms on, was a kind of religious ritual," according to Lans. "This was about playing *this* game tonight and winning."[27]

The difficulties Keith Hernandez had with drugs prior to his trade from St. Louis are well known, and he distanced himself from the evils of New York by first living in Connecticut, the better to avoid the nefarious temptations of the Big Apple. But he was drawn to the city and its many positive aspects by Staub, who took Hernandez and other players under his wing to show them the culture, refinement, and taste that were available in New York to the discerning eye. This transition was instrumental in helping Hernandez adjust to his new home—he eventually did move into the city—and it positioned him to assume a leadership role with the Mets.

But the major problem, in both the societal and economic sense, that had the harshest impact on the Mets was substance abuse. Even more pernicious in the 21st century than in the 1980s, "You see that drugs are ruining America," noted Lans. "Rural America, city America, wherever you go in America. Suburb and exurb, drugs have just destroyed this country."[28]

Exacerbating the substance abuse problem is the huge disposable income enjoyed by professional athletes, which facilitates transactions for obtaining drugs. "You take a kid who's making $500 a month [in the minor leagues] and then the next year, the next day, he's making a million dollars a year," bemoaned Lans. "When you were 19, what would you do with a million dollars? Then you throw them into a world where there are a lot of predators...."[29] The outcomes of these conditions usually do not end well, and several Mets players failed to avoid the pitfalls inherent such a climate.

When alcohol, which was present at the birth of baseball, is added to the toxic blend of drugs, a person's downward spiral can be career-inhibiting if not fatal. The effect on the Mets was to short-circuit their aspirations both individually as players and collectively as a team, thus derailing the plans for a dynasty. Not only were Gooden and Strawberry sidetracked into desultory careers but another prospect "who should have been the shortstop for ten years with the Mets," Kevin Elster, "spun out of control" and lost out on a promising career.[30]

Lastly, the Mets were not immune from the pressures exerted by racial divisions. The most vocal of the players was George Foster, the African American outfielder who was once one of baseball's most feared sluggers and an All-Star with the Reds but was only a notch above mediocre in his years wearing a New York uniform. When Davey Johnson finally benched him in 1986 due to poor production, Foster told a reporter that he perceived racial overtones in the manager's decision to replace him with a platoon of Mookie Wilson—also African American—and Danny Heep, who was white. When Wilson was injured earlier in the spring, Johnson installed Lenny Dykstra, another white player, in centerfield, and now Foster was upset that a mixed-race platoon was supplanting him in the lineup.

Foster aired his grievance to a reporter, broadly hinting that black players were being replaced by "a more popular player" who happened to be white[31]—the Mets had recently re-acquired former fan favorite Lee Mazzilli. Dykstra's wielding of a hot bat during Wilson's absence was also apparently lost on Foster, and Johnson was livid to learn of Foster's implication that the lineup and roster moves were besmirched by racial bias. The controversy reached its climax when a contrite Foster apologized to his teammates and broke down in tears during a private conversation with Ray Knight, his past teammate in Cincinnati. However, it was too late to salvage any hope of his remaining with the Mets, and within days Foster was given his release.

This last painful incident did not prevent the Mets from winning the NL East pennant in 1986, and the club still prominently featured a pair of the game's budding stars in Strawberry and Gooden, both African Americans. But Foster's perception that race was trumping sound judgment regarding personnel transactions was misguided—the Mets were comfortably atop their division when he voiced his opinion—and served as a continuing reminder that the flashpoint of ethnicity was always close at hand.

When the Mets were dismounted from their high horse, it marked the end of hubris and the onset of soul-searching at Shea Stadium.

Conclusion

The ephemeral reign of the New York Mets in the latter half of the 1980s became an object lesson in the pernicious effects that can attend the achievement of success. In the context of their times and under the influence of the sense of entitlement they believed they earned, the short trajectory of their rise and descent shocked those who had high expectations. By all accounts, they were positioned for a dynastic niche comparable to those forged at different times during the 1970s by the Oakland Athletics, Cincinnati Reds, and New York Yankees.

The Mets had been gifted with talent, depth, and youth. While every major-league roster is in constant flux due to benchings, injuries, and departures—via free agency, trades, and the like—the best teams find ways to cope in difficult times. But the Mets were unable to adjust in the way that two of their league rivals did. Divisional titles came to the Cardinals (1982, 1985, 1987) and Dodgers (1981, 1983, 1985, 1988), and Hall of Fame managers Whitey Herzog and Tommy Lasorda made the most with the players they had. At Shea Stadium, however, the foundation started to crumble before the champagne in the clubhouse even went flat.

Infected by solipsism, the Mets lost the opportunity to join the pantheon of greatest teams and instead took their place among the one-hit wonders. Their historic brethren of 1969 were thought to be miraculous overachievers, but with a retooling of the lineup, they were again competitive a few years later. It can only be left to speculation how the Mets would have fared in the 1970s under the stoic leadership of manager Gil Hodges, who died of a heart attack two days short of his 48th birthday, right before the 1972 season began. Yogi Berra was elevated from coach to manager and led the team to the 1973 World Series—a seven-game affair that ended with the A's defeating the Mets.

Yuppies who reveled in the moments—*any* moment—that were financed by credit cards in the 1980s—and were under the impression that the money would always come later to pay up—had an epiphany as the bills came due. The stock market crash of 1987, when the Dow lost more than 20 percent of its value in one day, reinforced this dread. The Mets had their own rude awakening when the realization set in that simply showing up at the ballpark did not mean an automatic win. Fewer wins meant less glory, although in baseball's salary structure, not a smaller paycheck.

The joy of 1986 yielded to a post–World Series reckoning marked by little accomplishment and much angst. In that glorious season, the Mets came, they saw, and they conquered. But at bottom they were human beings subject to the same vicissitudes as anyone else. It was morning again in Ronald Reagan's America, but the sunlight that shone on Shea Stadium was already quickly clouding over.

NOTES

1. Lou Cannon quoted in James T. Patterson, *Restless Giant: The United States from Watergate to Bush V. Gore* (Oxford, UK: Oxford University Press, 2005), 192.

2. Joseph Durso, "Mazzilli Is Emerging as a Symbol of Mets' New Winning Mood," *New York Times*, July 15, 1980: B13.

3. Joseph Durso, "Doubleday Hopes for Better Sequel," *New York Times*, September 14, 1980: S3.

4. Phil Pepe, "Lee Mazzilli an Innocent Victim of Madison Ave.," *Daily News* (New York), March 13, 1982: 62.

5. Charles DeMotte, *Baseball and American Society: How a Game Reflects the American Experience* (San Diego: Cognella, Inc., 2014), 176.

6. Mookie Wilson and Erik Sherman, *Mookie: Life, Baseball, and the '86 Mets* (New York: Berkley Books, 2014), 99.

7. Carter quoted in Dave Branon, *Safe at Home 2: More Winning Players Talk About Baseball and Their Faith* (Chicago: Moody Press, 1997), 4.

8. Keith Hernandez and Mike Bryan, *If at First…* (New York: Penguin Books, 1987; New York: McGraw-Hill Book Company, 1986), 439. Citations refer to the 1987 edition, which includes a section on the 1986 season, postseason, and World Series. The 1986 edition's full title is *If at First: A Season with the Mets*. It covers only the 1985 season.

9. Davey Johnson and Peter Golenbock, *Bats* (New York: G.P. Putnam's Sons, 1986), 82. The Mets players would vote Horwitz a three-quarter share of their 1986 post-season financial reward. Bruce Markusen, *Tales from the Mets Dugout* (New York: Sports Publishing, 2005), 136.

10. Hernandez and Bryan, 439.

11. *Ibid.*, 440–442.

12. J. Frank Cashen, *Winning in Both Leagues: Reflections from Baseball's Front Office* (Lincoln: University of Nebraska Press, 2014), 135–136.

13. Gary Carter and John Hough, Jr., *A Dream Season* (San Diego: Harcourt, Brace, Jovanovich, 1987), 62.

14. *Ibid.*, 63.

15. Mookie Wilson and Erik Sherman, *Mookie: Life, Baseball, and the '86 Mets*, 178.

16. *Ibid.*, 178.

17. Darryl Strawberry and John Strausbaugh, *Straw: Finding My Way* (New York: Ecco, 2009), 93.

18. Strawberry and Strausbaugh, 80.

19. Dwight Gooden and Ellis Henican, *Doc: A Memoir* (Boston: New Harvest/Houghton Mifflin Harcourt, 2013), 90.

20. *Ibid.*, 102–104.

21. Cashen, 184.

22. Mookie Wilson and Erik Sherman, *Mookie: Life, Baseball, and the '86 Mets*, 216–217.

23. Dr. Allan Lans, telephone interview with Paul Hensler, February 26, 2019. Dr. Lans's arrangements also included traveling with the team in September 1989, which created an uncomfortable situation for Davey Johnson and several players.

24. *Ibid.*

25. *Ibid.*

26. *Ibid.*

27. *Ibid.*

28. *Ibid.*

29. *Ibid.*

30. *Ibid.*

31. Foster's quote was initially reported by a Gannett newspaper reporter: "I'm not saying it's a racial thing, but that seems to be the case in sports these days. When a ballclub can, they replace a George Foster or a Mookie Wilson with a more popular player." Jim Corbett, "Foster Blasts Mets' Moves," *Journal-News*, August 6, 1986: 25.

More Than a Miracle

Mets Pitchers of the Early 1970s

SCOTT DOUGHTIE *and* DOUGLAS JORDAN

In 1969, Neil Armstrong and Buzz Aldrin were the first men to set foot on the Moon; war protests led to the initial troop withdrawals from Vietnam; the X-rated film and future Oscar winner *Midnight Cowboy*[1] premiered as did *Butch Cassidy and the Sundance Kid*[2]; major music festivals took place at Woodstock and Altamont; *The Saturday Evening Post* had its last issue; *Sesame Street, The Brady Bunch,* and *Scooby Doo, Where Are You?* premiered; the Manson Family murders took the lives of Sharon Tate and five others (one was shot and the others stabbed dozens of times); and The Beatles performed live for the last time and released *Abbey Road.*

Baseball offered a distraction from the tragedies and a complement to the popular-culture triumphs that Americans experienced as the 1960s faded into the history books. At the beginning of the 1969 season, anticipation filled the air as the latest expansion added the Montreal Expos, San Diego Padres, Seattle Pilots, and Kansas City Royals to Major League Baseball's roster of squads.

For Mets fans, there was hope for the team to post its first winning season. In 1967, the team went 61–101; 1968's record was 73–89. Though the Mets had improved in 1968 when new manager Gil Hodges brought an aura of seriousness to the team, it would have been outrageous to predict that the team would win the 1969 World Series. But it happened. And it was splendid. The word "miracle" became attached to the team, reminding people of its last usage to describe the 1914 Boston Braves, who swept the Philadelphia Athletics in the World Series.

Even people with a tangential knowledge of baseball could appreciate a great underdog story. They might not have known that Tom Seaver wore #41 or that Hodges used to play for the Brooklyn Dodgers, but they knew that

67

something special happened when Cleon Jones caught Davey Johnson's fly ball for the last out of 1969. Something miraculous.

The Mets' defeat of the Baltimore Orioles that year still has a hold on the popular imagination. From sportscaster Lindsey Nelson interviewing the team in the locker room while being drenched in champagne to the address change of Citi Field to 41 Seaver Way five decades later in 2019, the Mets' victory continues to resonate in popular culture. Tom Seaver made a guest appearance on *The Joe Namath Show* in October 1969.[3] In 1999, an episode of the popular situation comedy *Everybody Loves Raymond* featured *Newsday* sports writer Ray Barone and his brother, NYPD officer Robert Barone, traveling to Cooperstown to meet with members of the 1969 championship team.[4] Ray's brother had a bulldog named Shamsky, an homage to the dog they had when they were kids. For a non–Mets fan, it's an unusual name. For two kids growing up on Long Island in the late 1960s and early 1970s, it's perfect; Art Shamsky played for the Mets from 1968 to 1971. Comedians Ray Romano and Brad Garrett played Ray and Robert, respectively.

In 2009, *Sports Illustrated*'s "Where Are They Now?" edition featured Nolan Ryan and Tom Seaver on the cover.[5] The story discussed the status of 1969 team members 40 years later. In 2019, the Mets changed the address of Citi Field to 41 Seaver Way to honor "The Franchise," who wore number 41, and announced that a statue of the right-handed fireballer will be placed in front of the stadium.[6] Through the mist of 50 years, this baseball miracle in 1969 appears to be an island of Mets success in a sea of sometimes comically bad baseball performance. But our memories deceive us. The Mets' performance in 1969 *was* surprising based on the results from 1962 to 1968 (the combined record for those years was 394–737) but success was not limited to 1969—the Mets were competitive from 1969 through 1973, when the team made a second World Series appearance, because of a stellar pitching staff.

Tom Seaver

George Thomas Seaver was the 1967 Rookie of the Year when he went 16–13 with a 2.76 ERA and had 170 strikeouts. Two years later he went 25–7 with a 2.21 ERA. Seaver won the 1969 Cy Young Award that year, receiving 23 out of 24 votes. Phil Niekro got the other first-place vote but he came in a distant second in the voting with his 23–13 record and 2.56 ERA.

The 6'1" righty came close to winning the National League MVP in 1969, receiving the same number of first-place votes (11) as the winner, Willie McCovey, who led the National League in home runs (45) and RBI (126). He batted .320, good for eighth highest in the National League. Mets outfielder Cleon Jones surpassed McCovey with a .340 average and notched seventh place.

Despite coming up just short in the MVP voting, "Tom Terrific" won *Sports Illustrated*'s "Sportsman of the Year" award in 1969. The award is given to the athlete or team whose performance that year most embodies the spirit of sportsmanship and achievement. *Sports Illustrated* débuted in 1954—by 1969, the award was a topic for a national conversation.

The article that accompanied the award discussed both the surprising nature of the Mets championship and the contributions that Seaver made to it.[7] It reinforced as the evidence that nothing is impossible and "...it triggered an unexpected national response. From the Hudson to the hinterlands people turned the Met victory into a national cliché of hope: 'If the Mets can win, anything can happen.'" Although Gil Hodges was given some consideration as who was most responsible, the magazine chose Seaver: "Their achievement must be attested to by other terms: by youth, by verve, by personality, by conviction, by naiveté and finally by rare talent where it counted most—on the field. That is why George Thomas Seaver, a 25-year-old man-child from Fresno, Calif., is 1969's Sportsman of the Year." The article also pointed out that Seaver "became the youngest National League pitcher in 34 years to win as many as 25 games (Dizzy Dean was the last). He won the Cy Young Award as the best pitcher in the National League and had more victories than anyone through a season that produced 15 pitchers with 20 wins or more."

One of Seaver's highlights from the 1969 season occurred on July 9, when he threw 8⅓ perfect innings against the Chicago Cubs, who led the NL East. More than 59,000 were at Shea Stadium for this heartbreaking event. Seaver's opportunity for what would have been the only perfect game of his career was broken up when rookie outfielder Jim Qualls lined a single to left center. The 4–0 Mets win would go down in history as "Tom Seaver's Imperfect Game."[8]

Seaver pitched 18 complete games during the 1969 regular season, so it was not completely unexpected that he would throw another one that postseason. And he did so in Game 4 of the World Series, an extra-innings contest. Seaver gave up six hits and one earned run in 10 innings. He also struck out six Orioles in the Mets' 2–1 win.

Seaver and the Amazin' Mets looked like they could win it all again in 1970. On April 22, Seaver set a major-league record by striking out the final 10 batters in a 2–1 victory against the San Diego Padres at Shea Stadium. No major-league pitcher in the modern era (since 1903) has ever matched his feat of striking out 10 consecutive batters. His total K tally tied Steve Carlton's major-league record of 19 strikeouts in a nine-inning game. In mid–August, Seaver was 17–6 as the Mets battled the Pirates for first place in the NL East. However, he won only one of his last 10 starts; four happened on short rest. Seaver ended up 18–12 with a 2.82 ERA—which was the lowest ERA for the National League. He also led the senior circuit in strikeouts (283).

In 1971, Seaver continued to be one of the best pitchers in the major leagues, sporting a 20–10 record with a 1.76 ERA and leading the National League in strikeouts with 289 in 286 innings pitched. But his outstanding performance did not result in a second Cy Young Award, which is mind-boggling. The Cubs' Ferguson Jenkins, whose ERA was more than a full run higher per game at 2.77, won the award. Fergie's 23–13 record and exceptional control numbers (only 37 walks in 325 innings) are impressive, but those facts do not justify his winning the award over Seaver. If WHIP (Walks plus Hits per Innings Pitched) had existed then (it was invented in 1979) and been taken as seriously as it is today, Seaver would have had a 0.946 WHIP versus Jenkins's 1.049.

Seaver had a slightly down year in terms of ERA in 1972—2.92. He ended the season at 21–12 with 249 strikeouts, second most in the National League. In 1973, Seaver went 19–10 with a league-leading 2.08 ERA and 18 complete games. His superb performance in Game 5 of the 1973 NLCS against the Reds helped the Mets get to their second World Series—he pitched 8⅓ innings, giving up just two runs (only one of them earned) and striking out four in the 7–2 victory over the Big Red Machine.

It's no surprise that Seaver won his second of three Cy Young Awards that year. His 251 strikeouts led the National League for the third year out of four. A's slugger Reggie Jackson said, "Blind people come to the park just to listen to him pitch."[9]

Seaver is sixth on the career list for strikeouts with 3,640 and is the only major league player to strike out 200 batters in nine consecutive seasons (1968–76). Even Nolan Ryan and Randy Johnson did not accomplish this feat.

To the dismay of Mets fans, Seaver was traded to the Cincinnati Reds in 1977. He returned to the team for the 1983 season, pitching six strong innings in a 2–0 win over the Phillies on Opening Day. However, he was not protected in a free-agent compensation draft, so the Chicago White Sox claimed him for the 1984 season. He pitched for the White Sox for two-and-a-half seasons, getting his 300th win in New York against the Yankees. He almost returned to the Mets during the 1985 season, but manager Davey Johnson blocked it. The White Sox traded Seaver to the Boston Red Sox during the middle of the 1986 season. A knee injury prevented Seaver from appearing against his former team in the 1986 World Series. Roger Clemens attributes the time he spent with Seaver in 1986 as instrumental in helping him make the transition from thrower to pitcher.[10] Seaver's career ended after he declined Boston's offer of $500,000 for the 1987 season.

On June 24, 1988, the 12-time All-Star was at Shea Stadium when he became the first Mets player to have his number (#41) retired by the club. Mike Piazza (#31) is the only other Mets player to have his number retired by the team. Casey Stengel (#37) and Gil Hodges (#14) have had their numbers

The 1969 Mets went 100–62, beat the Atlanta Braves in the first NL Championship Series, and defied conventional wisdom by winning the World Series against the favored Baltimore Orioles. A formidable pitching staff was critical to the ascendance from the sub–.500 records in the team's early years. Pictured, left to right: Tom Seaver, Jerry Koosman, Nolan Ryan, Gary Gentry, Jim McAndrew (National Baseball Hall of Fame and Museum, Cooperstown, N.Y.).

retired by the Mets as managers. On January 7, 1992, Seaver's first time on the ballot, he was elected to the Baseball Hall of Fame with a then-record 98.8 percent vote total. Only Seaver and Walter Johnson have 300 wins, 3,000 strikeouts, and an under–3.00 career ERA.

On March 7, 2019, Seaver's family announced that he is suffering from dementia and will retire from public life.[11]

Jerry Koosman

Jerome Martin Koosman certainly did his part to help the Mets win the 1969 World Series in his second season in the big leagues. He was a key factor in helping the Mets overtake the Cubs, who were 9½ games ahead on August 14—Koosman won eight of his final nine decisions. Dating from August 14, the Mets won 38 out of 49 games.

The left-handed pitcher won 17 games, lost nine, and struck out 180 batters with a 2.28 ERA that season. His performance in the beginning of the season warranted selection onto the National League All-Star team for the second straight year.

Koosman was the pitching star of the 1969 World Series too, winning both games that he started. After Seaver took the loss in Game 1, Koosman held the Orioles hitless until the seventh inning in Game 2, allowing only one run in 8⅔ innings. After the Mets won Games 3 and 4, Koosman was on the mound when the Mets closed out the Series in Game 5, pitching a complete game and allowing three runs; no Oriole scored after the third inning. After Jones caught Johnson's fly ball, he gave it Koosman. He kept the game balls from Games 2 and 5 in a safe at home until the early 1990s, when he sold the ball bestowed by Jones. But he retained the Game 2 ball.

Koosman went 12–7 with a 3.14 ERA in 1970 and 6–11 with a 3.04 ERA in 1971. His 1972 performance went below .500, yielding an 11–12 win-loss record and 4.14 ERA.

In 1973, Kooz improved his ERA to 2.84, winning 14 games and losing 15. From late August to early September, he set a Mets record by pitching 31⅓ consecutive scoreless innings. (R.A. Dickey broke Koosman's mark with 32⅔ consecutive scoreless innings in 2012.)

Koosman won Game 3 of the NLCS against the Reds; he started Game 2 of the World Series but gave up three runs by the second inning. Berra pulled him in the third with two men on and one out against the defending champion A's. In Game 5, Kooz held them scoreless for 6⅓ innings and got credited with the victory, which gave the Mets a 3–2 lead in the Series. But Oakland won the next two games to repeat as World Champions.

In 1976, Koosman, then in his 10th major-league season, finished as a runner-up to Randy Jones for the National League Cy Young Award. He went 21–10 with 200 strikeouts in the Bicentennial year. After going 8–20 (and leading the major leagues in losses) in 1977 and a 3–15 record in 1978, Koosman got traded to his native state—Minnesota—and compiled a 36–26 record ·for his two full seasons with the Twins. In the strike-shortened season of 1981, he notched 3–9 before going to the White Sox, where he went 1–4 in the remainder followed by an 11–7 record in 1982 and again in 1983. Koosman closed his career in Philadelphia, going 14–15 in 1984 and 6–4 in 1985.

Jerry Koosman has the third most wins in Mets history (140) behind Seaver (198) and Dwight Gooden (157); his career win-loss record is 222–209. He is 33rd on the MLB Career Leader for Strikeouts with 2,556. For Mets fans recalling or studying the days of yore when the Miracle Mets surprised the world and the 1973 team inspired with its "Ya Gotta Believe!" mantra, the career of Jerry Koosman will be prominent for his 4–0 postseason record and his dutiful performances that brought joy and hope to Shea Stadium's crowds.

Nolan Ryan

Lynn Nolan Ryan was just a hard-throwing right-handed pitcher before he became a legend. His pitches were so hard at Alvin (Texas) High School that they sometimes broke bones in catchers' hands.[12] Ryan was drafted in the 12th round of the 1965 Major League Baseball draft by the Mets, and pitched for them in the 1966 and 1968 seasons; he was in the minors in 1967. Unable to break into the Mets starting rotation in 1969, Ryan became a reliever and a spot starter, winning six games and losing three with a 3.53 ERA that season. Ryan pitched well for the Miracle Mets in the 1969 postseason, winning a game against the Braves in the NLCS and not allowing a run in 2⅓ innings in the World Series.

Unfortunately, this is the only World Series that the "Ryan Express" ever got to play in during his 27-year pitching career, an astounding achievement that ties him with Cap Anson for the most seasons by any player. In 1970, Ryan tied a then-record for the Mets by striking out 15 batters in one game against the Phillies. His 1970 record was 7–11 with a 3.42 ERA. Ryan won 10 games and lost 14 with a 3.97 ERA for the Mets in 1971.

But the Mets gave up on Ryan too soon, very unfortunately for Mets fans. After the 1971 season, they traded him to the California Angels for Jim Fregosi, who only played two seasons for the Mets. There is little doubt that Ryan could have helped the Mets win in 1972 and 1973, as he was an All-Star with the Angels and led the major leagues in strikeouts in both of those seasons. In the 1972 season, Ryan pitched 20 complete games and nine shutouts, struck out 329 batters, and ended the season at 19–16 with a 2.28 ERA.

In 1973 season, Ryan set a major-league record that still stands: 383 strikeouts. His stamina was unparalleled, resulting in 26 complete games and 326 innings pitched. His 21–16 record included four shutouts and 2.87 ERA. But he got eclipsed in the Cy Young Award voting for the American League. Instead, it went to Jim Palmer.

Ryan's career is full of superlatives. It's a shame for Mets fans that he didn't spend more time with Seaver et al. In addition to the single-season strikeout record, Ryan has the records for career strikeouts (5,714) and career walks (2,795). Ryan struck out ten or more batters in a game 215 times and threw seven no-hitters (another MLB career record).

There will always be debates about pitchers. But it would be hard to question the theory that Nolan Ryan is the best pitcher never to have won a Cy Young Award.

Jon Matlack

Jonathan Trumpbour Matlack was the fourth overall pick by the New York Mets in the 1967 MLB draft. After four years in the Mets farm system, he became one of the "Big Three" with Seaver and Koosman. The lefty made the team after Spring Training in 1972, getting off to a 6–0 start with a 1.95 ERA in the first two months of the season. He ended the season at 15–10 record and a 2.32 ERA to win the NL Rookie of the Year Award. But he has another distinction from his rookie year—on September 30, 1972, Matlack gave up Roberto Clemente's 3,000th and final career hit.[13]

Matlack had a tough start to the 1973 season. On May 8, a vicious line-drive off the bat of Marty Perez of the Atlanta Braves struck his head so hard that the ball rebounded into the dugout. Matlack suffered a hairline fracture of his skull but recovered quickly enough to return and pitch six shutout innings in Pittsburgh on May 19.[14] He ended up winning 14 games and losing 16 with a 3.20 ERA for the National League Champion Mets. Though Matlack had a losing record in 1973, he was 5–1 from August 18, helping the Mets capture the NL East crown. On October 7, 1973, he held Cincinnati to just two hits in Game 1 of the 1973 National League Championship Series.

Matlack was equally impressive in the 1973 World Series, giving up just three hits in six innings in Game 2. However, the Oakland A's scored a run on Felix Millan's error in the third and another run later in the inning. Oakland won 2–1. Matlack won Game 4, giving up just one run in eight innings. However, he lost the seventh game of the series, 5–2. In the third inning of that game, he gave up two-run homers to both Bert Campaneris and Reggie Jackson, the only two home runs that Oakland would hit the entire series. It's likely that Matlack was not as effective as in Game 4 because he pitched Game 7 on only three days' rest.

Tug McGraw

Frank Edwin "Tug" McGraw, Jr., was the best relief pitcher for the Mets during this five-year window. He got the nickname "Tug" from his mother because of the particularly aggressive way that he breastfed.[15] Without ever playing Double-A or Triple-A ball, the southpaw made the Mets squad out of 1965 Spring Training. That same year, when asked if he preferred the new Astro Turf on the field at the Houston Astrodome to real grass, he showed his sense of humor: "I dunno, I never smoked AstroTurf."[16]

McGraw was a starting pitcher from 1965 to 1967, but spent all of 1968 in the minor leagues. When he returned to the Mets in 1969, they did not need him as a starter until Koosman went down with an injury in May, so he pitched in relief. McGraw went 1–1 with a 5.23 ERA filling in for Koosman, whose return prompted McGraw's primary role to be a closer. He earned his first save on May 31 by pitching the final two innings against the Giants. McGraw finished the season with 12 saves, an overall record of 9–3, and a 2.24 ERA.

McGraw's first postseason experience came in Game 2 of the 1969 NL Championship Series. After the Atlanta Braves tallied six runs in 4⅔ innings, Hodges replaced Koosman with Ron Taylor and then McGraw. The duo held the Braves scoreless for the remainder to secure an 11–6 victory. McGraw did not appear in the 1969 World Series against the Baltimore Orioles. But this is not too surprising given how long managers stayed with their starters in those days.

McGraw emerged as one of the top closers in the National League in the early 1970s. He was 4–6 with a 3.28 ERA in 1970, but turned things around the next year when he went 11–4 with a 1.70 ERA in 1971. In 1972 he was an All-Star, giving up just 71 hits in 106 innings pitched and setting a Mets record with 27 saves. That club record stood until Jesse Orosco saved 31 in 1984. His '72 record was 8–6 with a 1.70 ERA.

Although 1973 wasn't as good statistically for McGraw (his ERA was 3.87), the team valued his leadership. When the Mets fell into last place in the NL East and remained there through August 30, it seemed that '73 would be an unmemorable season. McGraw was the winning pitcher for the Mets on August 31 when the team emerged from last place with an extra-innings victory over the St. Louis Cardinals. For the rest of the season, McGraw went 3–0 with a 0.57 ERA and had 10 saves. The Mets, meanwhile, went 20–8 from that point forward to pull off the stunning achievement of capturing the division title.

One of the most famous aspects of the 1973 campaign is the slogan that the Mets used during the latter part of that season. At a July 9 team meeting, where Mets Board Chairman M. Donald Grant was trying to encourage the team, McGraw shouted the words, "Ya Gotta Believe" in response to Grant's entreaties.[17] The phrase became a popular rallying cry for the Mets. He uttered the famous phrase when only he believed the Mets could actually get to the World Series. But soon enough, hearing McGraw say it again and again, and seeing him do his magic on the mound, his Met teammates came to believe. They pulled into first place on September 21 with a 10–2 victory over the Pittsburgh Pirates, and clinched the division crown on the final day of the season.

McGraw continued his dominant pitching into the postseason, when he pitched five innings over two games in the 1973 NL Championship Series against the Cincinnati Reds without giving up a run. He appeared in five of the seven games of the 1973 World Series against the Oakland A's. McGraw blew his first opportunity to save Game 2 by allowing back-to-back singles to Reggie Jackson and Gene Tenace in the bottom of the ninth inning. But he blanked the A's for the rest of the 12-inning game to earn the win.

McGraw got traded to the Phillies after the 1974 season, leaving the Mets as the club's all-time leader in saves, games pitched, and games finished. McGraw died on January 5, 2004, from a brain tumor. The Mets played the 2004 season with the words, "Ya Gotta Believe" embroidered on their right shoulders in McGraw's honor.[18]

Gary Gentry

Gary Gentry was drafted by the Mets in the 1967 Major League Baseball draft. He spent two years in the minors before making the Opening Day roster at 22 years old for the 1969 season and pitched the third-most innings (233⅔) for the '69 squad, behind Seaver and Koosman. Gentry posted a 3.43 ERA and a 13–12 won-loss record. In Game 3 of the World Series, Gentry kept the Orioles scoreless into the seventh inning before handing the ball off to Nolan Ryan for the save. Gentry started 1970 with a 4–1 record but couldn't sustain that excellence. He finished the season with a 3.68 ERA and a 9–9 record. In 1971, he went 12–11 and had a 3.23 ERA. Following the 1971 season, the California Angels inquired about Gentry, offering third baseman Jim Fregosi for him. The Mets were unwilling to part with Gentry, so they sent Nolan Ryan in arguably the worst trade in Mets history. Gentry won seven games and lost 10 in 1972. His ERA was 4.01. Following the 1972 season, Gentry and relief pitcher Danny Frisella were traded to the Atlanta Braves for All-Star second baseman Felix Millan and lefty George Stone.

Sports Illustrated

The Mets have been on the cover of *Sports Illustrated* 33 times, additional evidence of the team's prominence in popular culture. The first issue with a Met on cover was the March 5, 1962, issue, with the caption "Casey of the Mets" accompanying a photo of Casey Stengel during Spring Training before his first season managing the Mets. That issue cost 25 cents.

Other Mets featured on the cover include Ron Swoboda, Ron Gaspar, Jerry Koosman, Bud Harrelson, Jerry Grote, and Willie Mays. Seaver's return in 1983 led to the cover of the April 18, 1983, issue, with the caption "You Can

Go Home Again." During the 1981 strike, baseball fans found solace when they picked up the July 27 issue and found Seaver smiling on the cover. The caption read: "Hey, baseball fans, need a quick fix? Want a little instant nostalgia? We bring you Tom Seaver...." Though he was in a Reds warmup jacket, the nostalgia factor ignited memories of Seaver in a Mets uniform throwing fastballs with an incredible leg extension that caused his right knee to hit the dirt as he released the ball. *SI* writer Frank Deford wrote, "It's especially revealing that though he was an instant success on the field when he first joined the Mets, he seemed to make an even greater impression with his attitude. He had never even heard of Marvelous Marv Throneberry, and he refused to laugh at the team's reputation for inept high jinks. This was the first right turn toward the world championship, and Gil Hodges, New York's strong new sobersided manager, was perhaps the first, save Seaver himself to notice that the Metsies always seemed to play a little better when young Tom took the mound."

Seaver. Koosman. Matlack. Ryan. McGraw. Gentry. Their names receive recognition as being key players on the '69 Mets. But their performances during the 1969–1973 period merit attention for being a formidable staff that, with a few more breaks, might have added more division titles and World Series championships to the roster of Mets achievements.

NOTES

1. *Midnight Cowboy*, directed by John Schlesinger (MGM; 1969)
2. *Butch Cassidy and the Sundance Kid* (Campanile Productions; 1969).
3. *The Joe Namath Show*, Syndicated, October 6, 1969.
4. Zuckerman, Steve, dir. *Everybody Loves Raymond*. Season 3, episode 19, "Big Shots." Aired March 1, 1999, on CBS.
5. *Sports Illustrated*, July 13–20, 2009.
6. "Mets Planning to Unveil Tom Seaver Statue During 2019 Season: Report," SNY, https://www.sny.tv/mets/news/mets-planning-to-unveil-tom-seaver-statue-during-2019-season-report/304957164/ (last accessed November 10, 2019).
7. https://www.si.com/vault/1969/12/22/618802/sportsman-of-the-year
8. Kristen Gowdy, "Tom Seaver Nearly Perfect," National Baseball Hall of Fame and Museum, Cooperstown, NY, https://baseballhall.org/discover/inside-pitch/tom-seaver-nearly-perfect (last accessed November 10, 2019).
9. "Tom Seaver Quotes," Baseball Almanac, http://www.baseball-almanac.com/quotes/tom_seaver_quotes.shtml (last accessed November 10, 2019).
10. "Clemens Rockets His Way Past Seaver," Associated Press, *Los Angeles Times*, July 24, 2001, https://www.latimes.com/archives/la-xpm-2001-jul-24-sp-26007-story.html (last accessed November 10, 2001).
11. "Tom Seaver, New York Mets Great, Diagnosed with Dementia," NBC, https://www.nbcnews.com/news/us-news/tom-seaver-new-york-mets-great-diagnosed-dementia-n980766 (last accessed November 10, 2019).
12. "This Day in History, August 22, 1989, Nolan Ryan Registers 5000th Strikeout," The History Channel, https://www.history.com/this-day-in-history/nolan-ryan-registers-5000th-strikeout (last accessed November 12, 2019).
13. Thomas Lawrence, "Roberto Clemente Record 3,000th Hit in Final Regular-Season At-Bat," National Baseball Hall of Fame and Museum, https://baseballhall.org/discover/inside-pitch/clemente-final-hit (last accessed November 10, 2019).

14. Joseph Durso, "Mets' Koosman Beats Braves, 8–1: Triumph His 5th—Matlack Out Indefinitely," *New York Times*, May 10, 1973: 59.

15. Michael Carlson, "Tug McGraw," *The Guardian* (London, UK), *The Guardian*, https://www.theguardian.com/news/2004/jan/08/guardianobituaries.sport (last accessed November 10, 2019).

16. "I Never Smoked Astroturf," https://quoteinvestigator.com/2011/02/14/smoke-astroturf/ (last accessed November 10, 2019).

17. Marty Noble, "Starting to Believe? Recall Mets of 1973," Major League Baseball, https://www.mlb.com/news/1973-mets-coined-ya-gotta-believe-mantra/c-141082310 (last accessed November 10, 2019).

18. The phrase appears on a patch with the name "Tug" and outlines of a batter and pitcher. For part of the season, the patch on the left shoulder depicted Bob Murphy's name above the traditional Mets logo (scripted name, bridge, and city skyline). The longtime Mets announcer passed away on August 3, 2004.

Straight Up NYC, Like a Mets Fitted

How the New York Mets Influenced Hip-Hop Music and Culture

JEMAYNE LAVAR KING

Jay-Z made it clear; he can make the Yankee hat more famous than a Yankee can, and he may have. Thus, hip-hop has a plethora of references to that "other" franchise residing in the Bronx. In the same manner, there is a strong connection between the New York Metropolitan Baseball Club and hip-hop; there are lines in songs comparing one's ability to Rey Ordonez's fielding adroitness and donning team paraphernalia. Consequently, the Mets have a permanent place in hip-hop culture. In the early 1980s, hip-hop began to establish itself as a stand-alone genre of music. Its style—the B-boy look—morphed from a funk/punk rock esthetic, to what would dominate the decade. Brands like Levi's, Lee, Wrangler, Ralph Lauren, Le Tigre, and Lacoste became fashionable during the period. In addition, these garments typically featured baseball caps that not only signaled professional sport franchise support, they also alerted—for those who subscribed to hip-hop culture—which borough the wearer represented. In more instances than not, hailing from Queens, New York, meant donning a Mets cap. In spite of the staunch traditions associated with Major League Baseball, wearing a cap of a particular franchise does not guarantee allegiance to specific clubs within hip-hop culture. The wearer may not always be a Mets fan, however, the interlocking curlicue-style "NY" represents more; it exemplifies Queens and its place in hip-hop history, literature, and culture.

Considering hip-hop's sub society and its global influence, how did the New York Mets influence hip-hop culture, thus influencing global popular culture? Hip-hop music began as an implement that gave a voice to the voice-less. Constructed—mainly—by African Americans and Puerto Ricans in the Bronx in the 1970s, the genre evolved to party motifs, and compositions that boasted of sexual conquests and financial spoils. Practitioners of hip-hop culture did not need to look beyond their borough for inspiration. Yet, they did.

Hip-hop has been concerned with Queens since its inception. In "The Bridge Is Over"—a dis to MC Shan and the Juice Crew—KRS-One proclaimed the Bronx to be a superior borough to Queens, especially in regard to the origin of hip-hop music and culture. This manifested into a battle of boroughs for hip-hop supremacy. Supporters of MC Shan—and hip-hop municipal the Juice Crew—aligned themselves with the Queensbridge Houses—a public housing development in the Long Island City locality of Queens, New York—by wearing New York Mets paraphernalia. Hip-hop aficionados in line with the KRS-One and Boogie Down Productions—a name acquired from the nickname of the South Bronx segment of the Bronx—wore Yankee caps to signify their allegiance. Hence, the winners of conflicts traditionally write history. The history concerning "The Bridge Wars" reports the Bronx as the birthplace of hip-hop, thus cementing it in an apex status when compared to the home of the Mets.

In a similar fashion, the rivalry between the New York Yankees and New York Mets would later manifest in one of hip-hop's most notorious misun-derstandings, which turned into a full-fledged rap beef. Like Queens rapper MC Shan, Nasir Jones—commonly referred to by his stage name Nas—also hails from Queens. Known for his New York Mets references, Nas typically pays homage to the club by wearing their paraphernalia. He is synonymous with the Mets cap, though in lesser instances, he has worn a Yankees cap. In the same manner that "The Notorious B.I.G." intertwines with Tupac Shakur, Nas intertwines with Jay-Z. Within hip-hop culture, one would have a difficult time identifying two emcees who are as complex and impactful as Nasir bin Olu Dara Jones "Nas," and Sean Corey Carter "Jay-Z." Over time, each poet acquired a cult-like following by producing legendary works analyzed by the-orists while at the same token, inspiring future artists and practitioners. Despite critical mauling, Nasir Jones and Jay-Z are considered two of the greatest rappers in hip-hop's history. Due to a perceived misapprehension, the two engaged in a conflict—complete with Mets and Yankees merchandise in tow—that rivaled the Subway Series rivalry games betwixt the Yankees and Mets.

Nas was born on September 14, 1973, in Brooklyn. While still a youth, his family migrated from Brooklyn to Queens. Due to a lack of funds, the family moved into the Queensbridge housing projects. His mother, Fannie Ann Jones, worked a postmaster and his father, Olu Dara, was a jazz musician.

Though he traveled the world performing during his son's formative years, Dara had a profound influence on Nas. As a result, Nas initially wanted to become a comic book artist or a jazz musician like his father once he reached adulthood. Similarly, Jay-Z, born Sean Corey Carter on December 4, 1969, earns recognition as a global—and cultural—icon. Born and raised in Brooklyn—specifically, the Marcy Houses development in the Bedford-Stuyvesant neighborhood—he is considered among the best rappers of all time.

Concerning his feud with Nas, the two entities began openly disrespecting each other in 2001 on recordings, after passive-aggressive allusions to each other in songs since 1996, after Nas received an invitation to record on Jay-Z's debut album *Reasonable Doubt* but no-showed the recording session. As the 21st century opened, the Mets and Yankees caps took on new significance within hip-hop culture. For example, Jay-Z wore a Yankees cap for the cover of his 2003 retirement effort, *The Black Album*. The recording symbolized Jay-Z's career fading to black. Therefore, to achieve this aesthetic, everything in the cover's artwork appeared as a film negative. The Yankees' interlocking cap insignia experiences the blacked-out treatment, though its presence is implied.

The cap symbolized Jay-Z's positioning as the apex rapper in New York, and the world. In retrospect, on his 2001 release *Stillmatic*, Nas wears an orange velour tracksuit, white and orange Air Force 1 low-top sneakers, and an orange baseball cap emblazoned with the words, "New York" in the Mets trademarked font appearing on their road uniforms. In a season where the Mets would finish in third place in the National League East with an 82–80 record, Nas supporters and hip-hop aficionados alike understood the hat to represent Queens and not the New York Mets. Nas was signaling that—in this conflict—he was also defending the honor of the Queensbridge Houses, Queens, and all portions of New York that sided with him and opposed Jay-Z in the skirmish. For Nas, *Stillmatic* rejuvenated his career, and brought significant attention to his rhyming prowess. The album also reminded the hip-hop community of the marketability of the New York Mets color scheme.

Like the Mets, rappers from Queens had to prove themselves worthy of adulation. Jay Hook—who earned the first-ever victory for the Mets—spoke of this mindset during the club's inaugural season of 1962. He quipped, "Don't give up a run because you'll lose the chance for a tie" (Topel 6). In brief, this characteristic fosters a massive following; the Mets have influenced everything from television and movies to novels and music, namely, hip-hop. Therefore, practitioners of hip-hop music and culture pay homage to the Mets as if doing so was mandatory.

To understand the hip-hop culture's fascination with the Mets and the ball club's influence on hip-hop music and culture, one must first examine hip-hop's origins. Specifically, hip-hop music is the offspring of the Jazz and

Disco genres. Black Arts Movement artists such as Nikki Giovanni, Sonia Sanchez, and Amiri Baraka, and countless Soul, Funk, Rock and Punk artists also provide hip-hop music and culture with influence. Through gang strife, horrible economic conditions, and a lack of entertainment/expression outlets, hip-hop began in the South Bronx—as a form of locution, and later, social activism. The genre's lore dates the origin to 1520 Sedgwick Avenue on August 11, 1973, at Cindy Campbell's basement party. That season, the Yankees finished at 80–82—relegating them to 4th place in the American League East, and an afterthought when compared to the scrappy Mets. At the time, "The Amazins" set a major-league record for the lowest win percentage for a pennant winner, finishing slightly better at 82–79. The Mets went to the World Series and lost in seven games to the Oakland A's. That season served as a microcosm for the relationship Queens would maintain with the Bronx in hip-hop culture. No matter how impactful a Queens rapper would be, the snide manifested that they were not from the Bronx. This equated the Queens rapper as a second-rate MC. Regarding New York's baseball franchises, The Mets—no matter how bright they played in spurts—their light could not outshine the luminance of—at the time of hip-hop's inception—20 World Series titles belonging to the Yankees. It is ironic that hip-hop music and culture began during one of the Mets most memorable seasons.

Regarding the basement party, Cindy intended to use proceeds from the gathering to purchase new school clothes. To achieve this destination, she rented the recreation room in her apartment building, purchased alcoholic beverages and other refreshments, and convinced her brother, Clive (Kool Herc), a proficient DJ, to perform. She manufactured hand-written fliers to distribute throughout the neighborhood and publicize the extravaganza. Knowing that women would attract a multitude of men, she charged women 25 cents, while charging men double the admittance. Hip-hop historian Joseph C. Ewoodzie, Jr., recounts the evening. He explains:

> Hence, the events of August 11, 1973, birthed hip-hop music and culture; the subculture and genre begin with DJ Kool Herc. The socioeconomic conditions of the Bronx combined with the desires and lifestyles of the borough's youth to begot what would eventually become a multi-billion-dollar industry. Contrary to popular belief, Kool Herc did not intend to create a new music genre; he—like others—filled a cultural nihility.

Considering New York's urban decay of the period, the Bronx's youth distracted themselves with a multitude of social activities, of which hip-hop stood paramount. Filled with exploits the mainstream could not imagine, the reality of inner-city life helped propel hip-hop music, culture, and literature into national and international spaces. For these outsiders, the detailed African American enterprises provided a view into a biotic community that—

prior—did not exist. This is largely due to the success and impact of the Sugar Hill Gang's song "Rapper's Delight," the first example of epic poetry in the genre. It became a Top 40 hit, legitimizing hip-hop as a music subculture outside Bronx neighborhoods and into majority-white towns like the ones in neighboring Westchester County. But the popularity contrasted with the lack of profit motive inherent in hip-hop's origins.

Record executive Sylvia Robinson—a singer who had reached number one on *Billboard*'s R&B Chart in 1973 with her single "Pillow Talk"—not only knew that hip-hop existed, but also recognized the earning potential of being an early exploiter of the then untapped genre. After Robinson's performing career subsided, she eventually became the co-owner of Sugar Hill Records. To capitalize on the hip-hop movement, Robinson envisioned a rap record and initially approached the infamous DJ Love Bug Starski about recording. But he declined the offer.

Robinson asked several others including Grandmaster Flash and the Furious Five, Eddie Cheeba, and DJ Hollywood. They all rejected her, because hip-hop music and culture was not previously recorded for monetary gain. Early practitioners simply refused to embrace the concept. Ultimately, Robinson formed the Sugar Hill Gang, a makeshift group that would change the course of hip-hop music and culture. The group's initial incarnation included Henry "Big Bank Hank" Jackson, Michael "Wonder Mike" Wright, and Guy "Master Gee" O'Brien. Robinson wasted no time piling the then unknown MCs into her studio.

As the Mets found success and swagger in the mid-to-late 1980s, so did hip-hop. MTV secured the genre's inclusion in mainstream entertainment with the show *Yo! MTV Raps.* The title pays homage to Public Enemy's 1987 album *Yo! Bum Rush the Show.* Black Entertainment Television followed with *Rap City.*

MC Hammer, Leaders of the New School, Young MC, Tone Loc, and Special Ed were among those hip-hop artists who penned tongue-in-cheek rhymes detailing teen angst coming-of-age lyrics. These artists displayed hip-hop music through rose-tinted glasses with albums that did not require stickers warning parents of potentially offensive lyrics. In turn, they were widely welcomed within America's suburbia. Hip-hop garnered acceptance outside the African American community partially because of sampling—the appropriation of a component of a larger recording. These elements include speech, rhythm, melody, and interpolations. One of the most popular samples in hip-hop is the breakbeat.

Therefore, examining hip-hop's trajectory during the last quarter of the 20th century, it is noteworthy that hip-hop music received little recognition from the Recording Academy. Unfortunately, it was not until 1989, when DJ Jazzy Jeff & The Fresh Prince won the inaugural award for Best Rap Performance for "Parents Just Don't Understand" that hip-hop artists begin to reap critical acclaim for their contributions. But the duo's lyrics spoke to a largely white, suburban audience weaned on reruns of family sitcoms airing on Nick at Nite. This paved the way for more serious offerings to follow, much like the 1950s, when white artists covered rhythm-and-blues songs originated by African American singers and sometimes softened the lyrics.

By then, hip-hop had subsisted for 16 years. In comparison to hip-hop's music, its culture existed as a "lack thereof" because the majority of music lovers did not embrace, or was not aware of, its precepts founded on urban pain turned into musical expression. But sportswear sales soared because of hip-hop influence. It became fashionable within the subculture for consumers to don sports apparel for their aesthetics rather than their affiliations. The apparel company Starter led this motility. Fueled by resplendent consumer support and fan loyalty, its apparel became synonymous with the hip-hop and urban community—fans of the NFL, NHL, NBA and MLB purchased Starter's merchandise, authorized by licensing agreements with the respective leagues. One of Starter's popular items was the Mets satin bullpen jacket. As the Mets enjoyed the patriarchal spoils of becoming the alpha New York baseball club during the 1980s, their on—and off-field—conquests created demand for their apparel.

To Mets fans, the phrase "Game Six" harkens the greatest moment in franchise history. During the 1986 Fall Classic, the Mets inexplicably won the sixth game in dramatic fashion against the Boston Red Sox, when Mookie Wilson's ground ball went through Bill Buckner's legs. Tying the World Series at 3–3, the teams had to play a seventh game. The final game was delayed by one day because of rain. However, the inclement weather did not "wash away" the team's gargantuan expectations.

These wins incited a boon in team paraphernalia sales. Hip-hop culture immediately embraced the satin jacket. Subsequently, the Mets Starter jacket featured prominently in catalogues, music videos, promotional album shoots, and sporting events.

Capitalizing on what would become a universal marketing technique, the upstart Starter embraced hip-hop culture, which, in turn, connected North American professional sports with the genre's demographic and its still untapped revenue potential. During this period in hip-hop history, singers—who once dressed in bizarre costumes in line with the garb adorning rock stars including but not limited to, Billy Idol, Kiss, David Bowie, and Van Halen—began to employ a look similar to street hustlers and stick-up (thieves) kids.

Starter's popularity reflected a growing awareness of black spending power. Mets paraphernalia, in turn, began appearing in urban-esque films marketed to African Americans. In Spike Lee's *School Daze*,[1] his character,

Half-Pint, dons a backwards Mets fitted cap the night he gains entry into Gamma Phi Gamma Fraternity. It symbolizes an edgier persona. For example, Half-Pint is the butt of jokes throughout the film and only appears in Mets apparel after his pledge experience. In the scenes where he wears the cap, Half-Pint is more assertive; he goes from observing patriarchal frat house antics to actively perpetrating them. Like the 1988 National League East champion New York Mets, Half-Pint becomes the alpha—dominant personality of his pledge class—in the same way that the decade's incarnation of the Mets was the alpha National League East franchise. During this period in the club's history, hip-hop culture embraced Mets products as their appearances in narratives concerning or related to hip-hop culture became commonplace.

From 1984 to 1990, the Mets enjoyed a seven-year period of winning baseball. Edgy in its expression, hip-hop concerns itself with the proletariat's ascension with many rap songs depicting gritty narratives of rising from a lower social class. Few teams personified this ascent better than the New York Mets; before their seven-year victory stretch, the club—and its fans—experienced seven consecutive years of losing baseball. From 1977 to 1983, the Mets finished no better than 5th place in the National League East. Hence, as proletariat rap became popular, so did the Mets.

Similarly, In John Landis's Queens-based *Coming to America*,[2] a cab driver wearing a Mets ball cap shouts a profanity at African Prince Akeem Joffer, played by Eddie Murphy, when the latter character steps into moving traffic, after "coming to America." Like Lee's Half-Pint, the cab driver appears overtly assertive while wearing the same Mets cap. Murphy's Prince Akeem dons a Starter Mets varsity jacket, which became famous because of the product placement in the blockbuster film. In 2016, New Jersey sneaker and streetwear boutique Packer Shoes collaborated with Starter to recreate the jacket. To promote its release, Packer employed Queens rapper Meyhem Lauren as a model for the product, further connecting the Mets and hip-hop culture.

Before this shrewd business model, alignment with hip-hop music and culture meant linking oneself with anarchy. All things hip-hop music and culture loomed as threats—sans capitalism—to traditional values that Americans held dear. By this period in hip-hop history, the New York Mets were synonymous with hip-hop music and culture.

One year after the Mets won the 1986 World Series, LL Cool J's "I'm BAD" kicked off his 1987 album *Bigger and Deffer*. During the album's success, it was common to see LL Cool J don a Starter Mets satin bullpen jacket, with his signature Kangol bucket hat. He became the poster child for hip-hop's evolution but was concerned with image and marketability, along with his artistry. So, LL took liberties with hip-hop's gritty reputation. Eventually, his sound bordered on a sound that featured—popular for that period—New

Jack Swing production cues. However, early on, his sound embodied new school topics rooted in hip-hop literature's patriarchy and tradition. While the Mets rebelled against the establishment, tradition, and status quo in the mid–1980s, so did LL Cool J in hip-hop.

LL Cool J's rebellious spirit helped usher in a "new era" for hip-hop artists. His brand of rap became the marquee hip-hop sound of the 1980s; his style of dress continued in the lineage of fellow Queens rappers Run-DMC. His stature made it cool for rappers to wear Mets paraphernalia—even if they did not hail from Queens. Rappers from other states including, but not limited to, André 3000 of Outkast, Rick Ross, Plies, Mac Miller, The Game, and ScHoolboy Q have all worn Mets' gear regularly. New York rappers from boroughs other than Queens who also wear Mets intellectual property include Diddy, Method Man, Fabolous, and Busta Rhymes.

Artists who have named dropped the Mets name in songs include Nas, Lil B, Rampage, Action Bronson, Artifacts, Big L, A Tribe Called Quest, and the Beastie Boys (Maseng). Whereas hip-hop music commonly utilizes professional sports as points of reference, baseball analogies, synonyms, and puns are not as common as the NFL and NBA. Because the New York Yankees and their intellectual properties transcend professional sports, they are heavily referenced in hip-hop music. On the contrary, the Mets—measurably—do not match the Yankees' history, nor their references in rap music. However, as the Mets have enjoyed a respectable presence within popular culture, they also enjoy appearances as hip-hop references within rap music. Players are also connected to hip-hop and not always as a topic for the lyrics. More well-known for his assemblage of fastballs and off-speed pitches, recently acquired pitcher Marcus Stroman leads a clandestine existence as a rapper. Stroman shared top billing in a video with former Duke University teammate Mike Seander, who currently raps under the moniker "Mike" (formerly Mike Stud). Previously, Stroman provided lyrics for Seander offerings.

Moreover, just as it has become commonplace for athletes to have aspirations and pursue hip-hop careers, recording artists have aspired to be athletes. In particular, NBA stars including, Danna Barros, Cedric Ceballos, Shaquille O'Neal, and Kobe Bryant have recorded and released commercial music. Conversely, legendary hip-hop mogul Master P was dangerously close to making the final roster of the NBA's Charlotte Hornets and Toronto Raptors on separate occasions. Whereas these types of instances are less popular in baseball, they still occur. Rapper Nelly grew up obsessed with baseball and excelled at the sport. Though garnering interest from several MLB franchises, he never fulfilled his professional baseball aspirations. Considering Marcus Stroman's MLB All-Star status, he does not fit the "traditional" profile of an athlete obsessed with hip-hop music and culture. Yet, he is an example of how hip-hop culture progressed beyond an existence as the "Psalm of the proletariat" and subsists as a "new school manifestation" of the Mets' influence on hip-hop culture and music.

The Mets represent hip-hop culture as much as they represent the interlocking insignia on their cap. In turn, the Mets are to New York, as New York is to hip-hop. All entities are one within the same.

NOTES

1. *School Daze*, directed by Spike Lee (1988; Columbia Pictures, 40 Acres & A Mule Filmworks).

2. *Coming to America*, directed by John Landis (1988; Paramount Pictures, Eddie Murphy Productions).

(900) 976–1313

DAVID KRELL

Joy cometh in the morning.[1] But only if your team wins the day or night before.

Dopamine rushes through a fan's nervous system like a raging river when learning of victories. Until the early 1970s, fans learned game results through late-night television newscasts, news-radio stations, or the local newspaper. Waiting for the scores increased the anticipation, or fear, of learning the outcome—the longer the wait time, the bigger the dopamine's effect. Technology reduced that time period to the few seconds that it takes to dial a phone number. (900) 976–1313. Sports Phone.[2]

Between "Ya Gotta Believe" and the 2000 Subway Series, Sports Phone's digits became as well-remembered as a best friend's home number. Mets fans rejoiced and recoiled when they dialed the digits because Sports Phone's success coincided with the "Ya Gotta Believe!" season of 1973; the mournful post–Seaver years of 1977–1982; the swagger of the mid–1980s; the hopeful Bobby Bonilla era of the mid–1990s; and the emergence of Mike Piazza as a Mets icon in the late 1990s.

Ever since the Town Crier went through the village square announcing news, we've craved information about the goings-on in our community. But the outcomes of contests have an emotional component. We rally behind a team, living vicariously through its exploits. Triumphs are celebrated, losses are mourned.

There's also a matter of civic pride, represented most obviously by the monikers of teams—Orioles for Maryland's state bird; Dodgers for Brooklyn's requirement to avoid trolleys; Mariners for the maritime activities in Seattle; Knickerbockers for a fictional character in Washington Irving's *A History of New York*; Ravens for Baltimore's connection to poet and "The Raven" scribe Edgar Allen Poe; Rockies for the West's mountain range; Padres for the missionaries who helped settle California; Pistons for Detroit's automotive industry; Dolphins for Miami's aquatic feature; Packers for Wisconsin's meat packing business; Steelers for Pittsburgh's steel trade; and, of course, Metropolitans for New York being the epitome of a city with culture, sophistication, and urbanity.

Sports Phone's announcers were telephonic versions of the Town Crier, dispensing the basic information of games in less than 60 seconds for an audience willing to shoulder the cost. For a data-dependent sports fan, it was a justified expense to achieve immediate gratification, emotional satisfaction, and improved speculation.

What began in 1972 as a service targeted to sports fans thirsty for immediacy became central to the information culture that led to the Internet's mass availability two decades hence, which prompted Sports Phone's demise. For fans, it was a novelty. Gamblers saw it as a necessity. Sportscasters, a launching pad. But there was no room for them to show, or even develop, a style. In 2015, Mets historian and announcer Howie Rose said, "What I was told on my interview was that they really wanted to make it a one-minute professional sportscast with commentary and scores."[3]

Indeed, it was a great foundation.

Rose recalls:

It was very exciting to get a legitimate credential and pretty good training. It was a great learning tool for an entry level job. We learned the fundamentals about speaking clearly, being succinct, and making sure we were grammatically correct. At the same time, we learned how to use the telephone as a device to track down stories during the day. I generally worked more when the games were going on. My first role was on Saturday night and Sunday night. Towards the last few months, I was a weekday host. Then I got a job at WHN and switched back and forth. The most memorable thing that I did was in February, 1976. Darryl Sittler for the Maple Leafs tied the record for goals in one NHL game. I called the Maple Leafts switchboard and got through to the locker room. I said, "Howie Rose, Sports Phone, New York. I want to do a quick interview." I got five minutes and cut it up into a million pieces. I sent to AP and UPI. We had the permission to sell the stories elsewhere and I got Sports Phone a scoop.

Some of us had different goals and agendas. The original daytime voice was Precision Peter Newman. He was one of the more recognizable voices. He didn't really work games unless they were baseball afternoon games. His interests far transcended sports. Sports Phone was a vehicle to get his name out. In the long run, he went into film production. Years later, he was involved in the movies *Smoke* and *Blue in the Face*. He needed a baseball announcer and used me to do the voice of the play-by-play guy.

I started in May, 1975. Bob Meyer ran it. The way I got the job was because I was the president of the Marv Albert Fan Club when I was a teenager in 1967. I was a big fan of Marv's and Bob was Marv's statistician. Marv became my mentor and friend. When I was the sports director and program director at WQMC at Queens College, Bob sent a letter to me. He asked Marv about entry level guys. My name came up.[4]

Technology had not caught up to the idea of an efficient pay-per-call service until Sports Phone. In 1964, Macy's leveraged its holiday-themed iconography with a program to dial Santa Claus. In the boardroom at the World's Largest Store, it seemed like a fine idea to add this gimmick to the other holiday markers—Thanksgiving Day Parade, *Miracle on 34th Street*. The failure was epic—an estimated two million calls "almost completely disrupted the Manhattan phone service."[5]

Off-track betting was the next step in the linkage between sports updates and telephony.[6]

When Sports Phone launched in 1972, the revenue structure was based on an advertising model—sell 15 seconds of every minute (actually, 57 seconds) to advertisers. Three years later, it adjusted to a pay-per-call template.[7] There's no doubt that the gambling community relied on the service, but Sports Phone also attracted the mainstream fan. "I've heard the gambling thing, of course," said Glenn Appleyard, President of Phone Programs. "I won't be so naive as to say there isn't some of that going on, but we do things that appeal to all people. The interviews. The features. The quiz."[8]

After being established in New York for a couple of years, Sports Phone extended its operations across the Hudson River to New Jersey. The Chicago office opened in 1977. One of the Windy City announcers was Fred Huebner.

My dad was working at a bank in Berwyn and he started a broadcasting company with the bank. They got permission to use the name Olympic Broadcasting Company.

I'd tag along with my dad to Cougars and Bulls games during high school because the company broadcast them. I knew that college math or science would be a struggle so I went to broadcasting school. The General Manager in Sports Phone's Chicago office was a guy that my dad had hired to be a color commentator on Bulls games.

It was tough for me because the guys I was working with were Northwestern or Loyola guys. Ron Gleason is still the Sports Director at WBBM. There was a lot of learning quickly and being able to reel off scores. I valued how to make sure that the callers were able to understand the scores and be succinct and exact so they would get reliable information.

At first, some people didn't know about Sports Phone unless they were die-hard sports fans or gamblers. There wasn't much sports talk radio back then and maybe one show here or there on TV. People were excited when they found out.

We had a 10–15 minute break after every update. We'd call the press boxes and be nice so that the PR directors or sports information directors would feed us information. Then, the teams got on board and helped us out.

It was old-fashioned journalism but a lot quicker. It wasn't just scores. We had press credentials and do 30-second wraps. We had to learn how to write them with eight-to-ten second cuts in the middle. A lot of stations don't do updates. They only want a sound bite if it's controversial.

I was there until 1990. I started as a part-timer, then became a full-timer, operations manager, and trainer.[9]

Gamblers' fealty to Sports Phone was acknowledged, though certainly not celebrated, or even highlighted, in the office. "We consciously try to stay away from that," said announcer Mike Walczewski. "You won't hear any betting lines or odds or things like that."[10] For that kind of information on football games, gamblers could tune in to NFL pre-game shows which were more laissez-faire concerning wagering on games.

For newsgatherers, Sports Phone was a vital arrow in their quiver. It's tough to beat the wire services—UPI, AP, Reuters—but Sports Phone did that. "The television sportscasters, guys like Ray Lane, Charlie Neal and Larry Adderly, tell me they sometimes call Sports Phone just before their broadcast," said John Cwikla, Michigan head of Phone Programs. "If they're waiting for a final score on a game, they'll run into the studio and do their headline on the air, then run out and call. We usually have the scores ahead of the wire services."[11] Sports Phone alumni became fixtures in sports announcing. In addition to Howie Rose and Fred Huebner, there were Gary Cohen, Al Trautwig, Michael Kay, Bob Papa, and Mike Walczewski ("King Wally"), to name a few.

In 1979, Sports Phone reportedly answered more than 50 million calls; stringers positioned at arenas and stadiums fed the information to the various Sports Phone offices. Though callers got a price break after 11:00 p.m. to 30–35 cents per minute, depending on the location.[12] Mets fans dialing the digits learned highlights of players who are still beloved decades later and others who are long forgotten to have worn the team's uniform.

Koosman wins 20th (Shea Stadium, September 16, 1976)

In 1976, the Mets finished third in the National League East with an 86–76 record. One of those 86 wins came on September 16, but it had a special meaning—for the fifth time in the team's history, a Mets pitcher won 20 games.

Jerome Martin Koosman.

The left-handed veteran did it with authority—13 strikeouts in the 4–1 contest against the St. Louis Cardinals. "It is the night of my life," said the southpaw. "This was the night I have waited for since I was 16 years old. It might seem like I started at the top, winning 19 games in 1968, playing in the World Series in 1969."[13]

Attendance was sparse—sportswriter Deane McGowen attributed the 7,820 attendance figure to a "day-long rainstorm" that offered a highly significant possibility of a rainout.[14]

Koosman's achievement capped an emotional season—his father died earlier in the year; he lost five straight games; and he received a demotion, though brief, to the bullpen.[15] When he took the mound, he had compiled a 14–2 record and 1.70 ERA since the All-Star Break.[16] 1976 was one of Koosman's outstanding seasons in a 19-year career: 21–10 win-loss record, 200 strikeouts.

The Cardinals went through five pitchers; Koosman pitched a complete game. Run support began in the bottom of the third inning—Pete Falcone walked Felix Millan and John Milner. Torre followed by getting on first, thanks to an error by shortstop Don Kessinger, which allowed Millan to score.

In the fifth, Torre doubled and Roy Staiger singled him home; Bruce Boisclair bashed a solo home run in the seventh.

St. Louis mishaps gave the Mets their fourth run of the night: Milner singled and advanced to second base on Doug Capilla's balk, then advanced to third on a wild pitch. Boisclair got his second RBI in the game with a single to score Milner.

The Cardinals' only run came from a two-out home run in the seventh hit by future Met and *Seinfeld* guest star Keith Hernandez.

Matlack Whiffs 10, Kingman Crushes 2 (San Diego Stadium, April 29, 1976)

When Jon Matlack left the Mets after the 1977 season, he left behind great memories—1972 National League Rookie of the Year; major-league leader in shutouts (1974); National League leader in shutouts (1976); and winning eight of his last 12 games to help the Mets secure the 1973 National League pennant and go to the World Series—an epic battle that went the full seven games and ended with a loss to the Oakland A's.

In his last tour of National League ballparks—before going to the Texas Rangers where he stayed for the remainder of his career, which ended with the 1983 season—Matlack gave an outstanding performance early in 1977 with a 10-strikeout performance against the San Diego Padres; slugger Dave Kingman boosted the score with two home runs, each three-run baggers.

Matlack hadn't seen the mound for nine days when he pitched, but he augured a tough contest for San Diego early—he struck out four of the first six batters. "I threw 72 fastballs out of 126 pitches. It seemed like a perfect mix."[17]

A lineup mistake went either ignored or unnoticed—the Mets batted out of order until Padres skipper John McNamara protested with two outs in the seventh inning. Roy Staiger and John Stearns had the #6 and #7 batting slots, respectively, in the Mets lineup but switched places. Stearns walked and went to third on Staiger's single. But the protest resulted in Staiger being called out.[18] McNamara claimed that he only found the switch in the seventh.[19]

Lee Mazzilli's Grand Slam and Swan's 13 Ks (Shea Stadium, July 4, 1978)

Nineteen seventy-eight was a magical year for baseball. Blissful, even. Gaylord Perry got his 3000th strikeout; Ron Guidry went 25–3; J.R. Richard notched more than 300 strikeouts; Pete Rose tied a National League record by hitting safely in 44 consecutive games and reached the 3000-hit plateau; the New York Yankees had an epic comeback to win the AL East from the Boston Red Sox, then won the World Series against the Los Angeles

Sports Phone began in 1972 and became a popular pay-per-call service for fans wanting current information about scores and stories. Mets fans dialing in 1975 would hear about Tom Seaver's explosive performance—leading the National League with 22 wins and leading the major leagues with a 2.35 ERA. Seaver won his third and last Cy Young Award that year (National Baseball Hall of Fame and Museum, Cooperstown, N.Y.).

Dodgers; and Mets legend Tom Seaver pitched a no-hitter a year after getting traded from the Mets to the Reds.

For the Mets, 1978 was a forgettable annum in their existence. With Seaver and Matlack gone, Koosman remained as the lone member of the celebrated trio of hurlers. He went 3–15; the pitching staff's ERA was 3.87; and the team placed sixth in the NL East with a 66–96 record. But there was one bright spot: Lee Mazzilli.

The Brooklyn native had the highest batting average on the team—.273 in 148 games; the second highest number of stolen bases (20); and the second highest number of walks (69). On July 4, Mazzilli gave fans a moment to celebrate when he crushed a grand slam in the first game of a twilight double-header against the Philadelphia Phillies. Pat Zachry pitched a complete game and got his 10th win of the season with a two-hitter. What made Mazzilli's home run a personal victory was the breaking of an oh-for-15 slump in recent games.[20]

The grand slam was responsible for all the runs in the 4–0 shutout. Alas, as often happened in late 1970s Mets games, the joy was short-lived. The Phillies took the second game 3–2, despite Craig Swan's phenomenal control—13 strikeouts, five hits. Ahead 2–1 in the ninth, Swan got Richie Hebner out on a 4–3 grounder and Tim McCarver on a foul ball to third baseman Lenny Randle. Bob Boone doubled and pinch-hitter José Cardenal banged a two-run homer to put the gentlemen from Philadelphia ahead for good.

Fog (Shea Stadium, May 25, 1979)

Charles Dickens likely would have cribbed from the beginning of his opus *Bleak House*, where he eloquently describes fog enveloping every nook and cranny of London if he were a sportswriter on May 25, 1979. The same weather condition forced an extra-innings contest against the Pirates to be stopped at 3–3 in the 11th inning and continued at a later date. The turning point happened when Pittsburgh left fielder Bill Robinson had more trouble finding the ball on a Joel Youngblood smash than Dorothy had finding the land of Oz. Youngblood scored a triple that probably should have been a fly out. After nearly an hour and 20 minutes waiting for the fog to lift, the umpires called the game.

There were no objections. Mets skipper Joe Torre said, "Fair enough. Youngblood would not have been on third if it hadn't been for the fog."[21]

The endurance for extra innings amounted to naught—MLB rules dictated that tie games had to be replayed from the beginning. So, the teams added a game to their June 25 meeting, giving fans a twi-night doubleheader. They split the games.

The Double That Wasn't (Shea Stadium, May 25, 1980)

On the Sunday of 1980's Memorial Day weekend, the Mets and Braves battled in a pitchers' duel that was scoreless until the eighth inning, when veteran hurler Phil Niekro gave up three runs to the fellas from Flushing.

Frank Taveras went four-for-four, with his last hit being a double to lead off the inning. Lee Mazzilli popped out to Braves catcher Bruce Benedict in foul territory; John Stearns followed with a double to score Taveras. Then, Mike Jorgensen, who smashed seven home runs in 1980, hit one into the right-field stands. Or did he?

Eric Gregg left his home-plate umpiring duties in the first inning after a foul tip whacked him on the forehead, which reduced the umpire crew to three and left a vacancy down the right-field line. *Daily News* scribe Bill Madden wrote, "This proved to be most fortunate when, on a 2–1 count, Jorgensen lofted a towering fly to right that appeared to many to have curved foul by about 15 feet."[22]

The 3–0 score gave Swan a nice cushion to maintain, which he did. Commenting on his three-hitter performance, Swan said, "With a one-run lead, I've got to be concerned about weak grounders and bunts etc. But with the extra two, I can challenge everyone like I did. There was no messing around, no walks, just getting them out."[23]

Washington Clouts 3 Homers (Dodger Stadium, June 22, 1980)

Claudell Washington came to the Mets in early June 1980, after playing in the American League—A's, Rangers, White Sox—since 1974. Any concerns about a lack of familiarity with National League pitching went the way of the mastodon on June 22. The right fielder went three-for-five and tallied five RBI against the Dodgers—all hits were home runs. "That was one helluva surprise to me, too, I'd been struggling and didn't know the pitching over in this league. This is my first time around, and I still don't know what to expect."[24]

The presence of Washington in the lineup was unexpected—an injury to Mazzilli's left hand required a substitute outfielder. Then, he suffered his own injury in the bottom of the first when he collided with Joel Youngblood, hoping to rob Davey Lopes of a hit by doing his best Ron Swoboda imitation. Instead, he caught Youngblood's shoe in the mouth and got "10 minutes of treatment"[25] for a cut lip.

Washington stayed with the Mets for one season, batting .275 with a strikeout ratio of less than one per game. After the stellar performance against the Dodgers, he talked about the vagaries of baseball: "I've been hanging in there. They can whip me all they want to, but I refuse to be broken. I've been through everything you can be through in baseball and I'll do the best I can until things get better. They can't get any worse."[26]

After the Mets, Washington played for the Braves, Yankees, and Angels. He ended his career in 1990 with a .278 batting average and nearly 1,900 hits.

Kingman's Grand Slam (Riverfront Stadium, August 22, 1981)

Dave Kingman's home runs were, quite often, mammoth, consistent with his 6'6" frame. In a 7–4 victory against the Cincinnati Reds, the man known as "Kong" sent Mike Cubbage, Mookie Wilson, and Hubie Brooks around the bases with a left-field, two-out blast. It's not as if Kingman could will the ball over the fence, but his power helped where other batters would have seen their efforts resulting in catches at the warning track.

Mets manager Joe Torre commented on Kingman's power after the game: "I didn't think he got a good piece of it, but I knew he was going for the long ball, and since he is so strong, I also knew that anything could happen when he swings that bat," said Torre.[27] Until Kingman's slam in the eighth, the Mets only managed three hits in this 1981 game.

Kingman was a career .236 hitter but his home-run total belies that figure—442. His knocks are fondly remembered by Mets fans during a period when there was not much to cheer about. He tied home-run kings Hank Aaron and Babe Ruth with 16 career grand slams.

George Foster Signs

After the 1981 season, truncated because of a strike, baseball fans looked forward to putting the controversy over the walkout behind them. Mets rooters, especially so. They got a clean slate for a new era—or so they hoped—when welcoming one of the National League's great sluggers of his era. George Foster. The Mets signed the Reds power hitter during 1982's Spring Training to a five-year contract at $1.7 million per season.[28]

"I'd like to warn the airplanes and the airport not to fly too low,"[29] joked the Cincinnati export.

It was exciting to be a Mets fan, knowing that the ownership was amenable to opening up the checkbook. There was a feeling that sunnier days were in store for Shea Stadium. "This deal might convince the hundreds of thousands of Met fans driven away by the Payson-DeRoulet-Grant regime that their team is on the way back. Nelson Doubleday is no George Steinbrenner, but he's not a piker, either,"[30] wrote Doug Gould and Henry Hecht in the *New York Post.*

The Mets finished 65–97 in 1982; Foster hit 13 home runs in 151 games. He stayed with the Mets for four full seasons—the Mets sent him to the White Sox in the middle of the 1986 season, eclipsing Foster's chance to be on another pennant-winning, World Series contender.

Will You Be the Mets' Valentine? (Shea Stadium, September 5, 1982)

When Ellis Valentine injured his wrist, it sent him to the bench for three games at the end of the 1982 season. When he returned, the baseball gods must have healed it. In a 10–2 victory marking the first time in a month that the Mets won two consecutive games, Valentine had a double, a three-run bash, and a catch reflecting his fielding excellence. The Reds used three hurlers to face the Mets, who scored seven runs in the second inning.

Mets skipper George Bamberger said, "He's playing great in rightfield [*sic*], really hitting, playing great all-round baseball."[31]

The joyousness eased some tension surrounding Valentine and his comments about the Mets being "the worst organization in baseball." Valentine wanted to play and, in his paradigm, wasn't getting sufficient opportunities. For the month leading to the game, Valentine hit .364. Whether he kept track or not, Valentine claimed the latter. "I didn't know that, but I do know I have been hitting the ball well. When you are a player like myself, you need to be in there every day to establish yourself."[32]

Ellis Valentine came to the Mets in the middle of the 1981 season and stayed through 1982. He played for the Angels in 1983, only saw two games with the Triple-A Edmonton Trappers in 1984, and finished his career with the Rangers in 1985.

Keith Hernandez Signs

Keith Hernandez is known as a leader of the 1986 Mets, a team broiled in controversy, swagger, and a seven-game World Series victory against the Boston Red Sox. After years as a broadcaster with SNY, his critiques and analyses with fellow alumnus Ron Darling and veteran announcer Gary Cohen have become the gold standard for color commentators. It is, thus and henceforth, difficult to conceive that Hernandez did not want to come to New York when the Cardinals traded him a year after winning the 1982 World Series. "I'm going home to check my contract to see if I can veto the deal,"[33] said the first baseman, who had won five straight Gold Gloves and had a career average of .299 up to that point.

Mets General Manager Frank Cashen saw an addition of power, leadership, and presence when conceiving a lineup with Hernandez. Pitcher Neil Allen had been floated as trade bait, igniting interest in teams. "One of the clubs that called me was the Cardinals," said Cashen. "Joe McDonald told me right off we could have Hernandez if we were willing to give up Allen. We've been working on the other player [pitcher Rick Ownbey] in the deal for about 10 days. I'd say they extracted a pretty fair price."[34]

Allen took it in stride, figuring that he would be remembered as the answer to a trivia question. "They'll remember this trade years from now and they'll say, 'Who was Keith Hernandez traded for?' I'm honored."[35]

Welcome Home, Tom! (Shea Stadium, April 5, 1983)

Thomas Wolfe was wrong.

Six years after being traded to Cincinnati—for Pat Zachry, Steve Henderson, Doug Flynn, and Dan Norman—Tom Seaver returned to Shea Stadium. He pitched six innings on 1983's Opening Day against the Philadelphia Phillies—led by southpaw Steve Carlton—and racked up a 2–0 win. It was, as Yogi Berra once said, déjà vu all over again. The 41 on his jersey. The long stretch that brought his right knee into the dirt with every pitch. The solid outing. Tom Seaver was back where he belonged.

Former Reds teammate Pete Rose was in the Phillies lineup that day. Seaver surprised him. "I didn't know he could still throw that hard," said Rose. "He messed me up. He threw it inside, too, and it established his fastball in the back of my mind. It's always in the back of your mind. The last three, four years he wasn't the blower he was when he was over here the first time, but he's still got that good No. 1."[36]

Seaver, the boyish-faced pitcher who mowed down the National League's fiercest batsmen in his prime, faced more than nerves and adrenaline common to Opening Day. "I knew it would be emotional," said the right-hander, "but I didn't think it would be that emotional. I had to block out a lot of it because I was pitching, but if I wasn't, I would have cried. I know my mother lost it."[37]

Gooden Breaks Rookie K Record (Shea Stadium, September 12, 1984)

For America, 1984 was a year of patriotism. Set in the early 1960s, the ABC show *Call to Glory* inspired audiences to remember a time when the country was unified in its defiance of communism, no matter in which end of the political spectrum one resided. Mary Lou Retton captured hearts and imagination when she won the Gold Medal in gymnastics at the Summer Olympics in Los Angeles.

For the Mets, 1984 was a year of renewal, building upon the NL East second-place finish in 1983. It was Dwight Gooden's rookie season, one that elevated Shea Stadium's citizenry and inspired the creation of the "K Corner" with a placard and a "K" signifying each strikeout. On September 12, he notched the most exciting one of the season—his 246th strikeout to break the record for a rookie pitcher, previously held by Herb Score in 1955 with the Cleveland Indians. Pirates center fielder Marvell Wynne has the distinction of being the prey for the record-setting whiff. "I'm a fastball hitter," said Wynne, who batted .266 in 1984, "and 90 per cent of what Gooden throws are fastballs. But the guy throws so hard it doesn't make a difference. All you can do is be patient and try to make contact."[38]

Gooden struck out 16 Pirates in the game, leading skipper Chuck Tanner to remark, "Our guys weren't saying anything at all in the dugout. They didn't have time. They were striking out so fast, they had to run back on the field."[39] The rookie hurler finished the season with 276 strikeouts.[40]

Conclusion

For people of a certain age who lived in the New York City metropolitan area during the last three decades of the 20th century, Sports Phone's television commercials are embedded in memory, along with those featuring "beautiful Mount Airy Lodge" in the Poconos; the Catskills' Nevele Hotel, where "there's so much to do"; Manhattan's Milford Plaza hawked by a staff singing custom lyrics that changed an iconic *42nd Street* song title to "Lullabuy of Broadway" ($43 per person); Apex Technical School with the allure of keeping your tools when you graduate; The Money Store promoted by Phil Rizzuto as an alternative to traditional banking; Mr. Coffee and the Bowery Savings Bank with Joe DiMaggio's mere presence indicating a high-quality product and service.

The rise of the Internet to mainstream availability and the consequent immediacy of obtaining information made Sports Phone obsolete. But it was a crucial source—and remains a nostalgic reminder—for sports-minded fans.

NOTES

1. Psalm 30:5.
2. This was a New York City number, though not the original one for Sports Phone. Also, the outlets in other cities varied in their phone numbers.
3. Joe Delessio, "That Was a Thing: Sports Phone, the 1980s Way to Get Real-Time Scores," February 24, 2015, https://grantland.com/the-triangle/that-was-a-thing-sports-phone-the-1980s-way-to-get-real-time-scores/.
4. Howie Rose, telephone interview with David Krell, September, 2019.
5. Charles Morey, "Dial Sports Phone," Associated Press, El Paso Times, December 3, 1972: 68.
6. Joe Henderson, "Sports Phone: If You Just Can't Wait," Tampa Tribune, October 7, 1978: 83.
7. Richard Hoffer, "Dial-It National Sports: Peace of Mind for the Sports Addict," Daily News (Lebanon, PA), July 25, 1981: 16.
8. Pat Calabria, "Sports Phone's profits are ringing off the hook," Asbury Park Press, July 25, 1982: 33.
9. Fred Huebner, telephone interview with David Krell, July 10, 2019.
10. Richard Hoffer, "New Dial-a-Score Service Has Caught on Fast," The Gazette (Cedar Rapids, IA), June 21, 1981: 52.
11. Judy Rose, "Sports People: There's Something 'Phoney' About This Sports Line," Detroit Free Press, October 13, 1980: 48.
12. Jay Frank, "Ma Bell Talking Sports," Daily Oklahoman (Oklahoma City), March 9, 1980: 25.
13. Bill Verigan, "Kooz' 20th, 13Ks Crush Cards, 4–1," Daily News (New York), September 17, 1976: 74.
14. Deane McGowen, "Koosman Gets 20th, and Fans 13 Cards," New York Times, September 17, 1976: D15.
15. Ibid.
16. Maury Allen, Life Begins at 20," New York Post, September 17, 1976: 76.
17. Maury Allen, "Matlack and Kong Cancel Mets' Goof," New York Post, April 30, 1977: 56.
18. Ibid.
19. Jack Lang, "King Conks Padres with 2 HRs," Daily News (New York), April 30, 1977: 197.
20. Henry Hecht, "New Swan Song Leaves Mets Flat," New York Post, July 5, 1978: 94.
21. "Mets, Pirates Tied in 11th; Fog Halts Game," New York Times, May 26, 1979: 13.
22. Bill Madden, "Swan Beats Braves 3–0 on 3-Hitter," Daily News (New York), May 26, 1980: 41.
23. Ibid.
24. Parton Keese, "Mets Top Dodgers to End Slide as Washington Belts 3 Homers," New York Times, June 23, 1980: C4.
25. Ibid.
26. Henry Hecht, "Claudell's Three Homers Power Mets Past Dodgers," New York Post, June 23, 1980: 62.
27. Parton Keese, "Mets Rally to Beat Reds, 7–4, on Grand Slam by Kingman," New York Times, August 23, 1981: Section 5, Page 6.
28. Doug Gould & Henry Hecht, "The Mighty Met," Daily News (New York), February 10, 1982: 76. Bill Madden, "Swan Beats Braves 3–0 on 3-Hitter," Daily News (New York), May 26, 1980.
29. Dave Anderson, "The Anatomy of Biggest Trade," New York Times, February 11, 1982: B7.

30. Doug Gould & Henry Hecht, "The Mighty Met: Fence-Busting Foster Signs $8.5M Contract," *New York Post*: 76.

31. Hugh Delano, "'Red-Hot' Mets Clobber Cincy, 10–2," *New York Post*, September 6, 1982: 30.

32. Sam Goldpaper, "Valentine Returns with a Homer as Mets Win, 10–2," *New York Times*, September 6, 1982: 27.

33. Jack Lang, "Mets Send Allen, Ownbey to Cards for Hernandez," *Daily News* (New York), June 16, 1983: 87.

34. *Ibid.*

35. "Keith Hernandez Sent to Mets for Allen, Ownbey," *New York* Times, June 16, 1983: B17.

36. Henry Hecht, "Seaver Comes Out Smokin' vs. Phillies," *New York Post*, April 6, 1983: 60.

37. Steve Wulf, "It Was a Terrific Homecoming," *Sports Illustrated*, April 18, 1983: 38.

38. Bob Klapisch, "King of the Hill: Gooden Shatters Score's Rookie Mark with 251 Strikeouts," *New York Post*, September 13, 1984: 84.

39. Joseph Durso, "Gooden Fans 16 and Sets Rookie Mark of 251," *New York Times*, September 13, 1984: D23.

40. As of the 2020 publication of this book, Gooden's 276 strikeouts is the record for a rookie.

A Tale of Two Fans

Josh Lyman, Toby Ziegler
and The West Wing

DAVID KRELL

Post hoc ergo propter hoc.

When President Josiah "Jed" Bartlet inquires whether anyone in an Oval Office meeting knows the translation of this Latin bromide, Deputy Chief of Staff Josh Lyman understands "post" (after) and "ergo" (therefore).[1] Chief of Staff Leo McGarry—former Secretary of Labor and an old friend of Josh's father, Noah Lyman,[2] a litigator[3] and partner at the powerhouse law firm Debevoise & Plimpton[4]—reveals the complete translation: "After it, therefore, because of it."[5] B happens after A, so B must have been caused by A. It's one of many examples underscoring the fictional president's worldliness on *The West Wing*, which aired on NBC from 1999 to 2006, won 26 Emmys, and made political topics from census[6] to censure[7] palatable for prime time.

Using biographical details, it's apparent that Josh, a Mets fan, began his political career in the mid–1980s as the Mets emerged with swagger. So, it is quite possible that the "post hoc ergo proper hoc" syllogism applies. His body language as he walks through the White House corridors—head high and shoulders squared—conveys authority, confidence, and a take-on-all-comers attitude that Lenny Dykstra would admire.

A Fulbright Scholar[8] and a graduate of Harvard and Yale,[9] Josh is 38 years old when the series begins in 1999.[10] Though his "IQ doesn't break the bank," he invested sweat equity to build a political career[11] and is noted for possessing a "world-class political mind"[12] and being "the finest political mind in the party" aside from Leo.[13] His perspective is a "wide angle lens" for the president to factor the effects of a political decision. "It's not unusual for me to meet with the President in the Oval Office five or ten times a day."[14]

During an argument about political strategy with Bartlet re-election consultant Bruno Gianelli, Josh says, "I got two years as legislative director in the House, two years as Floor Director in the Senate, and thirty months as Deputy Chief of Staff. What do you got?"[15] It's also mentioned in a first-season episode that Josh was a Chief of Staff for a congressman and Floor Manager to the House Minority Whip.[16]

Josh's passion for the Mets is evident in at least three episodes. He books a Spring Training trip because he hopes for a potential head nod and one-word acknowledgment—"Dude"—from Mike Piazza. But his plans are dashed by a filibuster held by the elderly Senator Howard Stackhouse holding a filibuster to prevent a bill from being voted upon without expanded funding for autism.[17] His pleasure at being home with his girlfriend—women's advocate Amy Gardner—enhances with a nationally televised Mets game.[18] When the Mets lose, it can take him longer to focus on political matters the next day.[19]

Swagger as Bluntness

In the first-season episode "Five Votes Down," the Bartlet administration faces a boondoggle in getting a gun control bill passed. Josh seeks a fiat from Leo to confront Wisconsin Congressman Katzenmoyer over his intention to vote against the bill, even though the congressman is a democrat.

But Josh neither points out the positive effects of the bill nor the impact on Wisconsinites. He begins with numbers—Bartlet took the district with 59 percent but the congressman got 52 percent. Then, he threatens to run a challenger in the next primary with the president's endorsement.

Do you have any idea how much noise Air Force One makes when it lands in Eau Claire, Wisconsin? We're going to have a party, Congressman. You should come, it's gonna be great. And when the watermelon's done, right in town square, right in the band gazebo—you guys got a band gazebo? Doesn't matter. We'll build one. Right in the band gazebo, that's where the President is going to drape his arm around the shoulder of some assistant DA we like. And you should have your camera with you. You should get a picture of that. 'Cause that's gonna be the moment you're finished in Democratic politics.[20]

When First Lady Abbey Bartlet's agenda gets as much attention as Pepsi in Atlanta, Josh explains that her aide, who also happens to be her nephew, is an "idiot" because he has a fundamental misunderstanding about the political mechanisms that can get her agenda considered, funded, and approved. "The President and Leo make their decisions by listening to and participating in vigorous debate. This isn't school. I work with people who can play."

Showing neither indignation nor insult, she asks, "You're comfortable

Mike Piazza was mentioned in an episode of *The West Wing* when White House Deputy Chief of Staff Josh Lyman anticipated a trip to spring training and a potential encounter with the Mets' All-Star catcher (National Baseball Hall of Fame and Museum, Cooperstown, N.Y.).

being this condescending with me?" Josh explains, "Because I won. I always do. And you came here for my advice."[21]

Before joining Bartlet's first presidential bid, Josh was a member of Texas Senator John Hoynes's staff. With a war chest of nearly $60 million and no viable challenger, Hoynes was primed to be the Democratic nominee in the next presidential election. Increasingly concerned and about the campaign's lack of focus—"I don't know what we're for, and I don't know what we're against. Except we seem to be for winning and against somebody else winning."—Josh leaves to join Leo and the Bartlet campaign after hearing the New Hampshire Governor and Nobel Prize in Economics winner speak honestly to voters rather than tell them want they want to hear.[22]

Hoynes becomes Bartlet's Vice President. When Josh tries to convince the second-most powerful man on Earth that publicly opposing campaign finance reform—and by doing so, opposing against President Bartlet—is a bad idea politically, the veep posits, "You know something, Josh. Sometimes I wonder if I'd listened to you two years ago, would I be President right now? Do you ever wonder that?"

"No sir. I know it for sure."[23]

Swagger as Emotion

The mid–1980s Mets were a confrontational lot.

"The Mets lead the majors in self-congratulatory high-fives, curtain calls after homers, autobiographies, magazine cover stories and general swagger," wrote Thomas Boswell a few days after the team won the 1986 NL East pennant. "Their stars strut and their leaders don't mind a rumble. They will charge the mound if you dust them and talk a little trash in the papers, too."[24]

Neither was Josh afraid to mix it up, though his verbiage sometimes crossed into the red zone. In a television appearance with religious right-winger Mary Marsh on *Capitol Beat*, Josh has an encounter that places him on the precipice of being fired.

"Well, I can tell you that you don't believe in any God I pray to, Mr. Lyman. Not any God I pray to," says Marsh.

"Lady, the God you pray to is too busy being indicted for tax fraud."[25]

An exchange with Press Secretary Claudia Jean "C.J." Cregg gets quite confrontational as well.

"I really think I'm the best judge of what I mean, you paranoid Berkeley shiksa feminista! Whoa, that was way too far."

"No, No. Well, I've got a staff meeting to go to and so do you, you elitist Harvard fascist missed-the-dean's-list-two-semesters-in-a-row Yankee jack-ass!"[26]

Josh's indignation turns to intimidation when Leo's past addictions are vulnerable to exposure by a GOP operative. His target is Laurie, an escort who slept with a White House colleague but out of attraction—he didn't know she was a prostitute when they met in a bar and then spent the night together.[27] To counter the attack, Josh and Sam want embarrassing information about the sexual activities of Laurie's clients. When Josh learns that Laurie went to a White House event with a big-time Democratic donor, it leads to a tirade that demeans Laurie as a woman with no scruples who will sell out anyone for a buck. "If our tactics seem less than civilized, it's because so are our attackers. In any event, I don't feel like standing here taking a civics lesson from a hooker. We don't need your cooperation, Laurie. One of your guys wrote you a check and the IRS works for me. Just give me a name. What do you want? Money?"

Laurie stands her ground, making Josh realize that his bullying was not only demeaning, but also intentionally hurtful. He apologizes. The scene ends with Laurie giving the duo a comeuppance: "You're the good guys. You should act like it."[28]

Swagger as Hope

Mets fans are a hopeful lot. So, it's logical that Josh would be one of them. An ongoing story arc has Supreme Court Chief Justice Roy Ashland refusing to step down because the president can't get a sufficiently liberal justice confirmed. With 45-year-old conservative justice Owen Brady dead, Ashland won't relinquish even though he knows his mind is faulty at times. "I have good days. And bad. But on my worst day, I am better than the amped-up ambulance chasers you can get confirmed by the Senate."[29]

Josh pursues a novel angle—a balanced court. He proposes giving the Senate Republicans a conservative justice—Christopher Mulready—to get Evelyn Baker Lang nominated as Chief Justice.[30]

Swagger as Swagger

Boswell's interpretation mirrored that of many non–Mets fans. While the Yankees engendered animosity because of their victories without showboating in the Mickey Mantle era—which resulted in the 1954 novel *The Year the Yankees Lost the Pennant* and the Broadway show and film *Damn Yankees*—the Mets created a different kind of aura. "The brawlin', bragging, brainy, butt-kickin' Metropolitans may be one of the best ball clubs in a generation. But plenty of people in the game hope they aren't able to prove it."[31]

Josh, too, has confidence backed by political instinct, civic duty, and just plain chutzpah. When the GOP Senate Majority Leader calls with the intent to intimidate, Josh cuts him off at the pass: "Hi, Senator. Why don't you take your legislative agenda and shove it up your ass."[32]

The White House strikes a deal with Democratic Senator Lloyd Russell that requires abandoning a challenge to Bartlet in the next election. Josh declares, "Victory is mine! Victory is mine! Great day in the morning people! Victory is mine!" His diatribe to his staff concludes with chest thumping and arms raised in triumph.[33]

Clarifying his legislative impact for his assistant, Donna Moss, Josh's explanation might be fodder for a Barry Manilow lyric about politics: "I don't practice law? I help write the laws, I write the laws, I make the laws. I am the law."[34]

But sometimes Josh's swagger backfires. Terribly.

When Idaho Senator Chris Carrick holds on to more than 200 military promotions with the obstinance of a rhinoceros, Josh learns that it's a ransom for a missile launcher to be built in the Gem State. Bartlet's predecessor promised it, but neither he nor Bartlet made good on it. Carrick, who voted against the Bartlet administration's stimulus package, believes that even though the missile launcher—with a price tag of more than a quarter-billion dollars—doesn't work, it symbolizes military strength to adversaries who know not of its flaws.

A conservative Democrat, Carrick draws the White House into a battle, which escalates with another 50+ promotions in stasis. Josh, described as the "101st Senator" in a *Washington Post* story because of his legislative clout on Capitol Hill—which included sending a dead fish wrapped in newspaper to a congressman who "tried to bottle up the fisheries bill"—outflanks Carrick by leaking the situation to the Idaho newspapers.

Carrick, ultimately, has no choice but to yield to Josh. But there's a cost to the acquiescence; he resigns from the Democratic party and reveals to Josh that he'll run as a Republican in the next election. "I'm not leaving 'cause of you. But you made it a whole lot easier." Earlier, Leo underscored Carrick's importance to Democrats winning the Senate in the next election. Swagger turns to sullenness when Josh, just after Carrick's declaration, gets summoned to the Mural Room for his surprise birthday party.[35]

An epic fail occurs when Josh substitutes for C.J. at a press briefing because the novocaine hasn't worn off from her dentist appointment that morning. At a political lecture series featuring him as the guest speaker in an interview format, Josh recounts that he intended to "impos[e] discipline I felt had been lacking in C.J.'s briefings." To *Washington Post* reporter Danny Concannon right before the briefing, he condescends with the smugness of Lucy about to pull the football from away from Charlie Brown's attempt to kick it: "Let me tell you something, mi compadre. You guys have been coddled. I'm not your girlfriend, I'm not your camp counselor, and I'm not your sixth-grade teacher you had a crush on. I'm a graduate of Harvard and Yale and I believe that my powers of debate can rise to meet the Socratic wonder that is the White House Press Corps."[36]

With a sarcastic comment about the president's "secret plan to fight inflation," a barrage of questions follows, thereby making Josh look like the administration is hiding a crucial piece of economic news.

Swagger Silent, Confidence High

When Josh leaves the Bartlet administration because he finds Texas Congressman Matt Santos to be a compelling alternative to mainstream candidates vying to succeed President Bartlet—like former Vice President John Hoynes, who had resigned because of a scandal involving sex and revealing classified information, and current Vice President Bob Russell, a Colorado Congressman who replaced Hoynes—he is no longer the brash operative surrounded by like-minded, dedicated public servants. Quiet confidence replaces swagger. More Tom Seaver and Jerry Grote than Dwight Gooden and Gary Carter. More "Ya Gotta Believe!" than "Baseball Like It Oughta Be."

The Democratic National Convention appears to be heading back to the past with the delegates voting for a nominee from the convention floor, when Leo instructs Josh to have Santos accept a vice-presidential slot with Russell as the nominee. Though Leo accedes that Matt Santos's rise from three-term Democratic Texas Congressman to viable presidential candidate is "improbable, impressive," the party and the president want an organized convention with a decided nominee.

Josh counters, "You're not hearing me." It's a moment that secures Josh as matching, perhaps surpassing, Leo as a political operative with the strength to go against the grain as Leo did by convincing Jed Bartlet to run for president.

Josh acknowledges that he told Santos to accept the VP job, but Santos refused. "He's twice the man Russell is on his best day. Ten times. And Russell doesn't have that many good days."[37] Santos wins the nomination and the presidency; Leo is the VP nominee but dies on election night; and Josh steps into his mentor's shoes when he becomes President Santos's Chief of Staff. He has come full circle.

441

If Puerto Rico and Washington, D.C., achieve statehood, 441 may be an important number in politics. It's speculative, though conceivable, that each entity would get three voting members in the House of Representatives, thereby escalating the total number from 435 to 441.

For Toby Ziegler, it has a different meaning.

"I've been to 441 baseball games at Yankee Stadium. There's not a single person there who's ordinary," states Toby, the Bartlet Administration's Communications Director, to his deputy, Sam Seaborn, in response to a revelation that Republican presidential candidate and Florida Governor Robert Ritchie went to a Yankees game before a performance of *War of the Roses* to benefit Catholic Charities because "ordinary Americans" prefer baseball games for entertainment.[38] Though Ritchie's expected to come at intermission, Toby, ever conscious of the image of President Bartlet, takes umbrage at the opposition arriving after the president.

In a ploy to prevent, or at least delay, Ritchie's arrival, Sam follows a tactic used in a prior presidential campaign—during a primary, the staff of an incumbent president arranged for a motorcade to bring traffic to a standstill.[39] When Ritchie arrives, he tries his down-home, well-rehearsed statement about baseball only to have Bartlet challenge him by pointing out that the Yankees centerfielder (presumably Bernie Williams) is a classical guitarist. People can be literate and part of popular culture.

Toby points out that the Yankees were about to end a 12-game winning streak. The events of the show are skewed from real life—the election takes place in 2002, not 2000 or 2004. That year, the Yankees had a stretch where they won 12 out of 13.

Born Tobias Zachary Ziegler in Brighton Beach, a fact he lauds over Josh to somehow prove his Judaism is more authentic—"You know, the Ancient Hebrews had a word for Jews from Westport. They pronounced it 'Presbyterian.'"[40]—he does not have a good track record until he joins Bartlet's first presidential campaign. That is to say, he doesn't have any record to speak of. When Toby thinks that Leo will fire him, he passes time with the lubricant of liquor in a Nashua bar. Talking to a woman who appears to be a pleasant and curious barfly, Toby reveals his lifetime stats as a "professional political operative"—city council, two congressional elections, one Senate race, one gubernatorial race, one presidential race. All losing contests.[41]

Toby in the White House

Toby is the Billy Martin of the Bartlet White House. Combative. Passionate. Encyclopedic knowledge about his industry. He will not back down from an argument and will, when he believes that he occupies higher moral ground, ignite one. In the Oval Office, the sanctum sanctorum of the free world, Toby raises his voice to Leo and President Bartlet after they reveal that the president has relapsing, remitting Multiple Sclerosis. Agitated, Toby recounts what happened the night of the assassination attempt on the president and how the unclear lines of power were distorted further by the president's safeguarding his diagnosis. With the president under anesthesia, no way to know if the shooting was an act of war, and National Guard units in five states being federalized, there was a falsehood about leadership. "The Vice President's authority was murky at best! The National Security Advisor and Secretary of State didn't know who they were taking their orders from! I wasn't in the Situation Room that night but I'll bet all the money in my pockets against all the money in your pockets that it was Leo, who no one elected! For 90 minutes that night, there was a coup d'état in this country."[42]

When debating his ex-wife, Democratic Congresswoman Andrea "Andy" Wyatt, about the merits of a presidential speech (that he wrote) to the United Nations regarding freedom but targeting Middle East nations hell bent on rule by dictatorship, human rights violations, and "the crushing yoke of Islamic fanaticism," Toby is emphatic about the language clarifying America's role in the world. It's a result of exhaustion from being criticized by Arab nations for issuing economic sanctions against Iraq in the name of military restraint, advocating the land-for-peace option to Israel, and denounced by Arab media for "knowing nothing about Islam" even though the president called Islamic followers "faithful and hardworking."

It's a simple message from Toby's standpoint: "I don't remember having to explain to Italians that our problem wasn't with them but with Mussolini. Why does the U.S. have to take every Arab country out for an ice cream cone? They'll like us when we win!"[43] Toby's belligerence can be understated, though. Seth Gillette, an extreme-left, junior senator from North Dakota, threatens a third-party candidacy in the next presidential election. Toby, a wordsmith, responds with his own threat. A terse one. "Come at us from the left, I'm gonna own your ass."[44]

Toby and the Yankees

Toby's love for the Yankees transcends his relationship with Andy. Or at least comes pretty close. When she tells Toby that she was on a date with the Executive Advisor for the Baltimore Orioles, he admits confusion about the source of his disturbance—Andy on a date or a date with an executive for another AL East franchise.[45]

Andy and Toby reunite, though not in marriage; they have twins—Huck and Molly.[46] To Toby's dismay, his kids dress as Orioles players for Halloween; his daughter likes the Orioles' cartoon logo. His gifts of Yankees paraphernalia are relegated to ignominy in favor of Maryland's state bird. Later, he tucks the kids into bed, puts a Yankees cap on Huck's bed, and whispers to his sleeping son, "Trust me, you'll be happier."[47]

The scene aired in 2006, only one year after the Montreal Expos moved to Washington, changed the team name to Nationals, and ended the drought of Major League Baseball in the nation's capital since 1971. One can only speculate whether the Presidents Race would have changed her allegiance.

Richard Schiff and the Yankees

On the podcast *The West Wing Weekly*, Schiff explained that the genesis of his passion for the Yankees stemmed from his grandfather's love of the Brooklyn Dodgers and the National League exodus from New York leaving the city with one team from 1958 to 1961. When Roger Maris broke Babe Ruth's single-season home record in '61, Schiff was six years old—right about the time when fan devotion is formed. "And so there was no team, and he … played minor-league baseball, among many other things. So he took me to my first game [and] I saw Ted Williams's last year with the Red Sox."[48]

Like his alter ego, Schiff is an old-school fan. Wearing a Yankees cap on *The Rich Eisen Show*, Schiff broke down the differences between the way the game was played in eras past versus present day. "There are some great players in baseball that we don't see enough of. First of all, the fences have been all moved in since it was 461 to center field and 457 to left-center. You'd use to see triples. Triples to me is one of the most exciting plays. Also scoring from first on a double and the relay from left to short to home. That to me is the most exciting play. And the bunt. The suicide squeeze. That's baseball to me."[49]

Such is Schiff's devotion to pinstripes that he wore a Yankees cap to the 2001 Emmy Awards.[50] There's no word on whether Toby wore similar head gear to a White House Correspondents Dinner.

The President

Baseball is not limited to Josh and Toby. On Memorial Day, 2004, President Bartlet fulfills a ceremonial obligation by throwing out the first pitch at a Baltimore Orioles game.[51] "I could write a hundred speeches, and we'd never come close to the sight of you up on that mound,"[52] says Toby. But there's a problem—the president is "no Cy Young," the First Lady bluntly points out. With a well-used glove indicating affinity for the National Pastime, Toby consults the president on how to throw; Charlie Young, the president's body man, assumes the role of catcher. They practice in a hallway so it will be private, lest anyone see the president's inability. Though his first few throws hit the floor and the walls, Bartlet begins to focus on Charlie and pitch strikes.[53]

Initially, Toby believed that the president would throw from the stands but Josh alerted him that FDR did that in 1937 and hit one of his photographers. Though it's a fictional vignette, the tale has a factual basis—before the April 16, 1940, game between the Washington Senators and the Boston Red Sox, President Roosevelt threw out the first pitch from the stands and hit a camera from the *Washington Post*.[54]

Postmaster General James A. Farley got blamed without evidence that he "nudged the President's elbow" and caused the errant pitch. "Whatever the cause, there could be no doubt that the President's pitching arm was not in the best of condition," reported the *New York Times*. "Only a lens shade saved an expensive newspaper camera. Instead of looping the ball over the heads of the battery of cameramen grouped in front of his box, Mr. Roosevelt heaved it as though he were pegging to second and the near-accident resulted."[55] Forty-year-old Boston hurler Lefty Grove kept the Senators hitless through seven innings and allowed their only two hits in the eighth.

Throwing out the first pitch is a presidential tradition begun by William Howard Taft on Opening Day in 1910.

President Bartlet's Camden Yards appearance comes as he tries to negotiate a peace to the ongoing violence in the Middle East. A terror attack in Israel killed two congressman and a congressional aide; White House aide Donna Moss was researching the political climate and was severely injured. A suicide bombing wounded 100 people and killed an estimated 10–20 others.

Bartlet admits that his knowledge of baseball is lacking. He once thought that the name Stan Musial belonged to one of his wife's medical school classmates. But he does not dismiss baseball or any variation. When he realizes that an evening obligation will end in time to watch a softball game between Sacramento State and University of the Pacific, he explains to Charlie that it's part of the male ritual—work during the day, relax with sports at night.[56]

Had Bartlet been a more knowledgeable sports fan, he might have gotten in debates with Josh and Toby extending beyond politics. Being from New Hampshire, he would likely have been a Red Sox fan. Indeed, the president is a loyal New Englander. When the Granite State native discovers, to his dismay, that Alaskan crab puffs are being served at a White House function rather than New England crab puffs, the president is clearly surprised, though not outraged.[57]

One can imagine the high intellect of Jed Bartlet discussing the finer points of Game Six in the 1986 Mets–Red Sox World Series with Mets fan Josh and the tremendous Yankees–Red Sox rivalry with Yankees fan Toby.

NOTES

1. "Oval Office Meeting," Schlamme, Thomas, dir. *The West Wing*, Season 1, episode 2, "Post Hoc, Ergo Propter Hoc." Aired September 29, 1999 on NBC.

2. "Josh and Leo," Schlamme, Thomas, dir. *The West Wing*. Season 2, episode 1, "In the Shadow of Two Gunmen, Part I." Aired October 4, 2000 on NBC.

3. "Josh and Governor Bartlet at Airport," Schlamme, Thomas, dir. *The West Wing*. Season 2, episode 2, "In the Shadow of Two Gunmen, Part II." Aired October 4, 2000 on NBC.

4. "Joe Quincy is a Republican," Misiano, Christopher, dir. *The West Wing*. Season 4, episode 20, "Evidence of Things Not Seen." Aired April 23, 2003 on NBC.

5. "Oval Office Meeting," *The West Wing*, "Post Hoc, Ergo Propter Hoc."

6. Misiano, Christopher, dir. *The West Wing*. Season 1, episode 6, "Mr. Willis of Ohio." Aired November 3, 1999 on NBC.

7. Misiano, Vincent, dir. *The West Wing*. Season 3, episode 1, "H. Con-172." Aired January 9, 2002 on NBC.

8. "Josh and Mandy," Schlamme, Thomas, dir. *The West Wing*. Season 1, episode 1, "Pilot." Aired September 22, 1999 on NBC; "Josh and Mrs. Landingham," *The West Wing*. "Mr. Willis of Ohio."

9. "Josh and Danny," Misiano, Christopher, dir. *The West Wing*. Season 1, episode 15, "Celestial Navigation." Aired February 16, 2000 on NBC.

10. "Josh Lyman," The West Wing wiki, accessed December 7, 2019, https://westwing. fandom.com/wiki/Josh_Lyman. The pilot script posted on The Daily Script web site describes, "A youthful 38, Josh is Deputy Chief of Staff and a highly regarded brain." The Daily Script, accessed December 7, 2019, http://www.dailyscript.com/scripts/West_Wing_Pilot.pdf.

11. "Josh gets personal with Amy," *The West Wing*, "H. Con-172."

12. "Sam and Mallory," Misiano, Christopher, dir. *The West Wing*. Season 4, episode 2, "20 Hours in America: Part II." Aired September 25, 2002 on NBC.

13. "Will praises Josh," Misiano, Christopher, dir. *The West Wing*. Season 6, episode 11, "Opposition Research." Aired January 12, 2005 on NBC.

14. "Josh explains job to therapist," Schlamme, Thomas, dir. *The West Wing*. Season 2, episode 10, "Nöel." Aired December 20, 2000 on NBC.

15. "Josh and Bruno," Schlamme, Thomas, dir. *The West Wing*. Season 3, episode 1, "Manchester: Part II." Aired October 17, 2001 on NBC.

16. "Introduction for Josh Lyman," *The West Wing*, "Celestial Navigation."

17. Gordon, Bryan, dir. *The West Wing*. Season 2, episode 17, "The Stackhouse Filibuster." Aired March 14, 2002 on NBC.

18. "Josh and Amy at home," Schlamme, Thomas, dir. *The West Wing*. Season 3, episode 21, "We Killed Yamamoto." Aired May 15, 2002 on NBC.

19. "Amy talks about Josh," Misiano, Vincent, dir. *The West Wing*. Season 4, episode 4, "The Red Mass." Aired October 9, 2002 on NBC.

20. "Josh threatens political blowback," Lehmann, Michael, dir. *The West Wing*, Season 1, episode 4, "Five Votes Down." Aired October 13, 1999 on NBC.

21. "Josh and the First Lady," Graves, Alex, dir. *The West Wing*. Season 4, episode 17, "Red Haven's on Fire." Aired February 26, 2003 on NBC.

22. "Josh and Senator Hoynes," *The West Wing*, "In the Shadow of Two Gunmen, Part I."

23. "Josh and Vice President Hoynes," Schlamme, Thomas, *The West Wing*. Season 1, episode 22, "What Kind of Day Has It Been?" Aired May 17, 2000 on NBC.

24. Thomas Boswell, "The Mets: A Team Some Love to Hate," *Washington Post*, September 19, 1986: H1.

25. "Josh watches himself on television," *The West Wing*, "Pilot."

26. "Josh and C.J.," Buckland, Marc, dir. *The West Wing*. Season 1, episode 3, "A Proportional Response." Aired October 6, 1999 on NBC.

27. "Sam finds out Laurie is a call girl," *The West Wing*, "Pilot."

28. "Josh confronts Laurie," Graves, Alex, dir. *The West Wing*. Season 1, episode 10, "In Excelsis Deo." Aired December 15, 1999 on NBC.

29. "Chief Justice Ashland and President Bartlet," Graves, Alex, dir. *The West Wing*. Season 5, episode 7, "Separation of Powers." Aired November 12, 2003 on NBC. There's a continuity error in this scene. With Brady dead, there are seven other justices. But President Bartlet says, "The other eight are preparing to take it away from you, Roy."

30. "Josh, Toby, and President Bartlet," Yu, Jessica, dir. *The West Wing*, Season 5, episode 17, "The Supremes." Aired March 24, 2004 on NBC.

31. Thomas Boswell, "The Mets: A Team Some Love to Hate."

32. "Josh insults senator," Berlinger, Robert, dir. *The West Wing*. Season 1, episode 20, "Mandatory Minimums." Aired May 3, 2000 on NBC.

33. "Josh in the morning," *The West Wing*, "Post Hoc, Ergo Propter Hoc."

34. "Josh brags about influence," Coles, John David, dir. *The West Wing*. Season 4, episode 21, "Life on Mars." Aired April 30, 2003 on NBC.

35. "Josh and Carrick," Innes, Laura, dir. *The West Wing*. Season 5, episode 5, "Constituency of One." Aired October 29, 2003 on NBC.

36. "Josh's press conference," *The West Wing*, "Celestial Navigation."

37. "Josh and Leo," McCormick, Nelson, dir. *The West Wing*. Season 6, episode 21, "Things Fall Apart." Aired March 30, 2005.

38. "Toby and Sam," Graves, Alex, dir. *The West Wing*. Season 3, episode 22, "Posse Comitatus." Aired May 22, 2002 on NBC.

39. *Ibid.*

40. "Josh, Toby, and Donna," *The West Wing*, "20 Hours in America: Part II."

41. "Toby at the bar," *The West Wing*, "In the Shadow of Two Gunmen, Part I."

42. "Toby confronts the president and Leo," Graves, Alex, dir. *The West Wing*. Season 2, episode 18, "17 People." Aired April 4, 2001 on NBC.

43. "Toby and his ex-wife," Misiano, Christopher, dir. *The West Wing*. Season 3, episode 14, "Night Five." Aired February 6, 2002 on NBC.

44. "Toby meets with Seth Gillette," Misiano, Christopher, dir. *The West Wing*. Season 2, episode 14, "The War at Home." Aired February 14, 2001 on NBC.

45. "Toby and his ex-wife," *The West Wing*, "Mandatory Minimums."

46. "Toby and C.J.," Graves, Alex, dir. *The West Wing*. Season 4, episode 22, "Commencement." Aired May 7, 2003 on NBC.

47. "Toby puts kids to bed," Karrell, Matia, dir. *The West Wing*. Season 7, episode 15, "Welcome to Wherever You Are." Aired March 26, 2006 on NBC.

48. *The West Wing Weekly*, Episode 1:10, transcription on https://static1.squarespace.com/static/56e27eb82fe131d8eec3a4e3/t/59f0c64ff9a61eaaa713fd8a/1508951632588/1.10+-+In+Excelsis+Deo.pdf.

49. "Richard Schiff Talks 'The Good Doctor,' 'West Wing' Reboot & More w/Rich Eisen/Full Interview, *The Rich Eisen Show*, Audience Network, DIRECTV, You Tube, accessed on December 7, 2019, https://www.youtube.com/watch?v=rl581KAZKqo (published on February 27, 2019).

50. "Actor Richard Schiff Remembers 2001 Yankees & What Aaron Boone is Doing-4/18/18," *The Rich Eisen Show*, Audience Network, DIRECTV, You Tube, accessed December 7, 2019, https://www.youtube.com/watch?v=3RGruBWgkXs (published on April 18, 2018).

51. "President Bartlet throws out first pitch," Misiano, Christopher, dir. *The West Wing*. Season 5, episode 22, "Memorial Day." Aired May 19, 2004 on NBC.

52. *Ibid.*

53. The scene was filmed on April 23, 2004, before an Orioles-Blue Jays game. Roch Kubatko, "Sheen's wing is lacking on first pitch," *Baltimore Sun*, accessed December 7, 2019, https://www.baltimoresun.com/news/bs-xpm-2004-04-24-0404240377-story.html, April 24, 2004.

54. Christian Belena, Archives Technician, Franklin D. Roosevelt Presidential Library, National Archives and Records Administration, email to David Krell, July 30, 2019.

55. "Senators Blanked by Grove, Red Sox," *New York Times*, April 17, 1940: 34.

56. "Charlie and President Bartlet," *The West Wing*, "What Kind of Day Has It Been," NBC, Warner Brothers, May 17, 2000, Aaron Sorkin.

57. "Oval Office Meeting," Graves, Alex, dir. *The West Wing*. Season 2, episode 3, "The Midterms." Aired October 18, 2000 on NBC.

Meet the 19th Century Mets

BILL LAMB

Despite a colorful near-60-year history, a devoted fan base, and two World Series crowns, the New York Mets are often looked upon as being the Big Apple's *other* baseball club, playing a decided second fiddle to the city's longer established, more celebrated, and perennially successful franchise, the 27-times world champion New York Yankees. This situation, however, is not without precedent. Back in the 1880s, the Mets' namesakes, the New York Metropolitans of the major league American Association, were accorded similar treatment. During their abbreviated life span—from formation in 1880 as an independent professional team through ascension to major-league status until its dissolution at the close of the 1887 season—the Mets had their moments, highlighted by the capture of an American Association pennant. That achievement notwithstanding, the Mets were mostly an afterthought to the Metropolitan Exhibition Company. For the majority of the Mets' existence, this closely held corporation operated the club but lavished its attention and resources on its other baseball holding—New York Giants.

Formation of the Ball Club

The founder of the original Mets and, indeed, of professional baseball in New York City proper, was John B. Day, a prosperous cigar manufacturer from Connecticut and amateur-baseball enthusiast.[1] In the late 1870s, Day relocated to Manhattan to oversee operation of a newly opened processing plant on the Lower East Side. Only in his early 30s, Day, who fancied himself a pitcher, devoted much of his leisure time to playing ball with various local nines. The transformation of Day from wanna-be player to professional ball club owner was the product of his meeting Jim Mutrie during the summer of 1880. Two versions of that encounter endure. According to lore, Mutrie,

116

then a marginally gifted shortstop between playing engagements but a man with organizational abilities and a keen eye for playing talent, introduced himself to Day after watching the cigar manufacturer's pitching get pounded by amateur opposition.[2] But according to the venerable Henry Chadwick, the Day-Mutrie meeting was prearranged by New York sportswriters. Whichever the case, Mutrie had a proposition for Day: if the well-heeled capitalist would finance the venture, Mutrie would recruit, sign, and manage a professional baseball nine that would play under Day auspices. Intrigued, Day agreed. Soon, Mutrie was busy stocking the roster of the new team—formally named the Metropolitan of New York—with first-rate talent, much of it coming from the Unions of Brooklyn and the recently disbanded Rochester Hop-Bitters.

On September 16, 1880, the Mets made a successful début, thrashing the depleted Unions 15–0 on the ball field of the Brooklyn club.[3] At the time, the absence of suitable playing sites in densely built-up and populated Lower Manhattan dictated that local professional teams, even those bearing the name *New York*, utilize grounds in Brooklyn, then a separate and distinct municipality from New York City and the nation's third largest metropolis, or elsewhere.[4] But Day was determined to find his club a home in Manhattan. In short order, prospective grounds were located uptown: a grassy meadowland situated just north of Central Park at Fifth Avenue and 110th Street. Occasionally used by the Manhattan Polo Association but mostly vacant, the grounds were flat and dry, had seating for several thousand spectators, and were already partially enclosed by fencing. Once a lease to the premises was obtained from property owner James Gordon Bennett, Jr., the socialite-sportsman who published the *New York Herald*, Day relocated his ball club to New York City proper.

The Mets' namesake is a 19th-century team with a five-year existence in the 1880s. John B. Day was the founder. But he also owned the New York Gothams, otherwise known as the Giants. Day's focus of time, energy, and financial resources on his other team was one of the reasons for the Mets' demise.

On September 29, 1880, the Mets inaugurated their new home field at the "Polo Grounds" with a 4–2 win over the Nationals of Washington, the contest being played before a crowd of 2,000 to 3,000 paying customers.[5] Years later, club owner Day revealed that the late arrival of the Nationals had been a cause of grave concern, the prospect of seeing the Mets play a hastily gathered pick-up nine instead of the advertised opposition prompting unrest among the crowd until the Nationals finally showed up.[6] By the time that its brief first season ended, the Mets had compiled a creditable 16–7–1 log, which included a 12–3 complete-game victory over Manhattan College pitched by Day himself.[7]

Smitten by ownership, Day quickly had bigger things in mind for the Mets. To underwrite his ambitions for the team, Day incorporated the Metropolitan Exhibition Company (MEC), with himself as president and dominant shareholder. Recruited as minority investors were coal dealer Joseph Gordon, stationer Charles T. Dillingham, and ne'er-do-well son of wealth Walter Appleton, all Tammany Hall-affiliated acquaintances of Day.[8] Over the winter, additional grandstands were erected behind home plate in the southeast quadrant of the grounds. But Day declined overtures to place his ball club in the National League for the 1881 season.[9] Rather, the Mets would play a taxing 151-game schedule, mixing contests with teams affiliated with the Eastern Championship Association (ECA) amid those against local independent, semipro, and college nines. And again, the Mets would have National League opponents. Managed by Jim Mutrie and with a lineup that included future major-leaguers Dude Esterbrook, Steve Brady, Ed Kennedy, and Chief Roseman, the New Yorkers continued to make respectable showings in head-to-head matches against the game's elite teams, winning 18 of 60 games played against NL clubs. The Mets also captured the ECA title handily, finishing 10½ games better than the Athletics of Philadelphia.[10]

The Mets' impressive showing against top-flight opposition drew the interest of a fledgling major league, the American Association. But Day declined the invitation to place his club in the new circuit. The 1882 Mets schedule would again consist of a mix of games against major-league teams, the clubs of other pro circuits, and local nines. The New Yorkers won 29 of 74 contests against NL foes while taking all but one game against AA teams. This brought the Mets' overall record against all comers—major leagues, League Alliance, ECA, independent, semipro, and college opposition—to a more-than-respectable 210–136–7 (.597).[11] MEC boss Day was now ready to enter the big time.

The New York Mets of the American Association—The First Seasons

In December 1882, Day unveiled his plan for major-league baseball in New York, the particulars of which to ensured the Mets of second-class status in MEC operations. To some surprise, Day declined the invitation to place the Mets in the National League. Rather, the Mets would play the 1883 season as an American Association club, with Jim Mutrie remaining as manager and MEC minority shareholder Joseph Gordon assuming the post of club president. Almost simultaneously, Day announced that the MEC would place an entirely different team in the National League.[12] The nucleus of this new club, called the Gothams or simply the New-Yorks and headed by Day himself, would consist of budding stars like Buck Ewing, Roger Connor, and Mickey Welch, plucked from the roster of the recently disbanded NL Troy Trojans. But in a player assessment that would soon be second-guessed, pitcher Tim Keefe, another Troy refugee, was deemed unworthy of a spot with the Gothams. Instead, Keefe would be relegated to the Mets.

The corporation's attitude toward its two ball clubs quickly became evident. In addition to the cream of the newly acquired playing talent being assigned to the Gothams, the Day nine also received preferential treatment when it came to the Polo Grounds. The established diamond with grandstands on the southeast quadrant of the property was designated the home field of the Gothams. The Mets, meanwhile, were consigned to a second, landfill-based diamond with separate grandstand and entrance turnstiles placed in the southwest corner of the grounds. The clientele intended for the two clubs was also stratified. The upper-crust clientele desired by the Gothams would have to pay 50 cents for general admission. The working-class fans of the Mets would get in for half that price.

The Mets roster was not talent-less. The right-handed pitching tandem of Tim Keefe and Jack Lynch was promising, while major-league veterans Candy Nelson (shortstop), Steve Brady (first base), Bill Holbert (catcher), and John O'Rourke (outfield),[13] plus rookie Dude Esterbrook (third base), provided respectable lineup material. But preseason exhibition play between the two MEC clubs indicated that the Gothams (with the Cooperstown-bound Ewing, Connor, Welch, and John Montgomery Ward) were the stronger nine—they topped the Mets in seven of eight intramural contests.[14] The Mets stumbled out of the regular-season gate, committing 13 errors behind Keefe in their major league début, a 4–3, 11-inning loss to Baltimore, played before a turn-away crowd of more than 5,000 at Oriole Park.[15] A day later, Lynch hurled the Mets into the win column with a 2–1 triumph over the Orioles.

On May 12, the club returned to New York and dropped a sloppily played (10 errors) 11–4 home opener to the Philadelphia Athletics before a Polo Grounds crowd of some 3,000.[16] Simultaneously scheduled Gothams and Mets games, however, presented a logistics problem for the MEC brass. The inelegant solution: erection of a temporary canvas fence to separate the outfields of the Polo Grounds diamonds from one another. Including Decoration

Day (May 30) doubleheaders, the two New York clubs played games at the Polo Grounds at the same time on 12 occasions that season.[17] The Mets' performance improved as the season progressed and, behind the pitching of Keefe (41–27) and the batting of Nelson (.305), the club finished the 1883 campaign with a respectable 54–42 (.562) mark. Home attendance, however, was a disappointment. Only 50,000 customers paid their way through the Southwest Polo Grounds turnstiles to see the Mets play.[18] The Polo Grounds attendance of the Gothams (75,000 at twice the general admission price) further cemented the NL club as the MEC's favorite, even if the Gothams' 46–50 (.479) sixth-place finish was less satisfactory.

The home game Gothams-Mets arrangement did not suit the MEC, either aesthetically or financially. During simultaneously played contests, the occasional spectacle of outfielders from one league hopping the canvas fence and chasing long hit drives onto the playing field of another league drew complaints from circuit executives, particularly those in the American Association. In the future, the AA wanted Mets home games decoupled from Gothams home games.[19] On joint home dates, moreover, the Gothams and Mets were, in essence, competing with each other for the patronage of New York's baseball fans. To remedy the situation, the Mets would be relocated.

On February 13, 1884, construction of the Mets' new ballpark, unoriginally named Metropolitan Park, began. The site chosen was situated about a mile east of the Polo Grounds at First Avenue and 107–109th Streets in East Harlem, something less than ideal. Bounded by the Harlem River, the two-block location had previously been a city garbage dump. The immediate surrounds were also unattractive, a mix of ramshackle Irish, German, Italian, and Jewish enclaves interlaced with factories, gas works, tar pits, stock yards, and other city dumps.[20] When ready for use early in the 1884 season, Metropolitan Park was a conventionally shaped and dimensioned wooden ballpark surrounded by 14-foot-high walls, and could accommodate up to 5,000 spectators (but would never have to).

Metropolitan Park was unveiled on May 13, 1884, before a reported crowd of 4,000–4,500 onlookers (including the NYC Board of Aldermen and about 1,000 other freeloaders).[21] Staff ace Tim Keefe broke in the grounds in handsome style, pitching the Mets to a 13–4 victory over the Pittsburgh Alleghenies. The triumph proved an augury of things to come, as New York would post a .743 winning percentage in the first 35 games played at Metropolitan Park. The only problem was that everyone—ballplayers, sporting press, and fans—hated the place. Particularly distasteful to Mets players was the landfill-based diamond. Resident wit Jack Lynch reportedly observed that infielders at Metropolitan Park may "go down for a grounder and come up with malaria."[22] Meanwhile, nearby refuse dumps regularly imbued the ballpark with foul odors, while billowing factory smokestacks often left those in attendance with soot-stained clothing. When the Mets took to the road for an extended trip in late June, the MEC pulled the plug on Metropolitan Park. Once the team returned to New York, home games would be played at the Polo Grounds, with Metropolitan Park employed only when there were simultaneous Gothams-Mets home games scheduled for a particular date.[23]

The New York Mets were the class of the American Association, posting an outstanding 75–32 (.701) record. Paced by the yeoman hurling of Keefe (37–17) and Lynch (37–15)[24] and the batting of burly young Dave Orr, the AA league leader in base-hits (162), batting average (.354), RBI (112), and total bases (247), and Dude Esterbrook (.314), New York cruised to the American Association pennant, finishing a comfortable 6 1/2 games ahead of the second-place Columbus Buckeyes. The Mets' bubble burst, however, when matched against the National League champion Providence Grays in a three-game post-season precursor of the modern World Series. Behind the pitching of 60-game winner (and future Hall of Famer) Hoss Radbourn, Providence swept the series with lopsided, poorly attended victories, all recorded at the Polo Grounds.[25]

The Decline, Sale and Relocation of the Mets

The club's tenure at the pinnacle of the American Association was brief, the Mets' fortunes being undone largely from the inside. Despite a championship season, attendance was again a disappointment, with only 68,000 at home games. The mediocre Gothams, meanwhile, had drawn 15,000 more fans (at twice the general admission price) without being a factor in the National League pennant race.[26] That winter, the MEC brain trust decided to enhance the prospects of the money-making Gothams, mostly at the expense of the Mets. First, manager Jim Mutrie, the man primarily responsible for putting the Mets' championship nine together, was reassigned to the Gothams. But the crippling blow was delivered just prior to the start of 1885 season. Ostensibly as a reward for their sterling performance the previous year, Mets mainstays Tim Keefe and Dude Esterbrook were dispatched to Bermuda for a preseason vacation at the onion farm owned by Gothams club president Day. Once the two were safely out to sea and incommunicado, the Mets released them. After the 10-day free agent signing period elapsed, Keefe and Esterbrook were promptly inked to contracts that made them members of Day's National League ball club.[27]

Upon discovery that star players had been slipped out of its league, the American Association executive board howled in protest. But all it could do was ban Mutrie from the circuit, an empty gesture as the erstwhile Mets manager had already left for the National League. The executive board also voted to expel the Mets franchise, but quickly reconsidered. Instead, the club was fined $500 for the manner in which Keefe and Esterbrook had been released. The Mets were also required to post a bond with the board, a sort of performance guarantee that the club would complete its 1885 AA schedule.[28]

The Mets fulfilled that obligation, but its time as a first-rate ball club was over. Under new manager Jim Gifford, the depleted Mets posted a non-competitive 44–64 (.407) log for the 1885 season, sliding all the way to seventh in AA standings. Although Dave Orr (.342 BA, with 56 extra-base hits and an AA-leading .543 slugging average), Candy Nelson, Steve Brady, and Chief Roseman still gave the club a decent everyday lineup, there was no replacing pitching ace Keefe. In fact, Jack Lynch's fall-off 23 wins exceeded the total posted by non-entities like Ed Cushman (8–14), Doug Crothers (7–11), Ed Bagley (4–9), and Buck Becannon (2–8), combined. At the same time, the addition of Keefe and former Buffalo star Jim O'Rourke put six future Hall of Fame inductees on the New York Gothams roster. Popularly called the *Giants* by mid-season,[29] the talent-laden club skyrocketed to an 85–27 (.759) record, only to lose the NL pennant to the even better 87–25 (.777) Chicago White Stockings.

The reversal in team fortunes, plus the fact that the 1885 Gothams/Giants had outdrawn the Mets by a near three-to-one margin in Polo Grounds attendance,[30] convinced the MEC to concentrate its holdings. To that end, the New York Mets were put up for sale. Enter Erasmus Wiman, a Canadian-born millionaire businessman-entrepreneur looking to add to the stable of attractions based in his adopted home of Staten Island.[31] In early December 1885, Day and Wiman closed on the $25,000 deal that transferred complete ownership of the New York Mets. Wiman's plan to relocate the ball club to Staten Island, however, encountered immediate resistance in the American Association. Rather than let that happen, circuit magnates voted to expel the New York franchise from the league and substitute one from Washington, D.C., in its place. Injunctive relief obtained by Wiman attorneys temporarily stymied the moves,[32] while the fledgling club owner blasted the now-stayed AA action. "In all my experience, I never heard of proceedings so unjustifiable…. Staten Island shall have a baseball club and I already have had offers to form a new and stronger association than the one just now guilty of the sharp game reflecting very little credit on baseball ethics,"[33] an indignant Wiman proclaimed. The vow to fight was reiterated by recently appointed club secretary George F. Williams, who directly blamed the AA opposition on Brooklyn Grays boss Charles Byrne, fearful of competition from nearby Staten Island and covetous of slugging Mets first baseman Dave Orr and fly hawk Chief Roseman, both reportedly in contract negotiations with the Brooklyn club.[34]

Other American Association magnates had little appetite for battle with the deep-pocketed Wiman, and the league soon capitulated. On December 28, 1885, the Wiman-owned New York Mets were recognized as a member club by the AA.[35] And pursuant to that recognition process, Byrne was compelled to relinquish any claim that Brooklyn may have had upon the services of Orr and Roseman.[36] Wiman then set about getting his St. George Grounds ready for baseball. Although a substantial property with a two-tier grandstand capable of seating about 4,100, the layout of the grounds was more suitable for the theatrical productions and cricket matches previously played there than it was for the national pastime. As aligned for baseball, the entire grandstand sat behind home plate perpendicular to the pitcher's box, with no seating along the foul lines or outfield. Nor did the new ballpark have any baseline or outfield fencing.[37] But as an incentive to entice distant customers to the grounds, admission to Mets games included round-trip ferryboat fare to and from Battery Park in Lower Manhattan or Jewell's Wharf in Brooklyn.[38]

Given that lightly populated Staten Island was then outside the borders of New York City (and Brooklyn),[39] the Mets were largely ignored by large-circulation dailies, prompting one out-of-town journal to observe: "Erastus Wiman ought to start a paper at his Staten Island resort, so that his club would receive occasional mention when they are at home. The New York papers are inclined to neglect the 'Mets.'"[40] It is unclear, however, how actively club president Wiman involved himself in the day-to-day operation of the franchise. Administration of routine club affairs was likely the duty of managing club director Walter Watrous and/or club secretary Williams. Wiman's time was consumed by his myriad other business affairs, particularly an ambitious project to transform sleepy Staten Island into a major commercial port and railroad terminus.[41] Nevertheless, making the grand gesture that he was fond of, Wiman donated an expensive solid silver trophy to be awarded to the American Association champion at season's end.[42]

On April 22, 1886, the New York Mets inaugurated play in their new Staten Island home by dropping a 7–6 decision to the Philadelphia Athletics. "Fully five thousand were in attendance," noted the *New York Herald,* but added that "judging from the inconvenience they were put to, it is not likely that the crowd will be so large every day."[43] The *Herald* proved prophetic. Only 1,500 showed up at St. George Grounds the following day to see the A's drub the Mets, 14–6. By late-May, Wiman had seen enough of his club's poor play. He discharged holdover field leader Jim Gifford for being "too easy on the boys," replacing him with crusty veteran Bob Ferguson.[44] The managerial change made little difference. The Mets' 53–82 (.393) seventh-place finish duplicated the previous season's result, while attendance at St. George Grounds was about the same (67,000) as the year before at the Polo Grounds, but spread over 11 more home playing dates.[45]

Endgame

The Mets got off poorly again in 1887, losing their first 10 games. By late May, the club was solidly ensconced in the AA cellar. At mid-season, Wiman was confirming reports that he might "give up baseball at Staten Island. The 'Mets' are certainly not a success."[46] Nor did things improve thereafter. By season's end, New York's dismal 44–89 (.331) record was good for a third consecutive seventh-place finish, some 50 games behind the AA champion St. Louis Browns. Shortly, Wiman divested himself of the Mets, selling the ball club for the same $25,000 that he had paid for it two years earlier.[47] Deducting his investment in player salaries and ballpark improvements, Wiman's dalliance with the game reportedly cost him some $30,000.[48]

The new owners of the New York Mets were Brooklyn club boss Charles Byrne and his partners in the Grays franchise. Byrne lost no time transferring Mets slugger Dave Orr, pitcher Al Mays, and outfielders Paul Radford and Darby O'Brien to the Brooklyn club. The remaining players on the Mets roster were released. Byrne then relinquished the player-less New York franchise to the American Association.[49] The franchise hulk was subsequently transferred to Kansas City, thereby bringing to a close Staten Island's run as a major-league baseball venue.[50]

During their five-season stint in the American Association, the New York Mets posted a cumulative 270–309 (.464) regular-season record, highlighted by the 1884 AA pennant. At various times during those years, the club roster included Hall of Fame hurler Tim Keefe, formidable batsman Dave Orr, everyday worthies Jack Lynch, Candy Nelson, Paul Radford, and Chief Roseman, and astute field leader Jim Mutrie. The Mets, of course, were hardly the only major-league club not to survive the 19th century. But the causes of the club's demise were somewhat unique. First and foremost, the Mets fell victim to internal decision-making, becoming secondary in the plans of its ownership, the Metropolitan Exhibition Company. Although he had founded and financed the Mets, dominant MEC shareholder John B. Day—whether for reasons of prestige, profit, or survivability—chose to prefer the National League New York Gothams/Giants over the Mets when it came to franchise investment, acquisition of playing talent, use of the Polo Grounds, or other advantage. Even the capture of the 1884 American Association pennant could not dissuade the MEC from focusing on the Giants. To the contrary, the Mets would be sacrificed (via the transfer of Mutrie, Keefe, and Esterbrook) to improve the NL club.

This is not to say that Day and his cohorts were wrong. As their respective attendance figures indicate, New York baseball fans preferred the Giants over the Mets. Perhaps more important, concentrating MEC attention on one ball club was shrewd business. When the Mets went belly up in 1887, the

Giants were on the cusp of back-to-back world championships (in 1888 and 1889) and shattered National League attendance records in the process.[51] The Giants ball club was also a cash cow, with one report placing the profits earned by the MEC during its first decade of existence at $750,000, almost all of it derived from revenues produced by the Giants, not the Mets.[52]

In retrospect, however, the event which sealed the doom of the New York Mets was the club's acquisition by Erastus Wiman. Unlike Day and Mets club president Joe Gordon, both one-time amateur players and genuine baseball enthusiasts, Wiman had no known interest in the game. Rather, he viewed ownership of a baseball team and its relocation as merely another addition to his already-existing Staten Island amusements empire and as a vehicle for increasing traffic on Wiman-owned ferryboat and rail lines. But Staten Island, sparsely populated and inconveniently located, was an unsuitable venue for a major-league ball club. Even a good team would have died there. Once the club did not produce the revenues that Wiman anticipated, he gave up the venture, leaving the Mets' fate to Brooklyn club boss Charles Byrne. And once he had title to the Mets, Byrne predictably reduced the unwanted rival to nothing but the franchise carcass, which the American Association then assigned to faraway Kansas City.

For the 1896 season, tempestuous Andrew Freedman, a successor to Day as Giants club owner, revived the New York Mets moniker, bestowing it on a short-lived farm club that he placed in the minor Atlantic League.[53] Thereafter, the name remained forgotten for well over a half-century, only to be resurrected when the National League decided to place an expansion franchise in New York for the 1962 season. Today, the New York Mets claim a fan base far larger and more avid than John B. Day or Erastus Wiman could have dreamed of. But few of the present-day Citi Field faithful likely appreciated that the name of their beloved team is not novel, or that a long-vanished 19th century major-league ball club was the original New York Mets.

Notes

1. For a more detailed profile of the Mets' founder, see Bill Lamb, "John Day," Society for American Baseball Research, Baseball Biography Project, http://sabr.org/bioproj/person/c281a493 (Last accessed November 16, 2019).

2. Peter Mancuso, "Jim Mutrie," Society for American Baseball Research, Baseball Biography Project, https://sabr.org/bioproj/person/430838fd (Last accessed November 16, 2019).

3. "Again Badly Beaten at Base-Ball," *New York Times*, September 17, 1880: 2. The unidentified *Times* correspondent reported that the "Metropolitans played a very brilliant fielding game throughout, making but one insignificant error in the entire game. They also did some very good batting."

4. Brooklyn was not incorporated into the City of New York until January 1, 1898. Among the Brooklyn-based clubs identified as a New York nine were the New York Mutuals, a member of the National Association (1871–1875) and National League (1876).

5. "Base-Ball on the Polo Grounds," *New York Times*, September 30, 1880: 8. The Mets

added four more runs in the top of the sixth, but the score reverted to 4–2 when darkness prevented the Nationals from completing their sixth-inning at-bats. The game's attendance was adjudged "by far the largest assemblage that has gathered on a ball field in this vicinity in three years."

6. See "John B. Day Tells of a Bitter Hour," *New York Times*, February 6, 1916: S3.

7. See "Metropolitan vs. College Players," *Brooklyn Eagle*, October 4, 1880: 2.

8. Although never active in NYC politics, Day become a member of Tammany Hall, the corrupt political machine that controlled Democratic Party affairs in Manhattan, shortly after his relocation from Connecticut.

9. As reported in "Base Ball on the Polo Grounds and Elsewhere," *The Sun* (New York), October 10, 1880: 6. The NL had just expelled the Cincinnati club and was in need of a replacement franchise for the next season. It is estimated that the Mets won one of every three games played against NL clubs in late 1880. See Richard Hershberger, "Memorable Games: Metropolitans 4, Nationals 2, September 29, 1880," in *The Polo Grounds: Essays and Memories of New York City's Historic Ballpark, 1880–1963*, ed., Stew Thornley (Jefferson, NC: McFarland, 2019), 177.

10. Per Robert D. Warrington, "Philadelphia in the 1881 Eastern Championship Association," *Baseball Research Journal*, Vol. 48, No. 1, Spring 2019, 83.

11. John J. O'Malley, "James J. Mutrie," *Nineteenth Century Stars* (Cleveland: Society for American Baseball Research, 1989), 98.

12. As reported in "The Sporting World," *Cleveland Leader*, December 8, 1882: 3, and elsewhere. New National League teams in New York and Philadelphia would replace just-disbanded ones in Troy and Worcester.

13. A holdover from the 1882 Mets, the 33-year-old O'Rourke had batted .341 for the NL Boston Beaneaters in 1879 and was the older brother of future Hall of Famer Jim O'Rourke.

14. As reported in "Baseball: The New Yorks Win Seven Out of the Eight Games," *New York Herald*, May 1, 1883: 4.

15. Per "Opened with a Victory," *Baltimore Sun*, May 2, 1883: 1.

16. The attendance estimate was published in "Baseball," *The* (New York) *Truth*, May 13, 1883: 6.

17. As calculated from 1883 game day logs published by Retrosheet. The Mets posted an aggregate 4–8–1 record playing on the Southwest diamond on dates when the Gothams were in action on the adjacent Polo Grounds field.

18. Per Robert L. Tiemann, "Major League Attendance," *Total Baseball* (Kingston, NY: Total Sports Publishing, 7th ed., 2001), 74. Spread over 46 home playing dates (including doubleheaders), the Mets drew an average of less than 1,100 fans per game date. Various sources refer to the Mets' 1883 home field as Polo Grounds (II), Southwest Grounds.

19. See Stew Thornley, *Land of the Giants: New York's Polo Grounds* (Philadelphia: Temple University Press, 2000), 19.

20. For more on Metropolitan Park, see Bill Lamb, "Metropolitan Park," Society for American Baseball Research, Baseball Ballparks Project, accessed November 16, 2019, https://sabr.org/bioproj/park-metropolitan-park-nyc.

21. See, e.g., "Metropolitan Park: Opening of the New Grounds of the Metropolitan Club," *Sporting Life*, May 21, 1884: 5: "Over 4,000 persons were present, one quarter of whom were there by special invitation." "Three Championship Games," *New York Herald*, May 14, 1884: 5. Some 4,500 spectators showed up and "the seating capacity was taxed to its utmost limit."

22. According to David Nemec, *The Beer and Whisky League: The Illustrated History of the American Association—Baseball's Renegade Major League* (New York: Lyons & Burford, 1992), 62.

23. Retrosheet game logs indicate that this necessitated Mets use of Metropolitan Park only seven more times during the 1884 season. No use, however, was made of the Polo Grounds' abandoned Southwest diamond during 1884.

24. On the final game of the 1884 campaign, Buck Becannon threw a six-inning complete-game victory for the Mets. This was the only game in which someone other than Keefe or Lynch pitched for New York during 1884.

25. The Grays outscored the Mets by an aggregate run count of 21 to 3, including a 12–2 match finale viewed by only 300. Radbourn is usually credited with 59 wins, rather than 60. That changed in April 2019, when Baseball-Reference.com announced that it had restored the 1884 record to 60–12 as it was originally, prior to the baseball records revisions adopted several days ago.

26. Tiemann, "Major League Attendance," 74.

27. As recounted in more detail by Nemec in *The Beer and Whisky League*, 91–92.

28. See the profile of John B. Day cited in note 1, above.

29. The nickname *Giants* is widely ascribed to new club manager Jim Mutrie, but according to Mutrie biographer Peter Mancuso, the iconic club name may actually have been coined by *New York Evening World* sportswriter P.J. Donahue.

30. After the 1884 season, the Mets discontinued use of Metropolitan Park. In 1885, the Giants drew 185,000 fans to home games at the Polo Grounds. The Mets attracted only 64,000 to the same ballpark.

31. In addition to operas, Wild West shows, theatricals, and other amusements staged at his newly constructed St. George Grounds, Wiman also owned Staten Island ferryboat and rail lines. For more on Erastus Wiman, see Bill Lamb, "Erastus Wiman," Society for American Baseball Research, Baseball Biography Project, https://sabr.org/node/54352 (Last accessed November 16, 2019).

32. As reported on December 11, 1885 in "Sporting Notes," *Dallas Morning News*: 3; "A Base Ball Sensation," *New Haven Morning Journal and Courier* (Connecticut): 4; "Erastus Wiman's Baseball Club," *New-York Tribune*: 1, and elsewhere.

33. As quoted in "Erastus Wiman Indignant," *New York Times*, December 9, 1885: 2.

34. Per "To Stand by Mr. Wiman," *New York Times*, December 13, 1885: 10.

35. As reported in "Mr. Wiman's Final Victory," *New York Times*, December 29, 1885: 1, and an untitled news item in the *New-York Tribune*, December 30, 1885: 4.

36. See "The Mets and Brooklyn," *New York Times*, December 30, 1885: 2.

37. The singular features of the St. George Grounds are depicted in a color lithograph reproduced on the back cover of *Base Ball: A Journal of the Early Game*, Vol. 1, No. 2 (Fall 2007).

38. Per Philip J. Lowry, *Green Cathedrals: The Ultimate Celebration of Major League and Negro League Ballparks* (New York: Walker & Company, 2006), 149. There are two 1992 versions of *Green Cathedrals*, each with differing numbers of ballparks in the subtitle (271 and 273). Lowry's first version was produced by Society for American Baseball Research and published in 1985 by AG Press in Manhattan, Kansas. SABR also produced the 1992 and 2006 versions, which greatly evolved from the first book as digital technology increased the availability of archival research. While the research was done under SABR's auspices, the books were published by third parties.

39. Like Brooklyn and the other outer boroughs, Staten Island was not incorporated into New York City until January 1, 1898.

40. "What the Players Are Doing," *Wheeling Register* (West Virginia), April 11, 1886: 2.

41. For more detail on the scheme, see the Wiman profile cited in endnote 31, above. The collapse of the venture would eventually lead to financial ruin for Wiman.

42. The glass-encased trophy was cast in the form of a 26-inch-high batter at the plate, and valued at between $1,000 and $2,000. For more, see Robert H. Schaefer, "The Wiman Trophy, and the Man for Whom It Was Named," *Base Ball, a Journal of the Early Game*, Vol. 1, No. 2 (Fall 2007), 44–54.

43. "Batting for Championships," *New York Herald*, April 23, 1886: 8.

44. Per David Nemec and David Ball, "James H. Gifford," *Major League Baseball Profiles, 1871–1900, Volume 2: The Hall of Famers and Memorable Personalities Who Shaped the Game*, ed. David Nemec (Lincoln, NE: University of Nebraska Press, 2011), 125–126.

45. As calculated from Retrosheet data. The 135 games that the Mets played in 1886 were 25 more than the previous year, but did not include any home doubleheaders.

46. "Mr. Wiman and the Mets," *New York Herald*, July 22, 1887: 9.

47. As reported in "The Metropolitans Sold," *New York Times*, October 9, 1887: 3. See also, "Big Surprise: Erastus Wiman Out of Base Ball," an unidentified news item contained

in the Erastus Wiman file at the Giamatti Research Center, National Baseball Hall of Fame and Museum, Cooperstown, New York.

48. Schaefer, 52.

49. Per Nemec, *The Beer and Whisky League,* 147.

50. Early in the 1889 season, the New York Giants, displaced from the original Polo Grounds, played 23 home games at St. George Grounds while awaiting the opening of the New Polo Grounds in far north Manhattan.

51. The 1889 New York Giants attracted 305,000 spectators to the Polo Grounds, per Tiemann, "Major League Attendance," 74. Interestingly, the AA Brooklyn Bridegrooms (né Grays) drew even better: 353,690.

52. See "An Offer for the Giants," *New York Times,* September 6, 1889: 3, reporting MEC rejection of a $200,000 bid for the Giants made by Polo Grounds landlord James J. Coogan.

53. By July, fellow Atlantic League club owners had grown tired of Freedman's antics and expelled the Mets. For more on the minor league version of the club, see Bill Lamb, "The Expulsion of the Andrew Freedman–Owned New York Metropolitans from the 1896 Atlantic League," *Beating the Bushes,* Spring 2018, 8–10. *Beating the Bushes* is the official newsletter of the Society for American Baseball Research Minor League Research Committee.

The Life and Times
of Mr. Met

Martin Lessner

What is a Metropolitan anyway? Let's start with what it is not. Of the 30 Major League Baseball teams, seven are named after animals—eight if you consider the Rays' stylized Sun to be secondary to the Devil Ray, a warm aquatic creature giving the team its original name and sitting prominently on the team's uniform sleeves. "Ace" (Blue Jays). "Fredbird" (Cardinals). "Clark" (Cubs). "Billy" (Marlins). "The Bird" (Orioles). "Paws" (Tigers). Though it does not take an incredible leap of imagination to link a mascot with a team, sometimes the origins are not immediately apparent. The Diamondbacks mascot is a bobcat named "Baxter," the choice of animal reflecting the initials of Bank One Ballpark—BOB.

The Angels are biblical characters, and it is easy to see some element of the fan base upset with a mascot who wrestles with shepherds, mimics killing a first born child, or goes around the stands telling female nonagenarians that they will shortly conceive a child. So, the Angels take a pass on the whole mascot thing. Nobody is really sure what constitutes a Giant, although legend has it that the manager of the 1885 New York Gothams referred to his players as "Giants" after a big win against the Phillies, a team founded two years earlier and presently with the longest contiguously used name in professional sports. A Golem of Prague would have worked for a small segment of the fan base, but the Giants went in a completely other direction with "Lou Seal." The "Jolly Green Giant" and "Wally the Green Monster" (Red Sox) are already taken.

Three teams are named for foot coverings, and their mascots do not even pretend to have relevance to the team nomenclature. The Reds' original mascot "Mr. Red" bears a striking resemblance to Mr. Met. Cincinnati's humanoid figure wears a Reds uniform with an oversized baseball for a head and a Reds baseball cap. The character first appeared in the 1953 Cincinnati Reds Yearbook, then two years later as a sleeve patch on the players' uniform. The costumed version began appearing at Riverfront Stadium in 1972. The White Sox have a green furry thing called "Southpaw," a reference to their ballpark on the South Side of Chicago.

Eight teams are named after human occupations, a practice often-times lending itself to mascot synthetization: Padres (the "Swinging Friar"); Pirates (a large green parrot shoulder riding a bucco companion); Royals ("Sluggerrr," a lion whose mane looks like a king's crown); Brewers ("Bernie Brewer"); Rangers ("Rangers Captain"—a horse once ridden by Texas lawmen); Mariners ("Mariner Moose"—surprising because a Moose is not normally known for his seafaring abilities); Athletics ("Stomper"—an elephant symbolizing a turn-of-the-last-century remark by Giants manager John McGraw that A's owner Ben Shibe [of Shibe Park fame] "had bought himself a white elephant"); and Astros ("Orbit"—a green space alien with antennae, sort of an astronaut from another planet).

Two teams are named for Native Americans: The Indians have "Slider," a large furry fuchsia-colored creature. The Braves ("Chief Noc-A-Homa" who lived in a teepee in the outfield bleachers). "Homer the Brave"—another baseball-headed mascot, suspiciously similar to Mr. Met and Mr. Red—replaced the chief and was himself replaced in 2019 by "Blooper" (described as "a very pale and lesser version of the Phillies Phanatic").[1]

One team is named after a geographic feature. The Rockies, honoring the slang term for the Rocky Mountains, created a mascot inspired by a triceratops skull unearthed during the construction of Coors Field—Dinger, a purple dinosaur.

And then there are the teams named after the people who live in the demographic area around the ballpark. The Dodgers reflect Brooklyn pedestrians who (sometimes unsuccessfully) attempted to avoid collisions with electric trolley cars. No mascot has ever been associated with the Dodgers, probably for good reason, though there was the unofficial bum character alluding to Dodgers fans calling the players "bums" during the team's less than prosperous years in Brooklyn.

And what exactly would a Yankee mascot look like? A Union solder from the Civil War? Probably not a real crowd pleaser, so the Yankees gave it a go from 1979 to 1981 with "Dandy" (as in "Yankee Doodle Dandy," a mustached character resembling Thurman Munson).[2] The Nationals could be considered citizens of the United States, but based in the home of the White House, has the Mt. Rushmore quad of racing presidential mascots—Washington, Jefferson, Lincoln and Teddy Roosevelt.

The Twins, named after the twin cities of Minneapolis/St. Paul created "T.C."—a bear modeled after the Hamm's Brewery Bear, the brewery being an early team sponsor. T.C.'s blatant commercialization contrasts with original name of the Toronto team. MLB made Toronto morph from Blue into Blue Jays because Blue was the name of the main beer for Labatt's, a major sponsor.[3] T.C. also avoids the Braves' Andy Messerschmitt impact, where MLB made the Braves change the nickname "Channel" from the back of his #17 uniform, to avoid the pitcher becoming a hurling advertisement for owner Ted Turner's Atlanta cable superstation.[4] WTBS was Channel 17.

Which brings us to the Mets.

Origin of Mr. Met

Mr. Met was an invention of the Mets' front office. Jim Thomson, the team's business manager, joined Tom Meany, an ex-sportswriter who brought his talents to the role of publicity and promotion manager, to create the famous mascot. Its costume was already known to fans—"based on a cartoon character that the organization had developed for use on its tickets and promotional materials."[5]

As of 1964, the idea of a team mascot was prevalent in college sports but not in MLB quarters. Mr. Met would be the first. Sort of. Before the 1964 season, the Mets had a little beagle named Homer sitting behind home plate at the Polo Grounds. But Homer was not actually a Mets mascot, rather, the canine was a mascot for Rheingold Beer, a key Mets sponsor. So, technically, Mr. Met was not the Mets first mascot.

Homer was not to be the only live animal affiliated with an MLB team. Charlie Finley, when he owned the Athletics in Kansas City, put a live mule on the field, named it "Charlie O.," and walked him around the field before each home game. On the July 3, 1965, Saturday night game between the A's and Twins, 32,503 fans saw starting pitcher Diego Segui transported to the mound by the mule mascot; later, the first reliever out of the bullpen—future Hall of Famer Catfish Hunter—rode Charlie O. to the mound.[6] But this idea of a mascot transporting starting and relief pitchers to the mound never caught on, and certainly was not what Thompson and Meany had in mind for Mr. Met.

In 1964, Dan Reilly was a young man in his early twenties, working in the Mets ticket office. One day, Thompson and Meany called Reilly into their offices, poured various items including ticket stubs and stationery on a desk, and quizzed Reilly on what these items had in common. Reilly nailed the correct answer by noting that all the disparate items had a caricature of a person wearing a Mets uniform with a baseball hat. Thompson and Meany then pitched the idea that Reilly would become a living, breathing Mr. Met. How about it, kid?

When offered the assignment as Mr. Met, Reilly had conflicting feelings. He realized he had a little bit of ham in him, and this might be an amusing gig. But he was a little concerned that the assignment might affect his aspirations as an up-and-coming baseball executive. Nevertheless, he decided to accept the assignment.

Thirteen years later, a parallel arc of mascot history played out. Legendary University of Delaware football coach Tubby Raymond used his influence to get his son, Dave, an internship with the Phillies. His two-pronged advice: (a) "You never know what might happen or where it might take you"; and (b) "Talk less."[7] In the spring of 1978, the Phillies hired Harrison/Erickson of New York City (now known as Acme Mascots), which had ties with Jim Henson's Muppets, to create a costumed mascot. Raymond got the call to suit up as the first Phillie Phanatic and asked what he was supposed to do. Phillies executive vice-president manager Bill Giles gave him a universal piece of mascot advice. "I want you to have fun." And as Raymond left, Giles yelled from his office, "G-rated, G-rated fun."[8] And of course, no talking.

Shortly after deciding in May 1964 to accept the assignment as the original Mr. Met, Reilly was introduced to his uniform—a huge papier-mâché head in the form of a baseball, with a big smiley face. Placing the object over his own head, the papier-mâché was a little unsteady, but it had a sweat band inside to provide stability, a mesh screen through the mouth for visibility, and arm straps so that it wouldn't come tumbling off. A uniform without a number soon replaced his business suit.

Mr. Met would appear only in pregame ceremonies and between games of a doubleheader, a concept of limited appearance that is unusual among contemporary mascots, who spend most of the game entertaining from the stands, in luxury boxes, or with on-field promotions. Even the 2019 version of Mr. Met appears on the field during the 7th inning at Citi Field, and monitors the squad of T-shirt gun holders shooting shirts into the stands while he tosses them.[9]

The tension between the present concept of a mascot who continually entertains during the game, and the original Mr. Met concept of a mascot making limited appearances during the game, has been harmonized by the Wilmington Blue Rocks, Single-A minor-league affiliate of the Kansas City Royals, playing in the Carolina League. The Wilmington Blue Rocks were founded in 1993. Its main mascot is a lovable moose named Rocky Bluewinkle, the name apparently being a combination of "Blue Rocks" and the characters "Rocky" and "Bullwinkle," as in the squirrel and moose from the 1960s cartoon show *The Adventures of Rocky and Bullwinkle and Friends*.[10] Rocky Bluewinkle is similar to Mr. Met, where the mascot is in a Blue Rocks uniform with the head of a moose, and the vision of the human dressed inside is through the costumed mouth. Rocky is in action through most of the game walking the stands, standing on top of the dugout, leading cheers, and generally shaking hands and having his picture taken with all of the young children in the crowd around.

Mr. Met's Debut

On May 31, 1964, the Mets had a Sunday doubleheader scheduled against the San Francisco Giants, a team that had left New York only seven years earlier. There were 57,037 paid in attendance at Shea Stadium, the largest major-league crowd of the season; the Giants were still quite a draw—they lost an epic seven-game World Series to the Yankees in 1962, boasted a lineup including icons Willie Mays and Willie McCovey, and had New York City fans who fondly remembered the team's years in the Polo Grounds. Mets baseball was not the reason for the crowd. The team had a 14–30 record, but the front office executives were thinking about other things, in addition to winning baseball games. The Mets marketing department was both anxious and eager to see what the reaction would be to their papier-mâché animated creation.

Dan Reilly was given a corner of the clubhouse where the box with his

Shea Stadium awaits the influx of fans who could always count on Mr. Met to bring joy, even during the Mets' down years. Mr. Met's popularity influenced other teams to develop mascots (courtesy of Bob Busser).

Mr. Met costume awaited him, and he dressed just as if he was a player about to go out onto the field. Reilly first went to the press room and then proceeded to a small section above home plate where the organist played and the scoreboard was operated along with the public address system. In a room called the "operations booth," Reilly waited, assisting with the out-of-town scores by verbally conveying the run totals off the ticker to the person in charge of updating the scoreboard. By the sixth inning of the first game, Reilly headed down to the clubhouse to prepare for his début.

When the Mets lost the first game of the doubleheader in a comparatively brisk time of 2:29. Unsure whether the reaction of the crowd would be different after a loss versus a win and unable to decide what to do when he emerged with the ground crew, Reilly ambled to the area behind home plate while the grounds crew got the infield ready for the second game. At some point, Reilly decided it would be best to head over toward friendly territory—the Mets dugout along the first-base side. With his bulbous head now in the natural light, Reilly began waving to the fans in the box seats, and then to his surprise, they started to wave back at him. Large groups of young fans started to swarm the area near the railing by the Mets dugout to get a better look. Mr. Met was a hit! Reilly signed autographs and posed for pictures. The number one question that the young fans asked him: "How do you see out of that thing?" Of course, one of the first rules of mascots, even the original mascot, is "no talking." That goes along with the other main mascot rule: never be seen with your head off.

But there is a fear of mascots not limited to children or the fictional fear/dislike from other team's mascots. Mets ace Noah Syndergaard is afraid of Mr. Met based on a condition called "masklophobia"—described as a "fear of people in masks and costumes, such as mascots, full-bodied costumed characters, masquerade costumes and Halloween costumes."[11] Syndergaard would rather not have Mr. Met, describing mascots as follows: "They're just creepy. They're very stealthy, but they're huge at the same time. I feel like they sneak up on me anywhere."[12] This dread of mascots would seem to eliminate a certain segment of the Met fan base, unless certain precautions are made, such as listening when a mascot-fearing fan says "We're going to the Mets game—can we just not sit next to the mascot so I don't need to give the mascot a hug?"[13]

About 20 minutes after Mr. Met made his first appearance, the Mets players emerged from the clubhouse to warm up for the second game of the twin-bill. This was Reilly's cue for Mr. Met to leave the field. But the players had a different idea—they decided to have a little fun with the kid wearing the papier-mâché head. The Mets soon began knocking on his head from behind. When Reilly turned around to see who was trying to get his attention, another player would tap his head from behind, with Reilly turning around to find the culprit. This turned into an amusing routine, which the fans were enjoying. Reilly pantomimed with his hands playfully as if trying to catch a baseball, which instigated the Mets players to test his vision by tossing hard-balls at him. No catches were made, and the only thing Mr. Met succeeded in doing was taking the lobbed baseballs off his papier-mâché forehead, with the fans laughing. This shtick was probably long forgotten by the time the second game ended, a 23-inning affair that lasted a major-league record seven hours and 23 minutes.[14]

Unlike Reilly's first interaction with the Mets players' soft tosses, mas-cots, and baseballs have not always gotten along so well. In the 1988 movie *Bull Durham*, the Bulls mascot was beaned by Ebby Calvin "Nuke" LaLoosh (played by Tim Robbins) on orders of catcher Crash Davis (played by Kevin Costner), simply to rattle the next opposing batter and emphasize LaLoosh's wildness.[15]

Tom Burgoyne—who began with the Phillies in 1989 as a back-up for Dave Raymond and took over the Phillie Phanatic outfit in 1994—got plunked during an out-of-town gig in 2011. Travelling the Pennsylvania Turnpike's Northeast Extension to Allentown for a Triple-A Iron Pigs game, Burgoyne's journey ended not at Coca-Cola Park but an emergency room in Lehigh Val-ley Hospital–Cedar Crest. The Phanatic was behind the first-base dugout when a foul ball from the Indianapolis Indians hit his neck—actually, Bur-goyne's head. Burgoyne acted wounded as the Phanatic, but was, in fact, injured. Though diagnosed with a concussion, Burgoyne showed how gritty (no pun intended) a Philly mascot can be, returning for the next day's action as the Phanatic.[16]

While the Mets players at Mr. Met's début were just funning around, and evidently realized that there was a real person underneath that head who could be injured if the horse play was taken too far, that has not always been the case for mascots. In 2002, Shawn Christopherson, who played "Raymond" for the Tampa Bay Devil Rays, had to limit himself to "basically signing auto-graphs" after a drunk tackled him and separated his shoulder.[17] Other mascots have been similarly abused by fans, as highlighted in an ESPN "Top 10 Mascot Abuse" segment, including a minor league mascot dressed like a tree being kicked in the groin by a kid who just lost a musical-chairs competition.[18] The Milwaukee Brewers have various sausages races as a promotion, or, more specifically people dressed up as various sausages racing around the field. Randall Simon of the visiting Pirates felled a young woman intently running to keep up with her fellow sausages. With a check swing, Simon caused her to knock over another woman dressed as the hot dog.[19] Simon later claimed that he was just kidding around, evidently he did not realize that sausages have feelings too.[20]

As the first baseball mascot, Reilly faced an unprecedented dilemma—

to resolving how much Mr. Met should interject himself into the on-field entertainment. Between games of doubleheaders, the Mets often hired renowned marching bands to play. In early June 1964, the Mets had the defending New York State marching band champions, the Hawthorne Caballeros, scheduled to perform. Mr. Met sat on the sidelines, but the band-leader had different ideas. He grabbed Mr. Met, pulled him out with the band, and gesticulated that Mr. Met should start dancing to the music. Mr. Met acquiesced, to the delight of the crowd. The fans didn't see this is upstaging at all, but as a real entertainment synergy. To this day, an integral part of the Phillie Phanatic's performance is to sidle up to any onfield performer, whether it's a dancer on Irish Heritage Night, marching bands playing before the National Anthem, or the klezmer band on Jewish Heritage Night.[21] Grabbing a band member's baton or mussing up an entertainer's hair is part of his schtick.

Mr. Met's First Father's Day

Father's Day 1964 was a test for the new mascot. During the first game of a doubleheader against the Phillies, Reilly prepared for his Mr. Met appear-ance but had to scramble when the game moved at a faster pace than he expected. Jim Bunning was pitching a very efficient game for Philadelphia—ultimately throwing 90 pitches—and heading towards perfect-game immor-tality. After Bunning retired the 27th Met, he went to the Phillies clubhouse but the Mets fans demanded an encore or at least a tip of the hat so they could recognize what he had accomplished. Mr. Met was then put in the unusual position of not only having to step aside for a visiting player, but to actually applaud him. He covered this traitorous deed by walking over to the Mets dugout and clapping along with the players in uniform.

Not all mascots show respect for the players on the opposing team. Los Angeles Dodgers manager Tommy Lasorda assaulted the Phanatic during a 1988 road trip at Veterans Stadium. The Phanatic ignited Lasorda's ire by showcasing a life-sized mannequin looking eerily like Lasorda and dressed in a Dodgers uniform. After retrieving the mannequin, Lasorda hit the Pha-natic in the head for good measure. Tom Burgoyne says that this was the closest the Phanatic (with Dave Raymond inside) has come to losing his head on field, a mascot no-no.[22] Twenty-seven years later, Lasorda still hates the Phanatic for this incident: "I was always upset about him always taking my shirt and putting it on some dummy and then running over it. I didn't par-ticularly like that, and I told him. I said, 'I don't want you to do that anymore.' The next time I saw him he still put my shirt on, so I went after him and I bopped him down a little bit. And I said, 'If there weren't all these people here I'd really rip ya."[23] Maybe Lasorda was just a hater, because almost a year later, he demanded the Montreal Expos mascot Youppi be ejected by third-base umpire Bob Davidson for dancing on top of the Dodgers dugout and bothering the players.[24] Davidson tossed Youppi.

Mr. Met and the Mascot Code of Silence

A first rule of mascots, with a precedent set by the original Mr. Met, is no speaking. Evidently, this was a good trait for a mascot off the field too, as Mr. Met kept the secret of a famous, but embarrassing after-hours baseball tale. On Saturday, July 24, 1965, the Mets celebrated manager Casey Stengel's 75th birthday with a cake and ceremony at Shea Stadium's home plate. Mr. Met stood beside Casey and led the fans in cheers. That part of the story is well-known. What wasn't well-known at the time was Casey's *real* party at Toots Shor's restaurant in Midtown Manhattan, courtesy of a celebrity cast of hundreds. Mickey Mantle, Whitey Ford, Yogi Berra, and Phil Rizzuto were all there, along with many ballplayers, celebrities, and old friends. Also, there was Mr. Met, although technically incognito as he was not wearing his big papier-mâché head. Towards the end of the evening, a commotion was heard in the men's bathroom. A headless Mr. Met rushed in, like Superman after changing from his Clark Kent clothes, to find out what happened. Casey seemingly slipped on whatever slickness was on the men's room floor and fell on his hip. The injury was a serious fracture that confined Casey to the hospital and sidelined him as the Mets manager, in favor of Wes Westrum, announced as the interim manager. The rumor spread that Casey had fallen off a barstool, but Mr. Met, true to the mascot creed of not talking, never revealed a rather unflattering story that Casey had slipped in the men's room on mystery slickness.[25]

Mr. Met and Biking

In 1966, the New York Mets had two main sponsors: Rheingold Beer and Borden Dairy. Rheingold sponsored the printing of schedules and brochures, in addition other promotions, including the short-lived Rheingold beer beagle who sat behind home plate at the Polo Grounds, the Mets' home in 1962 and 1963.[26] Borden was known for milk and ice cream; Elsie the Cow is the company mascot, so well-known that it had Borden's balloon in Macy's Thanksgiving Day Parade in Manhattan.[27] Its peer group included Popeye the Sailorman, Superman, and Bullwinkle.[28]

Borden decided to get some bang for its sponsorship buck, and asked the Mets front office if Mr. Met could accompany Elsie the Cow for the three-mile parade from Central Park West, down Broadway, to Macy's in Herald Square (34th Street and 7th Avenue). The Mets, of course, were excited about the idea, especially since the parade had a national audience. There was one condition, unusual and maybe unique for mascots. Mr. Met would have to ride a bicycle.

The assembly point was West 86th Street and Central Park at 8:30 a.m. on Thanksgiving. Problems developed almost immediately. The golden rule of mascots never removing their costumed head, especially in front of children, could be a promotional disaster if it were violated on national television. Biking with the huge papier-mâché head provided extremely limited peripheral vision, and it proved impossible for Reilly to turn his head side to side to see the crowds, much less take the hands off the handlebars to wave to the crowd. It was a very windy day, causing the big Mr. Met baseball head to get buffeted, which made remaining upright on the bicycle a difficult task. The parade spectators and a national TV audience were treated to the spectacle of Mr. Met weaving side to side with his hands clenched on the handlebars for a three-mile, slow-moving parade, looking like Mr. Met had indulged in one too many Rheingold beers the night before. Mr. Met, however, performed an athletic feat *par excellence*.[29]

Reilly rode his bicycle to Herald Square with almost no peripheral vision and heavy winds. Had he fallen or in any way lost his head, it might have spelled the end of Mr. Met as a viable mascot. Years later, a plastic figurine of Mr. Met riding a bicycle is a collector's item,[30] and the mascot shills for Citibank to promote the Citi Bike share in New York.[31] The Nationals have taken mascots promoting bike shares to a new level, with the Racing Presidents mascots using the big red Capital Bikeshare bikes in September 2010, shortly after Capital Bikeshare launched, and again in June of 2013 in a game at Nationals Park against the Mets.[32] The Phillie Phanatic has not been able to emulate Mr. Met's Macys Day Parade heroics. His only known cycling is at a Collingswood, New Jersey, post–Thanksgiving Parade, where he only rode a block or two, weaving in and out of the members of a high school marching band.[33]

Mr. Met Will Visit You!

According to the Mets official web site, "Mr. Met and Mrs. Met can visit you!" The array of possibilities is varied. "They both are available for Birthdays, Christenings, Weddings, Bar/Bat Mitzvahs, Corporate Affairs, Community Events, Fund Raisers, Grand Openings, ... and other occasions."[34] The "other occasions" are undefined and unmentioned, but possibly include visits to YMCA baseball clinics, where the kids get "high fours" (Mr. Met only has four fingers on each hand) and warned, "Don't touch his head, okay?"[35]

While the Mets advertise that Mr. Met is available for weddings, there is no proof that Mr. Met has actually participated in the wedding ceremony itself, walked the bride down the aisle, or served as a ring bearer. His role seems reserved for an appearance at the wedding party itself.[36] But Tom Burgoyne recalls the Phillie Phanatic being hired to attend the wedding of a particularly "phanatical" bride, who was kept in the dark about her special guest. During the wedding celebration, the DJ brought the proceedings, dancing, and the music to a halt. Then, he stated in a very serious tone that an ex-boyfriend showed up unannounced, making a huge fuss outside the ballroom and demanding that he would not leave until he got one final dance with his ex-girlfriend. The friends and family were quite taken aback, possibly suspecting some sort of violent incident. But before things got out of hand, the DJ declared that the groom okayed the dance for the sake of peace, and while the crowd groans, they then turn their heads to see the Phillie Phanatic race to embrace the bride, to the merriment of all.[37]

The Saint Joseph's University Hawk, while not an MLB mascot, follows the basic mascot code of behavior crafted by early adopters like Mr. Met. The Hawk is unique, though, in that he continually flaps his arms throughout an entire Saint Joe's basketball game, or anytime he is in public.

According to Timmy Parks, the student who was the Hawk from 2015 to 2017, the family of a deceased university booster requested the Hawk to attend his funeral. The Hawk showed up, but in a smart act of discretion, decided not to stand in the pews during the service flapping his arms, but instead stood behind the seated mourners during the ceremony. With the encouragement of the family, the Hawk took his place among the mourners as they walked from the church out to the hearse. While the family, or at least some of the family, may have thought it was a good idea, the other mourners were not quite sure what to make of the life-sized mascot walking beside them. Timmy describes this as extremely awkward, and probably the most uncomfortable moment of his two-year mascot career.[38] The famously outgoing Phanatic never got as far as the Hawk, but did stand in the receiving line at the funeral of a longtime game-day employee.[39]

Mr. Met and the Phanatic have cooperated to jointly celebrate religious ceremonies. On October 3, 2012, after both the Mets and the Phillies were confirmed postseason no-shows, Neil Wise, the Director of Programming of programing for the Princeton Jewish Center, sent out a most curious email:

> Phillie Phanatic and Mr. Met confirmed for TJC Simchat Torah! Yes, you have read this correct—The Jewish Center is excited to announce Mr. Met and The Phillie Phanatic, the official mascots of The New York Mets and The Philadelphia Phillies will

be attending our Simchat Torah celebration. Please join them this coming Monday evening, October 8 at 6:30 p.m., for a historic Simchat Torah celebration.

Due to the holiday, photographs, video, and autographs will not be permitted.[40]

Located in the middle of New Jersey, Princeton was the logical neutral ground for this joint appearance. This particular area is the borderline for Phillies and Mets fandom, with the fans south strongly favoring Phillies, while the fans north have their affiliations to the New York teams, and if not the Yankees then the Mets. This interesting fact was established when the *New York Times* cited a study of Facebook likes in order to draw a geographic map, color-coded, highlighting which ZIP codes supported which teams. Phillies support centers in downtown Philadelphia, but extends like fingers on a hand towards Harrisburg, Pennsylvania, south to Middletown, Delaware, and essentially follows the Atlantic City Expressway to the beach with a finger of support going up the Delaware River as far as Princeton.[41]

Mr. Met on TV

ESPN's humorous "This Is SportsCenter" television commercials have featured Mr. Met. In one clip, Mr. Met is driving while Mrs. Met says—with subtitles because mascots don't speak—that ESPN should make him a Sports-Center anchor because he is much sexier than Scott Van Pelt[42] In a similar clip she complains that that she should have married the San Diego Chicken after Mr. Met gets bumped from SportsCenter.[43] In the break room at ESPN's offices in Bristol, Connecticut, Mr. Met expresses his disgust for Josh Hamilton. ESPN anchor Stuart Scott explains that some of Home Run Derby balls that Hamilton hit were Mr. Met's "cousins."[44]

Mr. Met has also been the target of a Conan O'Brien sketch (clearly not authorized by the Mets), where the baseball-headed mascot is a male prostitute servicing a john in a car.[45] Conan also lampoons Mr. Met after the Mets' 2007 collapse, showing Mr. Met's suicide attempts, which failed because of his big head, and then his arrival at home to find Mrs. Met in bed with the Phanatic.[46]

Besides commercials and unauthorized satire, Mr. Met was featured in an episode of the 2015 remake of *The Odd Couple*. Oscar Madison was to throw out the first pitch. His estranged father is with him, making Oscar so mad that he hits Mr. Met in the head. As a publicity stunt, the Mets get Oscar to apologize to the mascot.[47] On a 2019 episode of *Madam Secretary*, President Elizabeth McCord has a nightmare about beaning Mr. Met when she prepares to throw out the first pitch at a Mets game.[48]

Mr. Met and Phillie Phanatic are mascots for rival teams, but that makes their collaboration in a Stand Up to Cancer commercial for MasterCard all the more effective. MasterCard's advertising agency selected Trenton Thunder Stadium, a midway neutral ground, for the location. The 2013 commercial shows Mr. Met and the Phanatic pranking each other, but then reconciling over lunch for the cause.[49] The two held up "Stand Up to Cancer" placards at the 2013 MLB All-Star Game at Citi Field and appeared on the red carpet in front of Radio City Music Hall before the 2013 All-Star Game at Citi Field, clowning with each other.[50]

The Phillie Phanatic's public rivalry with Mr. Met jumps to a new level in the ESPN commercial "The Phanatic Hates Waiting." Set to the introduction music for the FX comedy *It's Always Sunny in Philadelphia*, a frustrated Phanatic vandalizes and generally discombobulates the possessions in the cubicles of the ESPN staff. At one point, the Phanatic takes a yellow "Let's Go Mets" rally towel off a desk and uses it to wipe both his underarms and his green butt before throwing it over his shoulder and then taking a sledgehammer and silly string to the office furniture.[51] The Mets strike back, with a commercial showing Mr. Met driving a golf ball into a Phillie Phanatical doll with a resulting fireball explosion.[52]

Mr. Met Goes Rogue

In 2017, on the 53rd anniversary of Mr. Met's début, the Mets endured a 7–1 defeat at the hands of the Brewers. Whatever was left of the crowd relentlessly booed the Mets in the top of the ninth inning. Evidently, the loss was too much for Mr. Met, as he flipped the middle finger to a group of shouting fans who were apparently only seeking a "high four" from the mascot. The image of the bird-flipping Mr. Met went viral.[53]

Mr. Met Does Not Meet the Criteria for a World Series Ring

Steve Boldis wore the Mr. Met costume for 12 years (and played Mr. Met in the 2015 episode of *The Odd Couple*) but quit to take a construction job after the Mets lost the 2015 World Series. When he did not receive a National League pennant ring, Boldis said that donning the giant, ball-shaped head "was not just some job" and visiting sick kids, appearing on TV, at field days, and schools made the mascot gig "magic."[54] The Mets distributed more than 750 pennant rings and issues a statement revealing its reasons for Boldis not getting one: "He worked approximately half of the required hours last season, did not meet the criteria, and as such did not receive a ring."[55] Maybe Boldis would have gotten a ring if the Mets had actually won the World Series. On

October 31, 2008, more than one million people lined Broad Street for the Phillies' World Series victory parade. Who was in the flatbed truck leading the parade at two miles per hour? MVP Cole Hamels? Chase Utley? Ryan Howard? Jimmy Rollins? Nope. It was the Phillie Phanatic. Now that is some mascot respect.

Though the Phanatic is the nearest major-league mascot for baseball fans in northern Delaware, Rocky Bluewinkle has gained affection since his early 1990s début as the mascot for the Wilmington Blue Rocks, Single-A affiliate of the Kansas City Royals. But the team's beloved moose has a companion, of sorts, to entertain the crowd.

Mr. Celery.

The story goes that a conference of food distributors was held at the local convention center in the late 1990s. A celery-stalk costume was headed for the dumpster but a Blue Rocks executive took custody. It gathered dust in a warehouse for years, until a team executive saw an intern napping.

Rather than fire him or give him menial work, Blue Rocks management decided to give him what seems to be a hilariously embarrassing endeavor— wear the costume and run behind the batting screen at Frawley Stadium when the Blue Rocks score a run and CEL-ebrate.[56] "Song 2" by the English rock band Blue (a.k.a. "woo-hoo") accompanies him. It has become a Wilmington tradition, with some fans having brought signs that says he is "stalking" the opposition.[57]

Postscript

The Phillie Phanatic first appeared in public at Veterans Stadium on Tuesday night, April 25, 1978. Sitting in section 247, Row 1 were two 15-year-old boys from Claymont, Delaware, who had purchased a 15-game plan, at $9 per ticket.

Too young to drive, they rode the Greggs bus to the game. Excited to be independent for the evening, and excited to see a good Phillies team packed with expectations of another post-season appearance, they saw a 6'5" furry creature walking around before the national anthem. Turning to each other, they asked almost simultaneously, "What the **** is that?"[58]

I was one of those teenagers.

NOTES

1. Kit Anderson, "Atlanta Braves Reveal Disturbing New Mascot," ATL All Day, accessed November 10, 2019, https://atlallday.com/2018/01/28/atlanta-braves-reveal-disturbing-new-mascot/.

2. Jen Carlson, "The Short, Sad History of the Yankees 1980s Mascot, Dandy," Gothamist, accessed November 10, 2019, https://gothamist.com/arts-entertainment/the-short-sad-history-of-the-yankees-1980s-mascot-dandy.

3. Allen Tait, "Toronto Blue Jays Team Ownership History," Society for American Baseball Research, accessed November 10, 2019, https://sabr.org/research/toronto-blue-jays-team-ownership-history.

4. Paul Lukas (via ESPN), "Uni Watch's Friday Flashback: What's in a Nickname?," ABC News, accessed November 10, 2019, https://abcnews.go.com/Sports/uni-watchs-friday-flashback-nickname/story?id=39088122.

5. Dan Reilly with Bill Curreri, introduction to *The Original Mr. Met Remembers: When the Miracle Began* (New York: iUniverse, 2007), vii.

6. Roger Cormier, "The Idle Thoughts of the First Pitcher to Ride a Bullpen Cart in 2018," Fangraphs, accessed November 13, 2019,
https://blogs.fangraphs.com/the-idle-thoughts-of-the-first-pitcher-to-ride-a-bullpen-cart-in-2018/, March 9, 2018; Minnesota Twins at Kansas City Athletics Box Score, July 3, 1965, Baseball Reference, accessed November 13, 2019, https://www.baseball-reference.com/boxes/KC1/KC1196507030.shtml; see Edwin Shrake, "A Man and a Mule in Missouri," *Sports Illustrated*, July 19, 1965, 36–46, accessed November 13, 2019, https://www.si.com/vault/1965/07/19/606367/a-man-and-a-mule-in-missouri.

7. "The Man, the Myth and the Mascot," *University of Delaware Magazine*, August 2019, 36.

8. "History of the Phillie Phanatic: From Humble Beginnings to Crowd Favorite," *Daily Times* (Delaware County, Pennsylvania), accessed November 10, 2019, https://www.delcotimes.com/sports/history-of-the-phillie-phanatic-from-humble-beginnings-to-crowd/article_bbdf63da-f8b9–5851-aca3–9f4812c2138a.html, March 27, 2014.

9. Author's observation from Section 122, Citi Field, Mets v. Diamondbacks, September 9, 2019.

10. Paul Caputo, "Of Moose and (Celery) Men: The Story Behind the Wilmington Blue Rocks," Chris Creamer's SportsLogos.net, accessed November 10, 2019, http://news.sportslogos.net/2014/05/10/of-moose-and-celery-men-the-story-behind-the-wilmington-blue-rocks/, May 10, 2014.

11. Chris Thompson, "New York Mets Ace Noah Syndergaard Has an Actual Phobio of Mr. Met (Video)," Elite Sports NY, accessed November 10, 2019, https://elitesportsny.com/2017/04/09/new-york-mets-ace-noah-syndergaard-has-a-phobia-of-mr-met/, April 9, 2017.

12. Matt Monagan, "Noah Syndergaard, Expert Mascot Troll, Stole the Phillie Phanatic's ATV," Major League Baseball, accessed November 10, 2019, https://www.mlb.com/cut4/mets-noah-syndergaard-expert-mascot-troller-stole-the-phillie-phanatics-atv/c-223525990, April 11, 2017.

13. Lisa Esposito, "9 Phobias That Are Surprisingly Common," *U.S. News & World Report*, accessed November 11, 2019, https://health.usnews.com/wellness/mind/slideshows/9-phobias-that-are-surprisingly-common?slide=5, November 11, 2016; "Our Battle with Masklophobia," Forks & Folly, accessed November 11, 2019, http://forksandfolly.com/2012/12/our-battle-with-masklophobia/, December 3, 2012.

14. Alan Cohen, "May 31, 1964: Baseball's Longest Doubleheader," Society for American Baseball Research, Baseball Games Project, accessed November 11, 2019, https://sabr.org/gamesproj/game/may-31-1964-baseballs-longest-doubleheader.

15. "Throw it at the bull," *Bull Durham*, directed by Ron Shelton (1988; The Mount Company), You Tube, accessed November 11, 2019, https://www.youtube.com/watch?v=euHfP6X_axY; https://www.baseball-reference.com/bullpen/Nuke_LaLoosh.

16. Tom Burgoyne, telephone interview with Martin Lessner, August 28, 2019; Drew Magary, "Phanatic Hospitalized After Getting Hit by Foul Ball," WCAU-TV, accessed November 11, 2019, https://www.nbcphiladelphia.com/blogs/philthy-stuff/Phanatic-Hospitalized-After-Getting-Hit-by-Foul-Ball-124417434.html; "Phanatic Gets Hit with Foul Ball," YouTube, accessed November 11, 2019, https://youtu.be/_16E51cWi3c.

17. Jerry Guidera, "Baseball's Team Mascots Blame Heavy Costumes for Discontent," *Wall Street Journal*, accessed November 11, 2019, https://www.wsj.com/articles/SB103066294 3728822595, August 30, 2002.

18. "Top 10 Mascot Abuse," You Tube, accessed November 11, 2019. https://www.youtube.com/watch?v=TDZhetH_bwk.

19. "Sausage Incident," WTMJ-TV, You Tube, accessed November 11, 2019, https://www.youtube.com/watch?v=AkeygYiur9E, July 9, 2003.

20. Dayn Perry, "The Bobblehead Project: Randall Simon vs. Racing Sausage," CBS Sports, accessed November 11, 2019, https://www.cbssports.com/mlb/news/the-bobblehead-project-randall-simon-vs-racing-sausage/, July 11, 2013.

21. Keri White, "Phillies Celebrate 11th Jewish Heritage Night," *Jewish Exponent*, accessed November 11, 2019, https://www.jewishexponent.com/2018/05/09/phillies-celebrate-11th-jewish-heritage-night/, May 9, 2018.

22. Tom Burgoyne, telephone interview with Martin Lessner; "Phanatic All Up in Dodgers' Head," NBC Sports Philadelphia, accessed November 11, 2019, https://www.nbcsports.com/philadelphia/phanatic-all-dodgers-head-smash.

23. Gemma Kaneko, "Never Forget the Day Tommy Lasorda Got into a Fight with the Phanatic," Cut4, Major League Baseball, accessed November 11, 2019, https://www.mlb.com/cut4/video-tommy-lasorda-fights-phillie-phanatic/c-145738464.

24. "LA&MON: Lasorda Gets Youppi! Tossed from the Game," Major League Baseball, You Tube, accessed November 11, 2019, https://www.youtube.com/watch?v=pmzeK6oAtkk, August 23, 1989.

25. Dan Reilly with Bill Curreri, *The Original Mr. Met Remembers: When the Miracle Began,,* 80; Stengel announced his retirement in late August, 1965.Dick Young, "Casey Limps Out as Mets Maestro: He'll Scout Talent; Wes Carries On," *Daily News* (New York), August 31, 1965: 54.

26. Rodger Sherman, "Remembering Homer the Beagle, the Puppy That Was the Mets' First Mascot," SB Nation, accessed November 11, 2019, https://www.sbnation.com/mlb/2014/8/1/5957873/homer-the-beagle-new-york-metsmascot#targetText=Remembering%20Homer%20the%20Beagle%2C%20the,was%20the%20Mets'%20first%20mascot&targetText=Before%20Mr.%20Met%2C%20the%20Mets,though%2C%20because%20beagles%20are%20beagles.

27. "Elsie the Cow," Macy's Thanksgiving Day Parade Wiki, accessed November 11, 2019, https://macysthanksgiving.fandom.com/wiki/Elsie_the_Cow.

28. "Macy's Thanksgiving Day Parade 1966 Lineup," Macy's Thanksgiving Day Parade Wiki, accessed November 11, 2019, https://macysthanksgiving.fandom.com/wiki/Macy%27s_Thanksgiving_Day_Parade_1966_Lineup.

29. "Gallery: 50 Ridiculously Awesome Photos of Mr. Met," Complex, accessed November 11, 2019, https://www.complex.com/sports/2012/04/gallery-50-ridiculously-awesome-photos-mr-met/1.

30. "New York Mets MLB Mr Met Stranger Things Mascot on Bike Bobblehead," Sports Fan Island, accessed November 11, 2019, https://www.sportsfanisland.com/products/new-york-mets-mlb-mr-met-stranger-things-mascot-on-bike-bobblehead.

31. "Citi and Curtis Granderson Launch Mets-Themed Citi Perks Sweepstakes," Citigroup, accessed November 11, 2019, https://www.citigroup.com/citi/news/2016/160407a.htm, April 7, 2016; Mrs. Met, @mrsmet, accessed November 11, 2019, https://twitter.com/mrsmet/status/1021424123350863873, July 23, 2018; Citi Bike, @CitiBikeNYC, accessed November 11, 2019, https://twitter.com/CitiBikeNYC/status/884454124166709248, July 10, 2017.

32. Benjamin R. Freed, "Washington Nationals Racing Presidents Use Bikeshare," dcist, accessed November 11, 2019, https://dcist.com/story/13/06/05/washington-nationals-racing-preside/, June 5, 2013.

33. Tom Burgoyne, telephone interview with Martin Lessner.

34. "The Story of Mr. Met," Major League Baseball, accessed November 11, 2019, https://www.mlb.com/mets/fans/the-story-of-mr-met.

35. James Montgomery, "'Don't Touch His Head': A Day in the Life of Mr. Met," *Rolling Stone*, accessed November 11, 2019, https://www.rollingstone.com/culture/culture-sports/dont-touch-his-head-a-day-in-the-life-of-mr-met-165892/, August 21, 2014.

36. Shannon Shark, "Mr. Met Attends a Wedding," Mets Police, accessed November 11, 2019, https://www.metspolice.com/2010/08/17/mr-met-attends-a-wedding/, August 17, 2010.

37. Tom Burgoyne, telephone interview with Martin Lessner.

38. Timmy Parks, telephone interview with Martin Lessner, August 26, 2019.

39. Tom Burgoyne, telephone interview with Martin Lessner.

40. Neil Wise, email message to Princeton Jewish Center congregants, October 8, 2012.

41. Tom Giratikanon, Josh Katz, David Leonardt and Kevin Quealy, "Up Close on Baseball's Borders," "The Upshot," *New York Times*, accessed November 11, 2019, https://www.nytimes.com/interactive/2014/04/23/upshot/24-upshot-baseball.html?auth=login-email, April 24, 2014.

42. "Mrs. Met thinks Mr. Met should be an ESPN anchor," "This Is SportsCenter" television advertisement, ESPN, You Tube, accessed November 11, 2019, https://www.youtube.com/watch?v=rSnmOxUkZFE.

43. "Mrs. Met disappointed that 'SportsCenter' bumped Mr. Met," "This Is SportsCenter," television advertisement, ESPN, accessed November 11, 2019, https://www.espn.com/watch/player?id=17339569&lang=en.

44. "Mr. Met angry at Josh Hamilton," "This Is SportsCenter" television advertisement, ESPN, You Tube, accessed November 11, 2019, https://www.youtube.com/watch?v=VOc5kEY8AhU. Stuart Scott died of appendix cancer at age 49 in 2015.

45. "Mr. Met as Prostitute," *Late Night with Conan O'Brien*, Aired January 12, 2005 on NBC, You Tube, accessed November 11, 2019, https://www.youtube.com/watch?v=JuNQOFePQeM. The broadcast date is unavailable. But Beltran signed his seven-year, $119 million deal with the Mets on January 11, 2005. So, the date is approximated as the next day when the contract terms were reported in the New York City newspapers. See Jack Curry, "Beltran Brings Great Hope to 'New Mets," *New York Times*, January 12, 2005: D1.

46. "Mr. Met Attempts Suicide," *Late Night with Conan O'Brien*, Aired October 1, 2007 on NBC, Vimeo, accessed November 11, 2019, https://vimeo.com/7744420 (titled "Philly Fanatic [*sic*] vs. Mr. Met). See Ben Shpigel, "In Bitter End to Epic Skid, Mets Are Out," *New York Times*, October 1, 2007: A1.

47. Cendrowski, Mark, dir. *The Odd Couple*. Season 2, episode 4, "Madison & Son." Aired April 28, 2016 on CBS; "Thursday on TV: Garry Marshall Shows Up on 'The Odd Couple'—Along with Mr. Met!," *Salt Lake Tribune*, accessed November 11, 2019, https://archive.sltrib.com/article.php?id=3831988&itype=CMSID.

48. Mr. Met is positioned between the pitcher's mound and first base. When the time comes, McCord, played by Tea Leoni, pitches from the mound and hurls a ball slightly out of the strike zone. She filmed the scene before a Mets-Indians game on August 21, 2019, bouncing three pitches and getting one to reach backup infielder Luis Guillorme crouching behind the plate—that's the pitch used in the broadcast. The Mets won the game in the 10th inning on J.D. Davis's RBI single. Alcala, Felix, dir. *Madam Secretary/Madam President*. Season 6, episode 2, "The Strike Zone." Aired October 13, 2019 on CBS. McCord begins the series as Secretary of State, hence the show's title. Off camera between the fifth and sixth seasons, she gets elected to the presidency, so the title transforms in the show's opening. "Davis, Mets Helped by Indians Mental Lapse, Win 4–3 in 10," Associated Press, *USA Today*, accessed December 8, 2019, https://www.usatoday.com/story/sports/mlb/2019/08/21/davis-mets-helped-by-indians-mental-lapse-win-4–3-in-10/39994071/, August 21, 2019.

49. "Mascots for SU2C," You Tube, accessed December 6, 2019, https://www.youtube.com/watch?v=gVI7aqclKvE.

50. "Mr. Met and Phillie Phanatic in Midtown Manhattan," You Tube, accessed November 11, 2019, https://www.youtube.com/watch?v=xXrOBol9UUw, Major League Baseball All-Star Week, July 12–16, 2013.

51. "Phillie Phanatic Destroys ESPN Office," ESPN, You Tube, accessed November 11, 2019, https://www.youtube.com/watch?v=ZlItX63oo7A.

52. "Mr. Met Playing Golf," television commercial promoting July 28–30, 2014 New York Mets homestand against Philadelphia Phillies (feat. Phillie Phanatic), You Tube, accessed November 11, 2019, https://www.youtube.com/watch?v=yd5StSHHDzk.

53. Daniel Popper and John Healy, "Mr. Met Loses Head, Gives Finger to Fans!," *Daily News* (New York), June 1, 2017: 36; Cindy Boren, "Bevo vs. Uga: When Good Mascots Go Bad," *Washington Post*, accessed November 12, 2019, https://www.washingtonpost.com/sports/2019/01/02/bevo-vs-uga-when-good-mascots-go-bad/?utm_term=.575d7f215ed1&wpisrc=nl_most&wpmm=1\, January 3, 2019.

54. Brian Niemietz and Denis Slattery, "Mr. Met Loves the Mets, Despite Being Denied National League Championship Ring," *Daily News* (New York), accessed November 12, 2019, https://www.nydailynews.com/sports/baseball/mets/mr-met-loves-mets-ring-no-nl-championship-ring-article-1.2598604, April 13, 2016.

55. Brian Niemitz, "Mr. Met Claims He Was Snubbed by Mets, Who Denied the Beloved Mascot a National League Championship Ring," *Daily News* (New York), accessed November 12, 2019, https://www.nydailynews.com/sports/baseball/mets/mr-met-claims-mets-snubbed-denying-ring-article-1.2593971, April 8, 2016.

56. Paul Caputo, "Of Moose and (Celery) Men: The Story Behind the Wilmington Blue Rocks."

57. Author's observations from over 25 years of watching Blue Rocks baseball.

58. Author's first-hand recollection. See also "Remember the Phillie Phanatic Making His Debut Against Chicago Cubs in 1978," The Post Game, accessed November 11, 2019, http://www.thepostgame.com/blog/throwback/201504/remember-phillie-phanatic-making-his-debut-against-chicago-cubs-1978, April 25, 2015.

The Mets Baseball Hat and Human-Thing Entanglement in *City Slickers* and *Gone Girl*

DAVID M. PEGRAM

The New York Mets baseball hat has a unique history. In 1962, when the Mets began as an expansion team in the National League, their branding strategy capitalized on—or borrowed from—the legacy of the city's franchises that left after the 1957 season: the New York Giants and Brooklyn Dodgers. For team colors, the Mets chose royal blue (based on the Dodgers) and dark orange (based on the Giants). And for the all-important logo for the hat, the team adopted the interlocking NY design that the Giants had used for much of their existence. Indeed, the use of the hat and logo conjures up the old rhyme for brides: "Something old, something new, something borrowed, something blue…." In the case of the Mets, they seemed to walk into their marriage with the National League following those very words.

One could argue that by taking elements of other clubs' identities, the Mets immediately lacked their own. But almost 60 years later, the Mets hat and primary logo have remained unchanged. This commitment to the brand is commendable, considering that the Mets are in a market dominated by their neighbors, the Yankees. From a branding and marketing standpoint, the Yankees are in a class by themselves. There is no greater example of this than how the Yankees hat has become a piece of "cultural constancy."[1] In fact, the Yankees hat warranted an exhibit at the Museum of Modern Art in 2017. Even God wears a Yankees hat, as portrayed by Morgan Freeman in the 2003 film *Bruce Almighty*. (Although George Burns in the same role in *Oh, God!* proclaims that he was responsible for the 1969 Miracle Mets.)

In 1998, the Mets made one significant (and temporary) adjustment to their brand by changing the hat color to black. Mets Vice President for Marketing and Broadcasting Mark Bingham explained, "We want to be relevant. We want people to walk down the street with a Mets cap on, and felt that a black-based hat was a great look."[2]

But a baseball hat can serve a different purpose. When it establishes agency, it ceases being a hat and becomes something else. From this standpoint, the Mets' baseball hat offers examples of human-thing entanglement and identity in *City Slickers* (1991) and *Gone Girl* (2014). These films are radically different from each other, but a New York Mets baseball hat creates an entanglement in both films—for actors, characters, and audiences. Furthermore, the two films demonstrate how a baseball hat can become *transcendental*, gain *agency*, and open a discussion about our relationship with *things*.

Baseball Hats and Things

The baseball hat has become a staple of American fashion since the mid–20th century, accounting for approximately 80 percent of all hat sales in the United States, according to several sources.[3] The origins of the modern hat, with six panels and a visor, are rooted in the mid–19th century and the establishment of a hat as part of the team uniform. For this, the New York Knickerbockers of 1839 deserve credit: the team wore a stiff straw hat for their games.[4] However, the hat soon evolved, to feature rounded crowns and front visors (patterned after jockey hats). This style of hat, first worn by the Brooklyn Excelsiors,[5] became prominent in the 1860s.

Over the next 60 years, a "standardized" baseball hat was being worn by players in both the National and American League. The bill was longer and shaped by hard rubber, which provided greater shading for players' eyes.[6] Meanwhile, the hat also became recognized in popular culture as a normal piece of attire—though, at first, for *kids*. One of the earliest images of "baseball hat as apparel" is that Scotty Beckett's oversized backwards/sideways hat in the *Our Gang* short films. Scotty's image endures decades after viewing those episodes were first seen in movie theaters and later on television. In the late 1950s and 1960s, Jerry Mathers often wore a dark, generic baseball hat on *Leave It to Beaver*. On *M*A*S*H*, Jamie Farr portrayed Corporal (later Sergeant) Max Klinger and wore a Toledo Mudhens hat to honor his hometown; the producers made it Klinger's hometown as well. On the 1980s hit show *Magnum P.I.*, Tom Selleck was a combination of boyishness and machismo wearing his Detroit Tigers hat while tracking down bad guys and maintaining security on the Hawaii estate of best-selling novelist Robin Masters. Beaver, Klinger, Magnum and many prime-time television characters reinforce the viewpoint of CUNY media studies professor (and hat collector) Stuart Ewen:

baseball hats "embody a vision of manhood that is really about boyishness and the exuberance of youth."[7]

Soon, what went on the hat (as well as its colors), aside from the official stitching of a baseball team, became a statement. Baseball hats became "the new T-shirts."[8] Budweiser hats became in vogue for a younger demographic; gas station hats from Exxon, Sunoco, et al. are working-class symbols. Hip-hop culture in the 1990s situated the hat as an instrumental part of the "look." When the 21st century began, Von Dutch and other retailers made a highly styl-ized version of the mesh-backed version of the "trucker hat" seen prominently in the *Smokey and the Bandit* movies. Hats with "FDNY" or "PAPD" (Port Authority) stitched on the front demonstrated patriotism and unity after 9/11.

Once the baseball hat moved from functional (as a piece of baseball equipment) to an established piece of fashion or advertising, it gained agency. According to social anthropologist Alfred Gell, "things have agency because they produce effects, because they make us feel happy, angry, or fearful, or lustful. They have an impact, and we … produce them as ways of distributing elements of our own efficacy."[9] Anthropologist and sociologist Bruno Latour asserts that inanimate objects (*things*) can become "agentive," and *actors* that can help shape society.[10]

This shift into agency positions the baseball hat as a "thing." In 2001, critic Bill Brown proposed "Thing Theory," based on Martin Heidegger's sug-gestion that objects become things when they no longer serve their original function. Brown took Heidegger's philosophical stance a bit further: "The story of objects asserting themselves as things, then, is the story of a changed relation to the human subject."[11] In short, when an object moves beyond its intended purpose, humans begin to deal with its existence as a thing.

Archaeologists and sociologists have taken similar approaches, looking at how humans and things create an entangled relationship. Ian Hodder sug-gests that this entanglement leads to entrapment, the various degrees in which humans become "caught up" in a dependency on things, which, in turn, are dependent on us.[12] Humans become entangled in the need of things, produc-ing them and, as a result, fixing them. Though Hodder's theory is placed within the realm of practical objects, such as tools, produced for usefulness, it can also be applied to things in the theoretical sense, as put forth by Brown. An example of this entanglement, in terms of baseball, is the manufacturing of bats, gloves, and balls for the game to be played—particularly the baseball, and the amount of time and money spent to make sure that each ball desig-nated for game use meets specific requirements. Team merchandise is no dif-ferent. Jerseys and hats, along with T-shirts, are created with team logos so fans can show their team loyalty and identity. The entanglement is further complicated when humans depend on or become affected by the messaging (or optics) of the things they place on their bodies.

In popular culture, hats have often become things, with agency: a magician's top hat, for instance. Odd Job's bowler in *Goldfinger* and the Sorting Hat in *Harry Potter and the Sorcerer's Stone* are two examples. Likewise, the baseball hat has gained similar agency through films and television.

The Mets Hat in Film and TV

Mets hats appear in films for the sake of accuracy. *Rookie of the Year* and *Moneyball* (featuring flashbacks of a young Billy Beane) are two examples, with Mets uniforms and hats in full view. In the 1997 film *Men in Black*, the Mets hat is at the center of the shot, when Bernard Gilkey, tracking a fly ball, catches sight of a spaceship departing from the observation towers at Corona Park. Gilkey is so distracted that the ball hits him in the head. In this case, the use of the hat is central to the moment: audiences associate the team and its brand with the local geography, history, and culture. The third installment of the series, *Men in Black 3* (2012) features an overhead shot of Cleon Jones in a reenactment of his final catch in Game Five of the 1969 World Series.

One of the earliest appearances of a Mets hat on the head of a character occurred in the 1968 film *The Odd Couple*, starring Walter Matthau and Jack Lemmon. Matthau's character, Oscar Madison, wears the hat throughout the story. Madison is a reporter for the *New York Herald*, apparently assigned to the Mets beat. At the time of filming, the Mets were in the midst of a 101-loss season. Writer Neil Simon and director Gene Saks dismissed this and made a calculated decision to associate Madison with the Mets, as opposed to the Yankees. The reason, perhaps, is summed up by how former New York Mets broadcaster Howie Rose remembered the era: the Mets were young and hip and they "caught the city's imagination."[13]

The hat helps to set up Oscar Madison immediately. He first appears wearing it while serving food during a poker game. Later in the film, he wears the hat backwards: one of the first instances of this style choice caught on TV or film. On the TV version, Jack Klugman wore a Yankees hat in the first season but wore the Mets hat in subsequent seasons. However, it may be unusual, or even forbidden, for journalists to wear a hat of the team covered.

Former *Saturday Night Live* comedian Chevy Chase wore a Mets hat in the 1988 film *Funny Farm*. Like Oscar Madison, Chase's character, Andy Farmer, is a sportswriter. Farmer has moved to Vermont with his wife, to get away from the city and write a novel. In many ways, the hat represents Farmer's home and social leanings, as his life in the country begins to go awry. Chase's decision to wear the hat made sense: he was an avid Mets fan.

In the romantic comedy *Two Weeks Notice*, Sandra Bullock plays lawyer Lucy Kelson, who works for (and *falls* for) billionaire playboy George Wade

(Hugh Grant). The two attend a Mets game at Shea Stadium, with Lucy in a Mets hat and jacket. At one point, a pop fly comes to them, in their front row seats, but Lucy interferes with catcher Mike Piazza and she receives scorn from the Mets faithful. Piazza tells her, "Next time, go to a Yankee game."[14]

In each case, the hat gained greater agency simply by being worn for purposes other than baseball. It acted as a symbol or display of character in *Funny Farm* and *The Odd Couple*. It's viewed as an illegitimate attempt at fandom in *Two Weeks Notice*. But wearing the hat did not create controversy or criticism aside from Piazza's jawing at Lucy.

City Slickers: *The Mets Hat as Gesture of Gratitude*

The Mets hat became a problematic "thing" for Billy Crystal after he appeared in the 1991 comedy *City Slickers*. Crystal is known as a die-hard Yankees fan. He often joked that he idolized Mickey Mantle so much that for his Bar Mitzvah he delivered his Torah reading in an Oklahoma drawl. In 2000, Crystal honored his hero by directing the HBO TV-movie *61**, recounting the race between Mantle and Roger Maris to break Babe Ruth's single-season home-run record.

In *City Slickers*, Crystal played Mitch Robbins, a New York City radio executive and a big Mets fan. Mitch's love of the Mets is established in the first scene of the film when he and friends Ed and Phil attempt to run with the bulls in Pamplona. Mitch looks out of place, decked out in a Mets hat and warm-up jersey.

The film's plot revolves around Mitch's mid-life crisis, causing him to laments that at his age (39,) he is the best he will ever be.[15] Though it occurs when Mitch is on vacation, the Pamplona scene demonstrates Mitch's life: a race with no winners and being trapped on all sides. The traps are physical as well as mental and emotional. When Mitch returns to New York from Spain, we see him during his commute on a crowded Roosevelt Tram car and a crowded elevator in his office building.

To escape his existential angst, Mitch goes on another trip with Ed and Phil, to a working ranch in New Mexico for a real-life cattle drive. The idea is that open country and life as a cowboy might give Mitch some clarity—and it turns out that this search for clarity occurs mostly with a Mets hat on his head. Soon after arriving at the ranch, Mitch, Ed, and Phil try on gear: jeans, shirts, and, yes, hats. While Ed and Phil go for traditional cowboy hats, Mitch looks at himself in the mirror, trying on hat after hat before arriving at the only one that makes him feel like himself: his Mets hat, no matter that it is out of place. Mitch's desire to escape New York (whether it be in Spain or New Mexico) doesn't include his Mets hat. One is left to wonder if the Mets (and baseball, in general) are Mitch's only other escape.

Much like Andy Farmer in *Funny Farm*, Mitch Robbins is a city dweller and a fish out of water, or "city slicker" as western folks may derisively call those who have never ridden a horse, much less been part of a cattle drive. This time-honored trope is the impetus for the film's comedy. And as with *Funny Farm*, the hat carries symbolic weight: it is as much about Mitch's "New York-ness" as anything else. However, while Chevy Chase's allegiance to the Mets was also on full display, Crystal faced a different set of circumstances.

Since the film's release, Crystal has had to answer to his choice of wearing a Mets hat over a Yankees hat because his fandom was publicly in conflict with his character's. Crystal admits in his memoir, *Still Foolin' 'Em*, that the question of "Why a Mets hat and not a Yankees hat" was one he got asked "all the time."[16] As audiences saw it, the wearing of a Mets hat was reflexive and not merely a costume choice for a fictional character. The hat was not Mitch's; it was Crystal's. In fact, the idea that Crystal, the Yankees most vocal celebrity supporter, would wear a Mets hat was so incredulous that even the *New York Times* slipped up and reported Crystal as wearing a *Yankees hat* in the film.[17] They had to print a correction two days later.

In 2008, after Crystal played an inning for the Yankees during Spring Training, it became apparent that the issue still had not died down. Yankees players were asking why he wore a Mets hat in the film.[18] And one fan wrote to the *New York Post*: "I have one question for 'Mr. Ultimate Yankees Fan,' Billy Crystal: Why were you wearing a Mets hat in 'City Slickers'?"[19]

Four years later, the topic came up again in an ESPN online chat, when a viewer from Chicago said, "You're a big Yankees fan, so how could you wear a Mets cap in City Slickers? How could you Billy?" Crystal's explanation was rather brief: "I'm playing a character who rooted for the Mets, that's why."[20]

But the truth, as Crystal has later explained it, was that he wore the hat as a nod to the Mets organization. In the late 1980s, Crystal teamed up with fellow comedians Whoopi Goldberg and Robin Williams on the charity-based program and tour, Comic Relief. It was an annual tradition for HBO to air a performance. When Crystal approached the Yankees for donations, his beloved team turned him down. The Mets, meanwhile, donated handily. Furthermore, the Yankees refused to waive a licensing fee for the film, while the Mets did. Basically, Mitch Robbins wore a Mets hat, over a Yankees hat, because Crystal wanted to thank the Mets.[21]

Still, Crystal's own identity as a Yankees fan slips into the film when Mitch recounts his "best day" as the one when he saw his first baseball game, at Yankee Stadium. "The Mick" hit a home run. Mitch's recounting of the story here mirrors Crystal's personal story of Yankee Stadium in Ken Burns's documentary, *Baseball*,[22] and many other interviews.

Billy Crystal wore a Mets cap instead of a Yankees cap in the 1991 film *City Slickers* because the Mets contributed to one of the comedian's favorite charities. His beloved Yankees refused to donate. While audiences laughed at the western-themed, blockbuster comedy, Darryl Strawberry played in his eighth consecutive and last All-Star game (National Baseball Hall of Fame and Museum, Cooperstown, N.Y.).

Of course, his character's preference for the Mets in the film was established prior to release. In the official lobby poster, Crystal is depicted in a brown cowboy hat with the Mets orange, interlocking NY, stitched onto the crown. Mitch Robbins never wore this particular cowboy hat—and perhaps he should have—but from an advertising standpoint, his character was clearly depicted: a Mets fan about to face the wild west.

Crystal reprised the role three years later, in *City Slickers II: The Legend of Curly's Gold*, and again, Mitch had a fondness for a Mets hat. While *City Slickers* was the fifth biggest box office hit of 1991, *City Slickers II* fell short of expectations.

There was no significant pushback from Yankees fans about Crystal's choice. Five years earlier, he starred with Gregory Hines as Chicago detectives in the action-comedy film *Running Scared*. Crystal's character, Danny Costanzo, wore a Blackhawks jersey and a Cubs jersey; the lobby poster shows him in the latter. A Cubs hat was seen on his desk in the precinct scenes. If there were outcries from Yankees fans about betrayal, they were minimal and long forgotten.

Gone Girl: *The Mets Hat as Compromise*

The New York Mets hat is a far less visible component of David Fincher's 2014 film *Gone Girl*, appearing in only 10 seconds of footage. In this case, the hat solved a potential problematic "thing" for actor Ben Affleck, who wore it as a compromise to make sure his character's head gear did not become a major topic of conversation. It became one anyway.

Gone Girl stars Affleck as Nick Dunne, who is under investigation for the mysterious disappearance of his wife Amy, played by Rosamund Pike. Nick was raised in the small, fictional town of North Carthage, Missouri, near St. Louis, on the Mississippi River. (The real-life town of Cape Girardeau served as the filming location.) Through a series of flashbacks, we learn how he met Amy in New York, how he proposed to her at a book launch, and how financial and personal complications led them to move to North Carthage.

Amy's parents are writers of children's books and she is the inspiration (or subject) of the *Amazing Amy* series. Soon after Amy is reported as missing, the case goes viral across social media and makes national news. Under suspicion, Nick returns to New York to hire a prominent defense attorney, Tanner Bolt (Tyler Perry), and it is here that the Mets hat makes its brief appearance.

As Nick waits for his return flight, in a terminal at LaGuardia Airport, monitors are tuned to a talk show host's discussion of the case. Nick is prepared. He takes the Mets hat out of his bag and pulls it tight over his head, with the bill a little lower than normal. It's the best he can do to disguise himself as he heads to his gate. The hat is the black version, which makes sense given that the film is set in 2012, when the Mets did indeed still wear this on occasion. We then see Nick, head down, boarding the plane, the NY logo clearly visible.

Ten seconds. That is all. Yet the filming of this scene was so problematic that it caused production to be shut down for four days. At issue: the hat that Affleck would wear. Initially, Fincher desired to have Affleck wear a Yankees hat in the scene, something the actor, and die-hard Red Sox fan, refused to do. Affleck later recalled, "I said, 'David, I love you, I would do anything for you. But I will not wear a Yankees hat. I just can't. I can't wear it because it's going to become *a thing*.... I will never hear the end of it. I can't do it.' And I couldn't put it on my head."[23]

Affleck's emphasis on the hat becoming a *thing* is noteworthy. He publicly expressed and admitted that the hat had agency and that wearing it would transcend the film. In effect, he recognized that the line between actor and character would be blurred. Social media and Red Sox Nation would respond negatively. The four-day standoff ended with the Mets hat being a compromise, a form of neutrality. Fincher later questioned Affleck's professionalism, alluding to a perceived inability to separate self from character: "I really wanted it to be a Yankees cap but ... being from Boston and not being very professional as an actor, Ben refused to wear a Yankees cap."[24]

Fincher is a director known for his attention to detail, once described as the "master of the meticulous—famous for his obsessive research and endless takes, sometimes 50 or more per set-up."[25] Even in this relatively brief airport scene, Fincher had a clear image, even though his source material— Gillian Flynn's novel—does include this scene at the airport. In the novel, Nick does visit Bolt in New York, but his return flight home is not described. And while Fincher's reason for insisting on the Yankees hat was never revealed, it was likely rooted in getting a detail right, likely the basic truth that Yankees hats are the big sellers, more widely available.[26] He probably sensed that if Nick were picking up a hat at the airport gift shop, it would *have to be* a Yankees hat. It simply "smacks of *New York*."[27]

While the compromise might have ended the standoff, it only raised more questions. Whereas Mitch Robbins is from New York and his support of the Mets understandable, Nick Dunne's desire to pick up a Mets hat may be in direct contrast to his character, something Affleck didn't consider. After all, later in the film, Nick is seen wearing a St. Louis Cardinals T-shirt. In one of the film's early flashbacks, to the night Nick meets Amy, he introduces himself as a "corn-fed, salt-of-the-earth, Missouri guy," and we sense that this is not just a pick-up line, but a true description of his identity.

Given Nick's age, it stands to reason that he would have been a teenager during the eighties, when the Cardinals-Mets rivalry in the National League's

East Division had reached full tilt. For four straight seasons (1985–1988) either team won the division, with each also capturing an NL pennant. Would hypothetical love of the Cardinals prevent Nick from picking up a Mets hat in the gift shop? Quite possibly.

The Cardinals-Mets rivalry was elevated, in part, due to geography or culture: rural vs. urban, pastoral vs. metropolitan. As one Cardinal fan confessed, "New Yorkers can be very antagonistic. When you meet New Yorkers, you get the impression that they don't think there's any place but New York."[28] Turns out, Amy Dunne fit that New York stereotype, saying at one point that the "world ends at the Hudson."[29] It's an attitude also reflected in a mid–1970s cover of *The New Yorker*.

Though the "thing" that Affleck references is a Yankees hat, which never appears on screen, the fact that the Mets hat became a replacement, a compromise, categorized it as a thing, as well. Questions about Nick Dunne's motivation, about Affleck's stubbornness and Fincher's perfectionism only occur in a space where humans have become entangled and affected by their things.

Things and the Broken Fourth Wall

When is a Mets baseball hat more than just a Mets baseball hat? In the case of these two films, when that hat gains significance, to the point that it becomes an "actor" within an intricate "network."[30]

Andrew Kipnis reminds us that "agencies exist through entanglements and attachments—no agency exists as an isolate."[31] For both Crystal and Affleck, the very wearing of a Mets hat demonstrated such entanglement between human and thing, and that in both cases the hat had gained agency. Furthermore, in *City Slickers* and *Gone Girl*, agency and entanglement are dependent on the blurred line between actor and character. In Crystal's case, the line was blurred for him, after production, when the questions about the Mets hat began. In Affleck's case, he already saw the line blurred and recognized a Yankees hat as a *thing*. It was out of this concern, out of an awareness of the hat's agency, that he refused to wear it, even in the portrayal of a fictional character. Regardless, in both films, the illusion of the "fourth wall" was broken, implicitly. The dramatic needs, whims, and desires of Mitch Robbins and Nick Dunne were secondary (or viewed as such) to those of Billy Crystal and Ben Affleck.

Per Brown, a thing gains power (or agency) when it establishes multiple levels of significance.[32] A Mets hat, its material, its stitching, even its logo, have no less value than a Yankees hat. In terms of materials, they are equals. Where they become different is in the importance society places upon them, the agency they gain from our relationship with them. When Miami sports-writer Kevin Clark arrived in New York, he wrote about his process in choosing which baseball team—Yankees or Mets—to root for. Though he arrived on the Mets, the more important story was what occurred in this process. According to Clark, people responded to him quite differently, based on the hat on his head. He wrote, "But if you want a real New York experience, I suggest buying a Yankees hat and a Mets hat and wearing each of them around the city. You will experience very different New Yorks."[33]

If the characters of Mitch Robbins and Nick Dunne could truly speak, they might say that their experiences of "New York" differed quite a bit from the actors who played them. And all of it based on a hat on their head.

NOTES

1. Christine Flammia, "How the Yankees Cap Became a Cultural Icon," *Esquire*, https://www.esquire.com/style/mens-fashion/a13953190/yankees-cap-hat-history-new-era-moma/, December 11, 2017 (Last accessed November 11, 2019).

2. Clyde Haberman, "Mets Trying to Bridge the Cap Gap," *New York Times*, April 3, 1998: B1.

3. The 80 percent figure has been noted by several sources for at least 10 years.

4. Steve DiMeglio. "Baseball Cap Has Endured Generations as the All-American Hat," *USA Today*, http://usatoday30.usatoday.com/sports/baseball/2006–07–25-cap_x.htm, July 27, 2006 (Last accessed November 11, 2019).

5. James Lilliefors. *Baseball Cap Nation: A Journey Through the World of America's National Hat*. Cincinnati: Clerisy Press, 2009, 31–32.

6. *Ibid.*, 34.

7. Georgia Dullea, "Far from Home Plate, Baseball Caps Take Over," *New York Times*, July 10, 1991: C1.

8. *Ibid.*

9. Janet Hoskins, "Agency, Biography, and Objects," *Handbook of Material Culture*, Christopher Tilley, Webb Keane, Susanne Küchler, Michael Rowlands & Patricia Spyer, eds. (London: SAGE Publications, 2006), 76.

10. Bruno Latour, *We Have Never Been Modern* (Cambridge, MA: Harvard University Press 1991), 53.

11. Bill Brown, "Thing Theory," *Critical Inquiry* (University of Chicago Press) Volume 28, no. 1 (Winter 2001), 4.

12. Ian Hodder, "Human-Thing Entanglement: Towards an Integrated Archaeological Perspective," *The Journal of the Royal Anthropological Institute* (London: Royal Anthropological Institute of Great Britain and Ireland), Volume 17, no. 1 (March 2011), 163–164.

13. Anthony Rieber, "Neil Simon's Oscar Madison Nailed What New York Sports Was All About," *Newsday*, https://www.newsday.com/sports/columnists/anthony-rieber/oscar-madison-mets-neil-simon-odd-couple-1.20773037, September 1, 2018 (Last accessed November 11, 2019).

14. *Two Weeks Notice*. Directed by Marc Lawrence. Warner Brothers, 2002.

15. *City Slickers*. Directed by Ron Underwood. Columbia Pictures, 1991.

16. Billy Crystal. *Still Foolin' 'Em: Where I've Been, Where I'm Going, and Where the Hell Are My Keys?* (New York: Henry Holt and Company, 2013), 145.

17. Georgia Dullea, "Far from Home Plate, Baseball Caps Take Over."

18. Tyler Kepner, "Duncan, Defending His Slide," *Bats* (blog), *New York Times*, https://bats.blogs.nytimes.com/2008/03/13/duncan-defending-his-slide-meets-the-manager/, March 13, 2008 (Last accessed November 12, 2019).

19. "Dirty Pinstripes," *New York Post*, https://nypost.com/2008/03/16/dirty-pinstripes/, March 16, 2008 (Last accessed November 12, 2019).

20. "SportsNation Chat with Billy Crystal," ESPN. http://www.espn.com/sportsnation/chat/_/id/46500/actor-billy-crystal, December 19, 2012 (Last accessed November 11, 2019).

21. Crystal, 145.

22. Burns, Ken, dir. *Baseball*. "Inning 7: The Capital of Baseball." Aired September 24, 1994 on PBS. Florentine Films, 1994. DVD, 131 min. (2010).

23. Cara Buckley, "Ben Affleck and David Fincher's Spat in a Hat," *ArtsBeat: New York Times Blog, New York Times*, https://artsbeat.blogs.nytimes.com/2014/10/02/ben-affleck-david-fincher-spat/, October 2, 2014 (Last accessed November 13, 2014) (italics added).

24. Fincher, David. "Commentary." *Gone Girl*, DVD. Directed by David Fincher. Los Angeles, CA: Twentieth Century Fox Home Entertainment, 2015.

25. Stephen Galloway, "David Fincher: The Complex Mind of 'Social Network's' Anti-Social Director," *The Hollywood Reporter*, https://www.hollywoodreporter.com/news/david-fincher-complex-mind-social-95704, February 2, 2011 (Last accessed November 11, 2019).

26. Clyde Haberman. "NYC: Mets Trying to Bridge the Cap Gap."

27. Sam Borden, "Why the Yankees Hat Has Become a Global Fashion Sensation," ESPN, https://www.espn.com/mlb/story/_/id/27055049/sam-borden-why-yankees-hat-become-global-fashion-sensation, June 25, 2019 (Last accessed November 11, 2019) (italics added).

28. Ira Berkow, "Sports of the Times: The Revival of a Red-Tinged Rivalry Stirs Passions in the Midwest," *New York Times*, Oct 12, 2000: D3.

29. *Gone Girl*, directed by David Fincher (2014; Twentieth Century Fox, Regency Enterprises, TSG Entertainment, New Regency Pictures, Pacific Standard).

30. Bruno Latour, *Science in Action: How to Follow Scientists and Engineers Through Society*. (Cambridge, MA: Harvard University Press, 1987), 104.

31. Andrew Kipnis, "Agency Between Humanism and Posthumanism," *Hau: Journal of Ethnographic Study* (University of Chicago Press) Volume 5, no. 2 (Autumn 2015): 50.

32. Bill Brown, "Thing Theory," *Critical Inquiry*, 5.

33. Kevin Clark, "A N.Y. Transplant Chooses the Mets," *Wall Street Journal*, July 16, 2015: A13.

The Happy Cap

Blue Collar and Orange
in a Popular-Culture Context

Richard Pioreck

As one of the first four teams established in the TV age, the Mets are securely part of popular culture. The ubiquitously placed Met logo throughout the metropolitan tri-state area is a constant reminder of the team's presence baseball season or not. Met paraphernalia, especially baseball caps, allowed people to declare allegiance to the team before tradition established fan loyalty. In the past decade, loyalty has manifested with the Met 7 Line Army, a pop-cultural phenomenon organized by fans and named after the subway line to Citi Field. Members wear orange T-shirts and Met caps or other caps with a stylized NY.

Caps were not so readily available when the Mets began in 1962. But they have evolved in importance, availability, and variations. No longer restricted by the traditional blue-and-orange color scheme sporting goods stores as well as specialty shops like Lids offer a diverse line of caps. It is not unusual to see a Mets cap in green rather than blue, an item associated with Irish Heritage Night but presented for purchase at any time.

Hollywood has been a factor in putting a stamp of a more-than-sartorial nature on fans and burnishing the popular-culture image of the Mets. If movie making is the ultimate action for turning a sow's ear into a silk purse, many movies have contributed and burnished the popular-culture image of the Mets. Sporting goods stores sell all variations of caps. Caps make a statement about the person's relationship with the team. And it's not just pre-teenage fans who wear their team's caps everywhere. Men and women as well as boys and girls wear baseball caps in all sorts of situations. And while baseball caps had little importance when the Mets began, the cap began to put a stamp of a more than sartorial nature on their fans.

Without intending to do so, Tom Seaver changed the way the Met cap was perceived. Tom Seaver turned the franchise from a sow's ear into a silk purse. As Art Shamsky writes in *After the Miracle*, "Tom came up a star. As soon as he joined the ball club, he had that halo around his head."[1] And it's true that the cap created a hagiography of sorts and an important signal, not for Seaver alone, but for fans and players who wore the blue and orange cap. In contemporary New York baseball, the Yankees are Richard Cœur de Lion to the Mets' King John.

The cap's blue and orange colors come from the Mets' National League predecessors, Brooklyn Dodgers and New York Giants, who left the Big Apple for California after the 1957 season. These traditional colors are fine separately, but together they present a clownish mien on the Mets cap in sharp contrast to the Yankees cap in its traditional corporate midnight blue and white. And while both teams have traditional pinstriped uniforms, the Mets cap does not quite complete the ensemble as the Yankee cap does.

With more than 175 languages and dialects spoken in Queens, the Mets cap was a signifier of community even when language was a barrier. Cultural awareness spread from people wearing the cap on television and in films.

Beginning with *The Odd Couple*[2] in 1968, having a character wear the Mets cap depicts him an independent thinking New Yorker, not as the mark of a clown or lovable loser. *New York Herald* sportswriter Oscar Madison is neither lovable nor a loser, but a prize-winning New York sports columnist who lives in an eight-room apartment on Central Park West. Not to be condescended to by the established, patrician orders, Oscar wears the Mets cap because he identifies with the non-traditional Mets rather than maintaining the status quo embodied by his roommate, Felix Ungar. Felix is neat and orderly. Oscar is sloppy and carefree. The Mets cap is Oscar's badge of honor.

What is a Met cap to Mookie (Spike Lee) in *Do the Right Thing*?[3] Like Oscar, Mookie wears it as a badge of honor. The cap gives him a clownish appearance but becomes a noble talisman the longer he wears it. Mookie, like Don Quixote, loses his foolish demeanor as he continues his quest until it takes on a serious intent for him. This mirrors the Mets origin as lovable losers in 1962 to world champions in 1969.

Mookie wants Sal to change his pizzeria's wall of fame. His quest is to have a place for James Brown next to Frank Sinatra. Sal finds no entertainer better than Sinatra. He does not consider James Brown to be in the same league just as few non–Mets fans in 1969 considered the team to be peers with the Baltimore Orioles, who won 109 games. Nevertheless, the 100-victory Mets won that World Series in five games and new popular-culture heroes were born.

Jerry Koosman joined Seaver as did Bud Harrelson, Ed Kranepool, Cleon Jones, Tommie Agee, Donn Clendenon and Al Weis. Their pop-culture status is elevated each time the 1969 Mets exploits are remembered. And pop-cultural status, fleeting or enduring, was gained by other Mets in subsequent years. Among them—John Milner in '73; Gary Carter, Ron Darling, Keith Hernandez, and Howard Johnson in '86; Johann Santana for the first Mets no-hitter in 2012 and even Mike Baxter for his hit-saving catch in the no-hitter.

Lee uses the Mets cap to highlight what the Mets image means to the black community. In many ways, what being a Met fan means for black fans is the same for all fans. Sal's pizzeria's Wall of Fame represents the old order—Sinatra and DiMaggio's Yankees—heroes that appealed to the Italians, who have begun to move away from Bay Ridge by the late 1980s. Mookie's Mets cap represents the New Breed, who are demanding equal footing with the privileged old order. The Mets are supplanting the Yankees as the beloved team in New York during the 1980s. As the Yankees fall into irrelevance for the first time in 50 years, the Amazin' Mets are becoming New York's darlings. TV shots of Met games in these films give pop-culture texture to certain films.

Director Lawrence Kasdan's *Grand Canyon*[4] is a gathering of random events uniting the film's wildly divergent protagonists. Simon, (Danny Glover), an African American tow truck driver provides roving auto assistance on LA freeways, is the salt of the earth. His nature is signaled by the Mets cap he wears on his overnight rounds. Neither by happenstance nor coincidence does Simon wear a Mets cap, but as a choice about daily life of and for the common man. Like Met fans recognizing one another by their caps, Mack (Kevin Kline), sees Simon, a divorced, hard-working tow truck driver, as open and available, an honest and kindred soul, the rock upon which goodness and decency is built, and the goodness and decency of the people rests.

Mack, a wealthy immigration lawyer, is identified as elite by his allegiance to the NBA champion Los Angeles Lakers. Driving home from a Lakers game, Mack is stranded when his car breaks down. Gang members intent on extorting Mack come very close to their goal until Simon shows up and quietly confronts them. Mack, thankful, gets a tow to the service station. A few days later Mack seeks out Simon, "the guy in the Mets cap," for a cup of coffee because, he says, he wants to thank the man who saved his life. He doesn't want it to be just a chance meeting in the night. Simon offers Mack his friendship at the station and Mack's overture as fans meeting in the ballpark would welcome and accept one another. Simon confides he's worried about his sister's son, who seems to be getting involved with gangs. Mack may have a solution—he knows a man who owns an apartment building in a better neighborhood. But that neighborhood turns out to have its own sorts of dangers, including police who believe that the sight of a jogging young black man is automatically suspicious.

Mack also arranges a blind date between Simon and Jane (Alfre Woodard), a friend of Mack's secretary, Dee (Mary Louise Parker). Woven into this fabric are the tribulations of Mack's best friend, a pompous movie producer (Steve Martin) who emphasizes violence in his movies and is wounded in a robbery similar to the one threatening Mack at the beginning of the film; of Mack's wife Claire (Mary McDonnell), who adopts an abandoned baby; of their disenfranchised son, Roberto (Jeremy Sisto), named after Roberto Clemente; and of Simon's nephew (Patrick Malone), who is contemplating joining a street gang. The title is symbolic, referring to the class-imposed chasms which would normally separate the characters.

Although a Yankees fan, Billy Crystal chose to have his character, Mitch, wear a Mets cap in *City Slickers*[5] as a show of appreciation for the Mets donating to one of his charitable causes. It's appropriate in the story because his character tries to find meaning through fancy vacation experiences with his friends. There's something lacking, but he plods through his work as an advertising executive for a radio station hoping for a better day. His cattle drive experience is a parallel. Though unsure of himself at first, Mitch develops into the hero of the movie when he rescues a calf, Norman, after enduring teasing and taunting from the leader, Curly (Jack Palance). It is much like the Mets' experience. Years of frustration are followed by moments of glory. The Mets endured seven years of losing seasons before becoming 1969 World Series champions. After Tom Seaver got traded in 1977, the Mets played sub–.500 baseball until a resurgence in 1984, thanks to Dwight Gooden and Darryl Strawberry.

Frequency[6] uses the Mets cap iconography to establish popular-culture meaning that links generations, bringing understanding and closure to a father-son relationship. The 1969 World Series is a key part of the story about a man in 1999 communicating via ham radio with his father, an FDNY firefighter who died in 1969.[3] Working together, they kill a serial killer in self-defense in both timelines; the father survives because he takes his adult son's advice about a deadly warehouse fire that killed him in the original timeline. Using the knowledge, he gets out of the fire safely.

While baseball caps had little importance when the Mets began, they began to put a stamp of a more than sartorial nature on Mets fans. The cap has evolved from an accouterment at the ballpark and casual occasions into a pop-culture artifact because of its presence in movies.

Shea Stadium is a popular-culture symbol like the Mets cap. Much like Haight-Ashbury and Greenwich Village, Shea Stadium became a place that affected popular culture because what occurred there challenged and changed the traditional status quo. Events at Shea Stadium created a physical space that assumed a special place in pop culture. Mets fans wore their blue-and-orange hats with the intertwined NY paying homage to the New York Giants logo and experienced an abundance of high points and heartbreaks at Shea, from Ron Hunt driving home the winning run in the All-Star Game in Shea's inaugural season, 1964, to winning the 1969 and 1986 World Series, to the psychic pain of losing the 1973, 2000, and 2015 World Series, along with watching Kenny Rogers walking home the NLCS winning run in 1999, to Dan Uggla's eighth-inning home run in Shea's last game, which eliminated the Mets from the playoff race. Shea Stadium became a special place. From the landfill that the Brooklyn Dodgers rejected as the place for their new home, Shea Stadium as the Mets home became the place to be.

Perhaps Shea Stadium's most revolutionary important popular-culture event was the 10th inning of Game Six of the 1986 series World Series. The Red Sox physical prowess was overcome by the psychic popular-culture events during this game. With the Red Sox ahead 5–3 and one out from winning their first World Series since 1918, the fans exhorted the Mets not to surrender. Gary Carter and Kevin Mitchell singled. Ray Knight singled home Carter; Mitchell moved to third. Red Sox manager John McNamara pulled Calvin Schiraldi for Bob Stanley, who threw a wild pitch that allowed Mitchell to score and gave Knight second base.

And then Mookie Wilson came to bat with the score tied 5–5. Knight scored the winning run on Wilson's ground ball between first baseman Bill Buckner's legs.

I saw the game from the upper deck near the left-field foul pole. From my vantage point, Stanley became a spectator instead of covering first base for a toss from Buckner. Viewing the replay, however, there's doubt that either Stanley or Buckner could have beat Wilson to the bag.

Though McNamara had consistently replaced Buckner for defense during the season, he allowed the veteran to be on the field for the end of the World Series in a gesture of respect

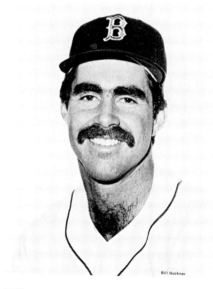

Bill Buckner

Bill Buckner became a part of Mets history when a ground ball went through his legs in Game 6 of the 1986 World Series and allowed the Mets to score the winning run. The victory forced a seventh game against the Boston Red Sox, which the Mets won. Buckner played himself in an episode of HBO comedy series *Curb Your Enthusiasm* and accepted the event with humor and grace (National Baseball Hall of Fame and Museum, Cooperstown, N.Y.).

for Buckner's production and leadership that season. This sentimental decision cost the game. But it did not cost them the World Series. The Mets
victory forced a seventh game. When the Mets won 8–5, it was fashionable
to wear a Mets cap again.

Hollywood expands Shea Stadium's popular-culture exposure with several films, including *The Odd Couple, Old Dogs,*[7] *Two Weeks Notice,*[8] *The
Wiz,*[9] *Men in Black,*[10] and even *Bang the Drum Slowly,*[11] which was about a
fictional New York team, used Shea to bring popular culture meaning to these
works which is special to the popular culture idea of the Mets. The importance
of Shea and the Mets seems counterintuitive to non–Met fans. But Shea's Hollywood presence is not limited to live scenes. The team's historical blue-collar
ethic is evident when characters watch the Mets on TV in *Fever Pitch*[12] and
Friends with Benefits.[13]

The Jumbotron, even though it didn't work reliably, is also part of the
Met legacy. Replaced by Diamond Vision, it was used to convey messages to
the fans, reinforcing the idea of community—*The Magic Is Back, Bring Your
Kids to See Our Kids,* etc. As part of the popular culture replacing traditional
culture, the TV-generation Mets have had a major cultural impact, allowing
it to equal traditional culture.

Iconic New York sports writers whose work was syndicated across the
country did much to situate the New York Mets in the popular culture. Before
the 1969 World Series, Jimmy Breslin and Dick Young helped establish the
new local National League team in the nation's conscience. Young often mentioned the Mets and their sometimes-dubious achievements in his nationally
syndicated newspaper column.

While sportswriters promulgated the cultural fabric and image of the
Mets, Bill Gallo's caricatures of Casey Stengel, Basement Bertha, and Yuchie
gave the newly formed Mets, also known as the New Breed, an identity in
popular culture. The Stengel cartoons, at first, were a sardonic look at Stengel
as the American League baseball genius in the National League cellar. Stengel
had won a string of World Series championships as the Yankees skipper before
taking on the same job with the Mets in 1962. Fans should have had no reason
to hold their heads up, but the Mets drew just under a million fans to the
Polo Grounds as the people of Queens and the rest of those in the tri-state
area who felt unwelcome at Yankee Stadium or betrayed by the Dodgers and
Giants flight to California, not only held their heads high, but attended games
at the Polo Grounds showered the team with loyalty and love.

Basement Bertha appeared when the New Breed seemed not to be able
to play this here game to the professional standards Stengel—who still possessed his dignity despite the team's incompetence and futility—and his
coaches tried to teach. Yet, gradually, the Mets started to gel after 1963, playing, with passion and heart not evident in the Polo Grounds teams. Bertha

began to feel like a plebian Queen, adored by her subjects, not always looked upon with pity and derision.

Later Yuchie, representing the unwelcome immigrants who flooded Queens, joined Basement Bertha. Yuchie found pride in the Mets accomplishments which mirrored the breakthroughs and strides that immigrants added to America's achievements. Yuchie could hold his head up high with Basement Bertha joining him on occasion, especially after 1968 when the Mets finished ahead of the Cubs in ninth place.

Then, in 1969, with the Mets in the newly created five-team National League East, Yuchie dreamed of a first-division finish. Basement Bertha held a more modest goal of reaching third place. As the season progressed, the Mets clung to second place, doggedly battling the Cubs for the division title. Yuchie was beside himself with pride and ambition. Popular culture seized upon the Mets as heroes representing what the underdog could do. Believing crowds filled Shea Stadium pulling for the Mets. Suddenly, Shea Stadium became a magical place where good things could happen. Once this idea took hold, it was only a matter of time and destiny before the Mets overtook the Cubs and seized the division title. Among those who believed in the power of popular culture, the 1969 World Series championship was safe in hand.

Ray and Robert Barone of *Everybody Loves Raymond* typify the Met fan born into and embracing the popular culture of the Mets. The CBS sitcom ran nine seasons and honored the Mets through dialogue, paraphernalia, and a guest appearance by several members of the 1969 Mets. Robert named his dog Shamsky, honoring his childhood dog of the same name. Set on Long Island, *Everybody Loves Raymond* is inspired by comedian Ray Romano's life. Romano is one of the Mets' long line of celebrity rooters, a list that includes Chris Rock, Kevin James, Jerry Seinfeld. Even one of the team's minority owners is a celebrity. Bill Maher.

The connection between the Mets and popular culture has never been stronger.

NOTES

1. Art Shamsky and Erik Sherman, *After the Miracle: The Lasting Brotherhood of the '69 Mets* (New York: Simon & Schuster, 2019), 121.
2. *The Odd Couple*, directed by Gene Saks (1968; Paramount Pictures).
3. *Do the Right Thing*, directed by Spike Lee (1989; 40 Acres & a Mule Filmworks).
4. *Grand Canyon*, directed by Lawrence Kasdan (1992; Twentieth Century Fox).
5. *City Slickers*, directed by Ron Underwood (1991; Castle Rock Entertainment, Nelson Entertainment, Face Productions, Sultan Entertainment).
6. *Frequency*, directed by Gregory Hoblit (2000; New Line Cinema).
7. *Old Dogs*, directed by Walt Becker (2009; Walt Disney Pictures, Tapestry Films).
8. *Two Weeks Notice*, directed by Marc Lawrence (2002; Castle Rock Entertainment, Village Roadshow Pictures, NPV Entertainment, Fortis Films).
9. *The Wiz*, directed by Sidney Lumet (1978; Universal Pictures, Motown Productions).

10. *Men in Black*, directed by Barry Sonnenfeld (1997; Columbia Pictures, Amblin Entertainment, Parkes+MacDonald Image Nation).

11. *Bang the Drum Slowly*, directed by John Hancock (1973; ANJS, Dibs Partnership, Paramount Pictures).

12. *Fever Pitch*, directed by Bobby Farrelly and Peter Farrelly (2005; Fox 2000 Pictures, Flower Films (II), Wildgaze Films, Alan Greenspan Productions, Mars Media Beteiligungs, ELC Productions).

13. *Friends with Benefits*, directed by Will Gluck (2011; Screen Gems, Castle Rock Entertainment, Zucker Productions, Olive Bridge Entertainment).

Hizzoner's Honors

The Mets, the Yankees
and the Mayor's Trophy

MATT ROTHENBERG

Despite the hubbub that surrounds the New York Mets and New York Yankees when they meet for their annual interleague match-ups, which started in 1997, there seems, more and more, to be fewer people who distinctly remember the games the teams used to play.

From 1963 through 1983, save for a two-year hiatus in 1980 and 1981, the Mets and Yankees faced off in the annual Mayor's Trophy Game. The game had its origins in the late 1940s, when New York City was a three-team town, but it ended when the Dodgers and Giants moved west after the 1957 season and left the Yankees as the sole team in the metropolis until the Mets débuted in 1962. Later, there was a preseason, rather than in-season, reprise from 1989 to 1990 and from 1992 to 1993.

Intra-City Series

After the American League's début in 1901, there soon became a desire among clubs in the same city to challenge each other on the field, rather than just the box office, following the conclusion of the regular season. Starting in 1903 and resuming in 1905, each league's pennant winner advanced to the World Series. Teams that failed to merit a postseason berth were not necessarily left in the cold.

City series occurred in New York, Chicago, Boston, Philadelphia, and St. Louis—cities with multiple major-league teams. Many of these games were contested in the postseason, though the Cubs and White Sox would have a preseason game that would last until 1971. Those two teams also held an in-season game between 1949 and 1972, the proceeds going to the Chicago Park District for boys' baseball.[1] Perhaps another close relative to the Mayor's Trophy Game was the competition in Philadelphia. Originating in the 1800s between the various major-league clubs in Philadelphia, it resumed with the Phillies and Athletics, ending in 1954—the latter team moved to Kansas City the following year. The winner took home the Ellis A. Gimbel Trophy, named after the department store magnate.[2] The Yankees and Giants faced each other for the first time in a postseason series in 1910[3] and did so once again in 1914. Each time, the National League club came out on top. Truly, John McGraw's Giants were the much better team at that time, although the Yankees had a few noteworthy players.[4] In 1913, the Dodgers opened Ebbets Field with a pair of preseason games against the Yankees, each team winning a game.

Origins

Just below John Drebinger's Yankees game story on the front page of the *New York Times'* sports section on June 9, 1946, was a small, unaccredited article with the modest headline "Yankees-Giants Set for Benefit Series." The story explained that the Yankees and Giants agreed to compete in a three-game series, with the prize being a trophy donated by New York City Mayor William O'Dwyer. The games' dates were July 1 at the Polo Grounds and August 5 at Yankee Stadium; details for the deciding third game, if needed, would be determined later. "A substantial portion of the receipts from these games will be allocated by the two clubs to aid in the promotion of sandlot baseball in the metropolitan area,"[5] explained the *Times*.

An article introducing the series in *The Sporting News* said the teams would "take advantage of the tremendous vogue of night ball sparked by construction of lights in [Yankee] Stadium." The Yankees averaged 55,000 fans during their night games. The article claims that "Mayor Bill O'Dwyer, a Dodger rooter, is giving a cup for the series," but offers no further details.[6]

There is no apparent indication of O'Dwyer's involvement in his subject file folders within the Office of the Mayor (William O'Dwyer) collection held by the New York City Municipal Archives. The *New York Journal-American*, owned by the Hearst Corporation, had a then-recent history of promoting sandlot baseball throughout New York City, but it is not clear whether the newspaper or its parent company was at the forefront of arranging these games.[7]

Louis Effrat perhaps sums up the entire concept of these exhibition games in the first paragraph of his game story in the July 2, 1946, *Times*. Effrat noted "[t]here was nothing at stake ... but it was as spirited a struggle as if a championship were involved" when both the Giants and Yankees met under the lights at the Polo Grounds. Both teams played many of their regulars— Phil Rizzuto, Joe DiMaggio, Joe Gordon, Tommy Henrich, and Snuffy Stirnweiss were all in the lineup for the Bill Dickey's Yanks, while Mel Ott and the Giants countered with Ernie Lombardi, Johnny Mize, Bill Rigney, and Sid Gordon, among other usual starters. Former National League umpire Bill Klem came out of retirement to help arbiter the tilt. The American Leaguers blanked their senior circuit counterparts, 3–0.[8]

The next game, on August 5 at Yankee Stadium, ended when the Yankees rallied from a 2–1 deficit to tie the game in the ninth inning and won in the tenth. With DiMaggio on third base, Willard Marshall caught Gus Niarhos's fly ball and threw the ball to home as DiMaggio tagged up. Lombardi fielded it and "lunged at DiMaggio," expecting home plate umpire Art Passarella to call the Yankee Clipper out. However, Passarella called DiMaggio safe, prompting protests from the Giants and a chorus of boos from fans, as the Yankees accepted the trophy from Mayor O'Dwyer.[9]

The series loss was minor for the Giants compared to their other loss that day. In the first inning, Mize, the Giants' slugging first baseman, was hit by Yankees hurler Joe Page. X-rays later revealed a fractured hand, Effrat wrote, and Mize would be lost for two to three weeks.[10] He would not return until September 13 against Cincinnati. Mize played that game and sat out the rest of the season.[11] The fear of significant injury in a meaningless game lingered among some players as the years went on.

The squads played a one-sided series—in seven games played between 1946 and 1950, the Giants only won once; the Brooklyn Dodgers became the Yankees' opponents in 1951. Attendance at the Polo Grounds reflected the Giants fans' attitudes towards the game, with fewer than 18,000 fans attending the 1948 and 1950 contests.[12] Yankee Stadium crowds were higher but still far below stadium capacity.[13]

A change in New York City mayors brought about a change in approach to the Mayor's Trophy Game. Mayor O'Dwyer resigned on August 31, 1950, when he was appointed United States Ambassador to Mexico by President Harry S. Truman.[14] Bedraggled by an ongoing police corruption scandal, O'Dwyer did not attend the 1950 game. Instead, Vincent R. Impellitteri, President of the New York City Council—and O'Dwyer's eventual replacement as interim and then fully elected mayor—went in his place.[15]

Impellitteri arranged for the Dodgers and Yankees to meet in 1951, and the teams would play for a brand-new trophy.[16] As before, receipts from the game would be donated to various sandlot baseball organizations throughout the New York City area. Although it is not known how much involvement O'Dwyer had in promoting the game during his City Hall tenure, it is clear that Impellitteri reached out to the teams and many media outlets, as well as city departments and agencies, to push ticket sales.[17] There was a recent and natural postseason rivalry between New York and Brooklyn, as the clubs met in the 1947 and 1949 World Series, the Yankees victors in each series. The 1950s would see four more postseason tilts between the two.[18]

The efforts by Impellitteri and others to boost ticket sales for the 1951 game at Yankee Stadium did not fall short. Over 71,000 individuals attended the game, which the Yankees won in 10 innings. This attendance figure would remain the high-water mark for any game in the competition of the Mayor's Trophy. Attendances were solid (48,000-plus) at Yankee Stadium for the next two years: an eight-inning game in 1952—the Yankees needed to catch a train to Cleveland, shortening the contest—and a 9–0 Dodgers shutout in 1953.[19] During the years of the Dodgers-Yankees games, half of the proceeds went to the Brooklyn Amateur Baseball Foundation and were ultimately distributed by the Dodgers.[20]

Under Mayor Robert F. Wagner, Jr., who took office in 1954, attendance dropped in half and further decreased in 1955, when the Giants replaced the Dodgers as the Yankees' foils.[21] No game was played in 1956, and the scene shifted to Ebbets Field in 1957, when the Dodgers returned to play the Yanks, drawing a respectable 30,000 patrons.[22]

The departures of the Giants and the Dodgers for greener pastures in San Francisco and Los Angeles, respectfully, meant the end of New York's intra-city series. The Yankees played the Dodgers for in-season exhibitions in 1959 and 1960 and the Giants in 1961.[23] The Mayor's Trophy was a relic about to be revived.

Mets v. Yankees

In 1961, under threat of the formation of a third major league, the Continental League, the National League admitted new franchises in New York (Mets) and Houston (Colt .45s, later Astros). The American League had expanded in 1960, growing from eight to ten teams, and now the National League would do the same.

The 1962 Mets were dismal on the field, finishing 40–120—dead last in the major leagues. Led by Casey Stengel and a motley crew of players, the Mets quickly gained the hearts of their fans, many of whom came from the ranks of the Dodgers and Giants faithful. The 1963 Mets would not be much better (they finished 51–111), but the time was right to renew the Mayor's Trophy contest.[24] On April 22, Mayor Wagner announced the return of the game on June 3 at Yankee Stadium. Keeping with tradition, proceeds benefited sandlot baseball in the New York City area.[25]

Mother Nature, however, had other plans, as rain forced the contest's postponement. The rescheduled date was June 20, forcing the Yankees into an unusual doubleheader. They would play their regularly scheduled game against the Washington Senators in the afternoon and then face off against the Mets that night. Using their regulars, the Bronx Bombers rallied for a 5–4 win over the Senators.[26] The nightcap would be a completely different story.

For Starters

Not only was the Mayor's Trophy Game a clash between intra-city teams, but it also represented a clash of generations, ideals, and perspectives.

"When the Mets and the Yankees agreed to play, the newspapers refreshed everyone's memory about [the Mayor's Trophy Game], and that first game in '63 was like a seismic cultural event in New York," said Marty Appel, former public relations executive for the Yankees. "No other game in the future of Mayor's Trophy games had the significance of that one because that really was the line in the sand that divided what the *Daily News* called the 'New Breed'—the young, vocal Mets fans—with the staid, old, conservative 'Old Breed,' the Yankees fans."[27]

The hapless Mets and their ever-passionate fans came into Yankee Stadium, "a forbidding and unfriendly place," described *Times* writer Robert Lipsyte. Over a lineup mostly consisting of Yankees bench players, the Mets came out of the stadium as victors by a 6–2 score.[28] More than 50,000 fans witnessed a five-run third inning that catapulted the National Leaguers, as Mets pitcher Carlton Willey shut down the Yankees over the final four frames. Starting pitcher Jay Hook, an original Met, earned the victory, allowing one run on three hits over five innings.[29]

Lipsyte perhaps best described the sensation: "A dream of pie in the sky became a reality last night at Yankee Stadium. It has to happen only once in a lifetime to make a dreamer happy."[30]

The game was Hook's first at Yankee Stadium and it proved to be a memorable one, as he recalled.

> The Mets fans were big at putting banners together and walking around the stadium with banners and holding them up and everything. They were called "banner people." They started coming to Yankee Stadium with their banners and the ushers wouldn't allow them to bring the banners in the stadium. … I think that probably agitated our fans … and they were extremely loud and cheering. Before the game, I was standing on the sidelines somewhere along the outfield … talking to I think it may have been Whitey Ford or one of the [Yankees]. And they said, "We've never heard noise like this at Yankee Stadium." It was terrific. I would say probably two-thirds of the fans in the stadium that night were probably Mets fans.[31]

Stengel had been released as the Yankees' manager after the team lost the 1960 World Series to the Pittsburgh Pirates in seven games. His tenure brought the Bronx 11 World Series appearances between 1947 and 1960. He left the Yankees with an 8–3 record in the Fall Classic. "I have no idea what was in Casey's mind that night," Hook recounted. "But if I were him, I would certainly feel a little upset that they released me as manager, probably because of his age. ... I'm sure it was in his mind that he would like to have a good performance that night."[32]

Ahead of Their Times

The concept of playing a team's regulars in an in-season exhibition was quickly becoming obsolete. The Mets and Yankees played many of their starters for part of the game, but the benches—and gradually, more minor leaguers—would receive plenty of work. Sometimes, players on the disabled list might use these games as a rehab stint of sorts. Plucking minor-league pitchers to bolster the roster became a common occurrence in in-season exhibition games, no matter the teams or the circumstances.[33]

Players on the way up might get an extra boost by playing in this game. In 1972, George "Doc" Medich was having an outstanding season at the Yankees' Double-A affiliate in West Haven, Connecticut. He was recalled for the August 24 Mayor's Trophy Game. Though he committed three balks, he shone nonetheless. Medich allowed one unearned run and scattered four hits in a complete-game victory, striking out six along the way. His West Haven teammate, Charlie Spikes, played the entire game in right field, going two-for-four.[34]

Medich would have to wait nearly two weeks for his actual MLB début, which turned out to be the complete opposite of his Mayor's Trophy Game performance. He started against the Orioles on September 5 and only lasted four batters, walking two and allowing two runs on two hits without recording an out.[35] He had a modest 11-year major-league career and was a member of the Milwaukee Brewers' 1982 American League championship squad.[36] Spikes made his major-league début on September 1 and played parts of nine seasons in the majors.[37]

In 1979, the Mets brought up Mike Scott from the Triple-A Tidewater Tides to start against the Yankees. He lasted two batters before leaving[38] what would be the only tie game in the series.[39] Unfazed by his premature removal, he made his major-league début two days later, providing relief against the Montreal Expos. Traded to the Astros in December of 1982 for Danny Heep, Scott won a Cy Young Award in 1986, leading the team to the National League West title and leading the major leagues in ERA and strikeouts.[40]

Experimentation

In certain circumstances, however, a player on his way out might receive an extra boost. Such was the case of one-time Yankees ace Whitey Ford in 1968. Ford, a two-time 20-game winner and a Cy Young Award recipient, pitched his final major-league game on May 21, 1967.[41]

According to Marty Appel, even though Ford was done as a starting pitcher, there were still those, such as Yankees public relations director Bob Fishel, who believed that he could become a short man in the bullpen, pitching an effective inning or two in relief.[42] In his autobiography *Slick: My Life In and Around Baseball*, written with the late, great New York sportswriter Phil Pepe, Ford explained his impact on batting practice during spring training and on the road. "I was throwing curveballs and sliders with no pain," Ford remembered, "and the hitters loved it, because I always could throw strikes."

"Some of them even said to me, 'Geez, Whitey, you're throwing better than half the guys on our pitching staff. Why don't you make a comeback?'"[43]

On May 27, 1968, Ford was the Yankees' first-base coach for the first four innings. Before the game, Yankees manager Ralph Houk asked, "'Would you pitch an inning if I need you? We're a little short of pitchers.'"[44] Sure enough, Ford agreed. When he took the hill at Shea Stadium, he tossed a scoreless sixth inning, retiring the side with a strikeout and two grounders. Houk got agitated at umpire Ken Burkhart, who twice called a ball when Ford placed his hand on his mouth while on the mound, something which had been outlawed for the 1968 season.[45] At 39 years of age, Ford had pretty much run out of gas, and the experiment was later scuttled.[46]

A year after Ford's appearance, Commissioner Bowie Kuhn used the Mayor's Trophy Game as a venue to test a baseball that was 10 percent livelier than the one already in use throughout the majors. To receive an "honest reaction," the five-dozen balls were used through the first five innings, unbeknownst to the participants.[47] Mets right fielder Art Shamsky—a .301 hitter going into the game on September 29[48]—took advantage of the rabbit ball, going three-for-three with a triple, home run, and five RBI.[49] Shamsky expressed surprise learning about the different ball some 50 years later.

"That's a new one for me! Maybe that's why I got three hits," said Shamsky, who did not receive more than four RBI in any meaningful game in 1969. "I'll take it."[50]

Tell-Alls

Erstwhile Yankees closer Sparky Lyle got himself and third baseman Graig Nettles in a touch of hot water with Bowie Kuhn in 1979. Lyle's book, written with Peter Golenbock, *The Bronx Zoo*, a tell-all on the 1978 season, revealed that as that season's Mayor's Trophy Game was going into extra innings, Nettles told Lyle that he'd throw the ball into the stands as a means of allowing the Mets the opportunity to score and end the game. As Lyle related:

> So we're in extra innings, and the ball was hit to Graig, and he bobbles it just like he said he would, and he threw it straight into the stands, a good ten feet over Chambliss's head. The batter ended up on second. And you know, those sons of bitches still couldn't score![51]

The Yankees won in 13 innings, the most innings played in a Mayor's Trophy Game. After the game, teammate Fran Healy approached Nettles and asked if he intentionally threw the ball away. Nettles replied, "Hell, yes, I did. I wanted to get the hell out of there."[52]

Reaction was swift by some in the media. *Daily News* columnist Dick Young felt that Lyle's betrayal of Nettles's confidence was worse than Jim Bouton's betrayal of his teammates in his 1970 book *Ball Four*. Kuhn reprimanded Bouton at the time and decided he would investigate the matter with Nettles and Lyle. Nettles denied any allegations of intentionally forcing an errant throw to end the game earlier.[53]

Joe Torre, Mets manager in 1978, did not seem fazed by Nettles' alleged actions, noting, "At that point, neither one of us cared who won. We had both run out of pitchers and they were trying to catch a plane. We felt we gave the fans their money's worth."[54]

Odds and Ends

A few players appeared on each side of the battle for the Mayor's Trophy: Phil Linz (Yankees, 1964–1965, and Mets, 1967–1968); Charley Smith (Mets, 1964, and Yankees, 1967–1968); Ron Swoboda (Mets, 1965–1970, and Yankees, 1971–1973); and Elliott Maddox (Yankees, 1974–1976, and Mets, 1978).[55] Yogi Berra was a coach and manager for the Yankees and the Mets at various times throughout the series. As the Yankees manager, he penciled himself into the 1964 game as a pinch-hitter.[56] Like Stengel four years earlier, Berra got fired after a seven-game World Series loss in 1964. Berra also appeared with the Yankees in earlier Mayor's Trophy games against the Dodgers and Giants.

Major-league umpires did not even bother to work what ended up being the final Mayor's Trophy Game in 1983. Receiving the nod instead were umpires who typically worked collegiate baseball games. The refusal to work stemmed from the firing of Bill Emslie, a minor-league umpire in the International League for the past four seasons. The Major League Umpires Association believed that neither the American League nor the National League would hire Emslie because "he was instrumental in keeping other minor league umpires from filling in for major league umpires when they were on strike for more than seven weeks in 1979." According to the union, Emslie was the only one of those umpires who was not hired by the major leagues.[57]

The replacement umpires for the 1983 contest were the same ones who filled in for the major-league umpires when the Mayor's Trophy Game was held during the seven-week strike in 1979. By all accounts, it appears that managers Billy Martin and George Bamberger, of the Yankees and Mets, respectively, had no complaints with the 1983 replacements. Martin, however, was disappointed that the regulars would opt not to show for an exhibition game whose proceeds assisted youth baseball.[58] It is not clear whether the 1979 replacement umpires drew any ire from the managers, but since the game ended in a rain-shortened five-inning 1–1 draw, the chances are probably slim.[59]

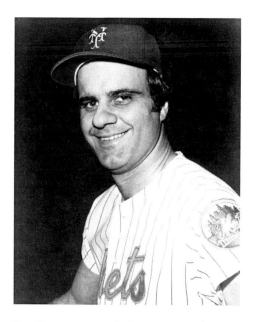

Joe Torre managed five teams in his career as an MLB helmsman, but his first stint was with the 1977–1981 Mets. During this period, the Mets and the Yankees played in the Mayor's Trophy Game three times. The interleague exhibition began in 1946 as an exhibition best-of-three series between the Yankees and the New York Giants (National Baseball Hall of Fame and Museum, Cooperstown, N.Y.).

The Long Goodbye

Following three years of sub–16,000 attendance figures, a two-year break in the series occurred in 1980 and 1981. The Mayor's Trophy Game reappeared on the schedule in 1982, with a robust 41,614 attendance figure at Yankee Stadium. Just over 20,000 attended the 1983 game, a 4–1 Yankees victory at Shea Stadium, the final Mayor's Trophy Game.[60]

Furthermore, in-season exhibition games such as these were gradually being bargained out of existence. The Basic Agreement, which governs relations between Major League Baseball and the Major League Baseball Players

Association, at one point allowed for a maximum of three in-season exhibition games. Eventually, that number dwindled to one—Cooperstown's annual Hall of Fame Game saw its death after the rained-out 2008 game.[61] Not only were in-season exhibition games on their way out, but so were scheduled doubleheaders, often played on holidays and Sundays. This led to fewer off days and condensed travel. During the second half of the 20th century, teams relied upon air travel rather than train travel. A flight from New York to Los Angeles could be accomplished in far fewer hours than a train trip from New York to Chicago.[62]

Attendance figures rarely approached sell outs—and were often higher at Yankee Stadium rather than Shea Stadium—but were fans bored? It is possible, especially by the late 1970s when the Yankees won back-to-back World Series titles amid three American League pennants and the Mets confronted their existence without Tom Seaver, who was traded to the Reds in 1977. Attendance figures reached their nadir in the 1978 game at Yankee Stadium, when fewer than 10,000 fans bothered to show up. By comparison, the Yankees drew over 2.3 million fans for the first time in 30 years, leading the American League.[63]

"There are a lot of reasons, I suppose, for the attendance decline," Mets General Manager Joe McDonald told the *Daily News*' Bill Madden at the 1979 game. "The scheduling has been a problem…. But the big thing seems to be the rivalry between the two teams and the fact that it just isn't what it once was." McDonald suggested that the amateur organizations involve themselves more in promoting the game and selling tickets.[64]

Promotion of the game is difficult to gauge. It is clear Mayor Impellitteri's office was active in getting city agencies, companies, the press, and the teams themselves involved in promoting ticket sales. Therefore, it should probably come as no surprise that the three games played during his tenure as mayor (1951 through 1953) had attendances among the top ten, including the highest, in the Mayor's Trophy series.

Indifference from the players and other team personnel toward the game may have played a part. This could be no more apparent than in Lyle's account in *The Bronx Zoo*. "I'll tell you, if I had been pitching against [the Mets] and it was extra innings, I'd have thrown the ball right down the cock," wrote Lyle, who did not pitch in any Mayor's Trophy Game. "After playing ten games in eleven days and traveling all around, we don't need this aggravation, especially to have to play extra innings."[65]

Yankees pitcher Ron Guidry perhaps put it most succinctly in a 2012 *New York Times* article, calling the Mayor's Trophy Game "a pain in the butt. It was supposed to be an off day and they made us play another game. It didn't mean anything, except to George [Steinbrenner]. Bragging rights? Who cared? A couple of times guys got hurt and we just said, forget it."[66]

Ron Hunt, a second baseman for the Mets from 1963 through 1966, who led the National League in being hit by pitches for seven straight seasons (1968–1974), including an astounding 50 times in 1971, was not chancing an injury if he did not have to.[67] Hunt told author Peter Golenbock that he "didn't like playing exhibition games too well. I had a reason. It wasn't that I was try-ing to snub the fans. I was programmed to get hit. When balls came inside, I didn't flinch from them, so when I was playing in an exhibition game, whether it was at Yankee Stadium or some minor league park, I worried that a pitcher would come inside on me and break my wrist. For an exhibition game? Because I'm programmed not to get out of the way. I just get hit and think about it later. That's the reason for me not liking exhibition games."[68]

Hunt retired third all-time in being hit by pitches. He now ranks sixth.[69]

Hook, a teammate of Hunt's, said playing in the game was "a civic service kind of thing," and Shamsky recalled little or no complaining among team-mates.[70]

"I think the only guys I ever heard of who might have [complained] were guys who were already injured," Shamsky recounted. "If you get hurt in an exhibition game and you miss time, that's when it really bothers you. For me, I didn't really mind playing in the game at all."[71]

In 1989, six years after the final Mayor's Trophy Game, the series was revived as two-game home-and-home preseason exhibition series. In 1989 and 1990, it was known as the Big Apple Series, and in 1992 and 1993, it was known as the Mayor's Challenge.[72]

Interest in the 1989 games was solid, with each game drawing over 50,000 fans, sell-outs in both stadiums. The 1990 matches were other matters, how-ever. Snow prompted cancellation of the game scheduled for Shea Stadium, and the following day's contest at Yankee Stadium drew just under 33,000 patrons. John Rowe of *The* (Bergen County, New Jersey) *Record* suggested "[i]t's anybody's guess what caused the decline."[73]

The game was not played in 1991, yet attendance continued to drop in 1992 and 1993.

Soon, Major League Baseball would announce the start of inter-league play in 1997, and regular-season games between the Mets and Yankees would now mean something in the standings. Although these games have had some memorable moments, the series' culmination occurred in 2000, when both clubs met in the World Series, a five-game set that went to the Yankees.[74]

The whereabouts of the Mayor's Trophy are unknown. The Yankees won the final match in 1983, and Marty Appel said he "can picture [the trophy] sitting in a storage area at Yankee Stadium. It was not displayed; it was stored."[75]

In all, millions of dollars were raised to benefit sandlot and youth base-ball throughout the New York City metropolitan area, and if few people remember much about the Mayor's Trophy Game, it should be recalled that it was all for a good cause.[76] For some players, fans, and onlookers, though, there are some fun, fond memories to cherish.

NOTES

1. Emil H. Rothe, Assisted by Arthur R. Ahrens, "History of the Chicago City Series," Society for American Baseball Research, SABR Research Journals Archive, accessed November 18, 2019, http://research.sabr.org/journals/history-of-chicago-city-series.

2. Matt Albertson, "The City Series: A Philadelphia Baseball Tradition," Sports Talk Philly, accessed August 22, 2019, https://www.sportstalkphilly.com/2017/09/the-city-series-a-philadelphia-baseball-tradition-.html, September 16, 2017.

3. The Giants won a best-of-seven series in 1910, four games to three. Christy Mathewson appeared in each Giants victory. See "Greater New York Championship" in *The Tribune Almanac and Political Register* (New York: The Tribune Association, 1910), 617, accessed August 10, 2019, https://books.google.com/books?id=WB4XAAAAYAAJ.

4. The Giants took the 1914 series, four games to one. See "The New York City Series," in John B. Foster, ed., *Spalding's Official Base Ball Record* ("Red Cover" Series of Athletic Handbooks) (New York: American Sports Publishing Company, 1915), 57–61, accessed August 10, 2019, https://books.google.com/books?id=X1PzAAAAMAAJ.

5. "Yankees-Giants Set for Benefit Series," *New York Times*, June 9, 1946: 72. "Beneficiaries will include the New York Baseball Federation, the Police Athletic League and the New York Journal-American's city-wide baseball clinics and tournament."

6. "Yankees Will Play Giants in City Series Under Arcs," *Sporting News*, June 19, 1946, 7.

7. According to baseball historian and SABR member Alan Cohen, who has extensively researched the involvement of Hearst Corporation newspapers in youth baseball, there may not be any connection between the Mayor's Trophy Game and Hearst's efforts. Cohen said the *Journal-American* started the Sandlot Alliance, in which eight New York City leagues competed for a city-wide championship, in 1945. The following year, the concept went national with the Hearst Diamond Pennant Series, later known as the Hearst Sandlot Classic. In this series, an all-star team from New York City competed against teams from other cities in which Hearst had newspapers. Alan Cohen, Facebook direct messages to author, June 8, 2019.

8. Louis Effrat, "Yankees Set Back Giants, 3 to 0, in Benefit Game at Polo Grounds," *New York Times*, July 2, 1946: 28.

9. Louis Effrat, "Yanks Top Giants, 3–2, on Run in Ninth," *New York Times*, August 6, 1946: 18.

10. *Ibid.*

11. "Johnny Mize 1946 Batting Game Log," Baseball Reference, accessed June 17, 2019, https://www.baseball-reference.com/players/gl.fcgi?id=mizejo01&t=b&year=1946.

12. For annual Mayor's Trophy game attendance figures, see "Exhibition Games vs. Mets/Dodgers/Giants" in *New York Yankees 2018 Official Media Guide & Record Book* (New York: New York Yankees, 2018), 324.

13. Seating capacity for Yankee Stadium between 1948 and 1965 is usually listed as somewhere between 67,000 and 67,500. For more information, see Philip J. Lowry, *Green Cathedrals: The Ultimate Celebration of All 273 Major League and Negro League Ballparks Past and Present* (Reading, MA: Addison-Wesley Publishing Company, 1992), 60. There is also a 1992 version with the number 271 in the title. Lowry's first version was produced by Society for American Baseball Research and published in 1985 by AG Press in Manhattan, Kansas. SABR also produced the 1992 and 2006 versions, which greatly evolved from the first book as digital technology increased the availability of archival research. While the research was done under SABR's auspices, the books were published by third parties.

14. Dominick Peluso and Harry Schlegel, "History's My Judge, Says O'D. As 30,000 Broil, Gasp Adios," *Daily News* (New York, NY), September 1, 1950: 3.

15. Louis Effrat, "Yankees Crush Giants With 6-Run Fifth and Retain O'Dwyer Trophy," *New York Times*, June 27, 1950: 33.

16. "Mayor's Game Arranged," *New York Times*, April 12, 1951: 44.

17. Evidence of this can be found in several subject files microfilmed as part of the "Office of the Mayor (Vincent R. Impellitteri)" Collection, held at the New York City Municipal Archives, including: Box 65, files 788–789 (1951 Mayor's Trophy Game); Box 66, files 790–792 (1952 and 1953 Mayor's Trophy Game); Box 20, file 189 (1952 Mayor's Trophy Game); Box 21, file 195 (1953 Mayor's Trophy Game).

18. "World Series and MLB Playoffs," Baseball Reference, accessed June 17, 2019, https://www.baseball-reference.com/postseason/.

19. "Exhibition Games vs. Mets/Dodgers/Giants," New York Yankees, *2018 Official Media Guide & Record Book*, 324.

20. This was mentioned in a July 6, 1953, letter from John D. Tierney, Executive Secretary to the Mayor, to James H. Robert, secretary of the South Jamaica Community Council, who wished to know how to possibly receive funding from the game receipts. "Office of the Mayor (Vincent R. Impellitteri)" collection, Box 21, File 195. The Brooklyn Amateur Baseball Federation began in 1947 with receipts from the Brooklyn Against the World youth baseball competition. "Foundation Equipment Aids Sandlot Kids in B'klyn, Long Island," *Line Drives* (Brooklyn Dodgers newsletter), May 1952, 3. According to Alan Cohen, the Brooklyn Against the World competition was sponsored by the *Brooklyn Eagle* newspaper. Alan Cohen, Facebook direct messages to Matt Rothenberg, June 8, 2019.

21. Unlike Impellitteri, his predecessor, it is unclear how much Mayor Wagner was involved in the promotion of the Mayor's Trophy Game. Within the "Office of the Mayor (Robert F. Wagner, Jr.)" collection at the New York City Municipal Archives, there are a few subject files pertaining to the Mayor's Trophy game, but they ultimately had little noteworthy information. Similarly, such information was difficult to pinpoint in the subject files of Wagner's successors, Mayors John Lindsay, Abraham Beame, and Edward Koch.

22. "Exhibition Games vs. Mets/Dodgers/Giants" in New York Yankees, *2018 Official Media Guide & Record Book*, 324.

23. The Yankees defeated the Dodgers, 6–2, on May 7, 1959, before 93,103 fans—a one-time record for largest attendance at a major-league game—at the Los Angeles Memorial Coliseum. The exhibition game was a tribute to former Dodgers catcher Roy Campanella, who was paralyzed in a one-car accident in late January 1958. The Dodgers defeated the Yankees, 4–3, on June 27, 1960, at Yankee Stadium. The Giants defeated the Yankees, 4–1, at Yankee Stadium on July 24, 1961. See "Exhibitions Games vs. Mets/Dodgers/Giants" in *New York Yankees 2018 Official Media Guide & Record Book*, 324.

24. "New York Mets Team History & Encyclopedia," Baseball Reference, accessed June 17, 2019, https://www.baseball-reference.com/teams/NYM/index.shtml.

25. "Mets to Play Yankees in Trophy Game June 3," *New York Times*, April 23, 1963: 41.

26. "Washington Senators at New York Yankees Box Score, June 20, 1963," Baseball Reference, accessed August 10, 2019, https://www.baseball-reference.com/boxes/NYA/NYA1963 06200.shtml.

27. Appel called the differences between the fan bases as "kind of a beautiful thing to watch. The tabloids loved it. Dick Young especially embracing [the Mets fans] as the 'New Breed,' and the rally cry of 'Let's Go Mets' that kicked in." Marty Appel, telephone interview with Matt Rothenberg, June 7, 2019.

28. Robert Lipsyte, "Once, Just Once, Met Fans Find a Pie in the Sky Is a Tasty Dish," *New York Times*, June 21, 1963: 18.

29. Leonard Koppett, "Yanks Bow to Mets, 6–2, Before 50,742 After Outscoring Senators, 5–4," *New York Times*, June 21, 1963: 18.

30. Robert Lipsyte, "Once, Just Once, Met Fans Find a Pie in the Sky Is a Tasty Dish," *New York Times*.

31. Jay Hook, telephone interview with Matt Rothenberg, July 30, 2019.

32. *Ibid.*

33. Beginning in the 1970s, the teams playing in the annual Hall of Fame Game would call up pitchers and position players from minor league affiliates in order to preserve their regulars and to give starting pitchers a rest on what would normally be an off day. By the 2000s, rosters for teams in the Hall of Fame Game might resemble those of the New York–

Penn League affiliate just an hour or two away from Cooperstown. Unpublished research conducted by this author while employed by the National Baseball Hall of Fame and Museum shows that 17 of those who played in the 2007 Hall of Fame Game between Baltimore and Toronto were plucked from minor-league rosters, mostly from nearby Class-A affiliates. Thirty years earlier, in 1977, only one person who played between the two teams was a minor leaguer.

34. Deane McGowen, "Yanks Beat Mets, 2–1, on Rookie's Pitching and a Homer by Ellis," *New York Times*, August 25, 1972: 23–24.

35. "New York Yankees at Baltimore Orioles Box Score, September 5, 1972," Baseball Reference, accessed August 10, 2019, https://www.baseball-reference.com/boxes/BAL/BAL 197209050.shtml.

36. "Doc Medich," Baseball Reference, accessed August 10, 2019, https://www.baseball-reference.com/players/m/medicdo01.shtml.

37. "Charlie Spikes," Baseball Reference, accessed August 10, 2019, https://www.baseball-reference.com/players/s/spikech01.shtml.

38. According to *Daily News* (New York, NY) baseball columnist Bill Madden, Scott was "[t]he only person to depart the premises sooner than Mayor Koch (who left after one inning)." Scott suffered a ruptured blood vessel on one of his pitching fingers. Bill Madden, "Fans May Retire Mayor's Trophy," *Daily News* (New York, NY), April 17, 1979, 59.

39. Murray Chass, "Mayor's Game Ends at 1–1 in 5th," *New York Times*, April 17, 1979: B14. Rain stopped the game after five innings.

40. "Mike Scott," Baseball Reference, accessed August 10, 2019, https://www.baseball-reference.com/players/s/scottmi03.shtml.

41. "Whitey Ford," Baseball Reference, accessed August 10, 2019, https://www.baseball-reference.com/players/f/fordwh01.shtml.

42. According to Appel: "Fishel … really, really believed that Whitey would be an effective closer—the term didn't exist then—but he thought one of our best pitchers was sitting at home in Long Island while the Yankees were struggling along.… I'm sure Bob talked to Ralph (Houk) about that a number of times." Marty Appel, telephone interview with Matt Rothenberg.

43. Whitey Ford with Phil Pepe, *Slick: My Life in and Around Baseball* (New York: William Morrow and Company, Inc., 1987), 227.

44. *Ibid.* While it sounds as though Houk asked Ford just before the game, it may have been decided upon earlier, as news outlets reported Ford's availability in May 27 newspapers. See "Bomber Briefs" notes in Bob Kurland, "White Sox Steal Yanks' Chief Claim to Fame," *The Record* (Bergen County, NJ), May 27, 1968, D1, 57.

45. Leonard Koppett, "Mets Top Yankees, 4–3, on 'Bouncing' Triple," *New York Times*, May 28, 1968, 55. The details of Ford's appearance in *Slick* are incorrect. Ford actually faced (in order) Ed Charles, Tommie Agee, and Don Bosch. Ed Kranepool did not play, unlike Ford's claim. The game also did not end after Ford's appearance in the sixth, not ninth, inning. The home team Mets led after the top of the ninth, so there was no need to play the bottom half of the frame. Jim Bouton and Dooley Womack pitched the seventh and eighth innings, respectively, for the Yankees. See Ford and Pepe, *Slick*, 228.

46. For more information on Whitey Ford's pitching after his major-league playing career ended, see Bill Francis, "Ford's Pitching Skill Was Everlasting," National Baseball Hall of Fame and Museum, accessed August 10, 2019, https://baseballhall.org/discover/whitey-fords-pitching-skill-was-everlasting.

47. Leonard Koppett, "Mets Beat Yanks, 7–6, for Third Straight Victory in Mayor's Trophy Game," *New York Times*, September 30, 1969, 52.

48. "Art Shamsky 1969 Batting Game Log," Baseball Reference, accessed August 13, 2019, https://www.baseball-reference.com/players/gl.fcgi?id=shamsar01&t=b&year=1969.

49. Red Foley, "Mets Make the Most of Lively Ol' Ball, 7–6," *Daily News* (New York, NY), September 30, 1969: 79.

50. Art Shamsky, telephone interview with Matt Rothenberg, August 1, 2019.

51. Sparky Lyle and Peter Golenbock, *The Bronx Zoo* (New York: Crown Publishers, Inc., 1979), 64. It should be noted that the first baseman was actually Jim Spencer, according

to Michael Farber's game story in the northern New Jersey newspaper *The Record*. Farber quotes Nettles as saying, "That's the first time in my life I ever intentionally threw the ball away." See Michael Farber, "Mets, Yankees Would've Preferred a Night Off," *The Record* (Bergen County, NJ), April 28, 1978: C1, 20.

52. Lyle and Golenbock, 65.

53. Dick Young, "Yankees Betrayed by Sparky's Book," Young Ideas, *Daily News* (New York, NY), March 16, 1979: 72.

54. "Today's Quote," Sports Etcetera, *Daily News* (New York, NY), March 16, 1979: 59.

55. It can be assumed Charley Smith played for the Mets and the Yankees in the Mayor's Trophy game, however, it is at first unclear whether he or Dick Smith pinch-hit for the Mets on August 24, 1964. The box scores only say Smith. In 1964, Charley Smith played in 120 games for the Mets and Dick Smith only 20. Dick Smith would have been with Buffalo, the Mets' Triple-A affiliate at this point in time in 1964. On Sunday, August 23, Dick Smith is listed as Buffalo's left fielder in both games of an International League doubleheader against Atlanta. (See Joe Alli, "Merritt Earns Atlanta a Split," *Atlanta Constitution*, August 24, 1964: 11). Buffalo was scheduled off for August 24, and Dick Smith played both ends of an August 25 I.L. doubleheader against Toronto. (See Associated Press, "Homers, Tight Pitching Gain Bisons Sweep over Leafs," *Democrat and Chronicle* (Rochester, NY), August 26, 1964: 2D, 36.) According to Dick Smith's minor league contract card held at the National Baseball Hall of Fame and Museum's Library, he was optioned by the Mets to Buffalo on June 26, 1964 and returned to New York on September 1, 1964. (See "Richard Arthur Smith, Card #2," Microfilm Reel 231 [Smith, Ray–Snyder, Gary], Minor League Contract Card Collection, National Baseball Hall of Fame and Museum Library, Giamatti Research Center, Cooperstown, New York.)

56. After the 1964 game, Yogi joked, "I've been up two times this season and made four outs," referring to his having grounded into a double play that night and doing the same at the Yankees' annual Old-Timers Day on August 8, 1964. See Associated Press, "A Few More Yogis and Mets Would've Won," *Evening Press* (Binghamton, NY), August 25, 1964: 25.

57. "Umpires Boycott Mayor Game," *New York Times*, April 21, 1983: B21.

58. James Tuite, "Yankees Defeat Mets at Shea," *New York Times*, April 22, 1983: A21 & A24.

59. Murray Chass, "Mayor's Game Ends at 1–1 in 5th," *New York Times*, April 17, 1979, B14.

60. "Exhibition Games vs. Mets/Dodgers/Giants," *New York Yankees 2018 Official Media Guide & Record Book*, 324.

61. See "Article III (A)(1)(e)," *Basic Agreement Between the American League of Professional Baseball Clubs and the National League of Professional Baseball Clubs and Major League Baseball Players Association*, effective January 1, 1968, Major League Baseball, 2; "Article IV (D)(3)," in *Basic Agreement Between the American League of Professional Baseball Clubs and the National League of Professional Baseball Clubs and Major League Baseball Players Association* (1970, 3); (1973, 3); (1976, 4); (1980, 4); (1990, 4); "Article V (C)(3)," *2017–2021 Basic Agreement*, effective December 1, 2016, Major League Baseball, 6, accessed November 21, 2019, https://registration.mlbpa.org/pdf/Basic%20Agreement_english.pdf.

62. According to FlightAware's Flight Finder, flights between John F. Kennedy International Airport (JFK) and Los Angeles International Airport (LAX) last roughly six hours. (See "Flight Finder—John F Kennedy Intl [KJFK]—Los Angeles Intl [KLAX]—FlightAware," FlightAware, accessed August 21, 2019, https://flightaware.com/live /findflight?origin= KJFK&destination=KLAX.) This is about an hour or so less than a non-stop flight in the 1950s, according to a *Time* advertisement. (See "Leave New York at noon—Reach Los Angeles Before 5 p.m. on United Air Lines' DC-7s nonstop coast to coast," Ad*Access, Duke University Libraries Digital Repository, accessed August 1, 2019, https://repository.duke.edu/dc/adaccess/ T2242.) It is still a solid 19-hour train ride from New York to Chicago, even over 40 years after Lake Shore Limited service was introduced by Amtrak in 1975. (See "Lake Shore Limited Schedule—June 30, 2019," Amtrak, accessed August 2, 2019, https://www.amtrak.com/content /dam/projects/dotcom/english/public/documents/timetables/Lake-Shore-Limited-Schedule-063019.pdf.)

63. "New York Yankees Team History & Encyclopedia," Baseball-Reference, accessed

August 13, 2019, https://www.baseball-reference.com/teams/NYY/ and "1978 American League Attendance & Team Age," Baseball-Reference, accessed August 13, 2019, https://www.baseball-reference.com/leagues/AL/1978-misc.shtml.

64. Bill Madden, "Fans May Retire Mayor's Trophy."

65. Lyle and Golenbock, 65. "Right down the cock" is baseball slang for a good pitch. "Right down the pipe" and "Right over the plate" are similar terms.

66. David Waldstein, "Yankees and Mets Resuming Rivalry Down South," *New York Times*, April 3, 2012, B13.

67. "Ron Hunt," Baseball Reference, accessed November 18, 2019, https://www.baseball-reference.com/players/h/huntro01.shtml.

68. Peter Golenbock, *Amazin': The Miraculous History of New York's Most Beloved Baseball Team* (New York: St. Martin's Press, 2002), 150.

69. "Career Leaders and Records for Hit by Pitch," Baseball-Reference, accessed June 17, 2019, https://www.baseball-reference.com/leaders/HBP_career.shtml.

70. Jay Hook, telephone interview with Matt Rothenberg.

71. Art Shamsky, telephone interview with Matt Rothenberg.

72. "Exhibition Games vs. Mets/Dodgers/Giants," *New York Yankees: 2018 Official Media Guide & Record Book*, 324.

73. John Rowe, "Fans Show Less Interest in Yankees-Mets Contest," *The Record* (Bergen County, NJ), April 9, 1990: D3, 35.

74. "2000 World Series—New York Yankees Over New York Mets (4–1)," Baseball Reference, accessed June 17, 2019, https://www.baseball-reference.com/postseason/2000_WS.shtml.

75. Marty Appel, telephone interview with Matt Rothenberg.

76. Following the 1983 game, it was said the games raised over $2 million in total. See James Tuite, "Yankees Defeat Mets at Shea," *New York Times*, April 22, 1983, A24.

Come Out and See My Amazing Mets

Casey Stengel and the Selling of the New York Mets

WILLIAM J. RYCZEK

Baseball exhibition games are relaxed affairs played in the bright sun-shine of Florida or Arizona. They don't count in the standings, veterans go through the motions while trying not to get hurt, and the stands are filled with senior citizens who've migrated from colder climates. When the New York Mets played the Los Angeles Dodgers at Vero Beach one day in 1964, the sun weighed heavily on the wrinkled eyelids of one old man. He dozed off, woke up abruptly, shifted his position, and then promptly fell asleep again.

That old man was New York manager Casey Stengel. Met outfielder Frank Thomas was a notorious agitator, and when he saw Stengel snoozing, Thomas decided to have a little fun. He and Rod Kanehl slipped in on either side of the manager, and when veteran outfielder Duke Snider took a mighty swing and struck out, they jumped up and screamed, "Hey, Duke! Way to hit the ball! Way to hit it!" The clamor awoke Stengel, who yelled, "Yeah, Duke, way to hit the ball!" as Snider trooped back to the dugout and the Met bench collapsed in hysterics.[1]

That was not the first time Stengel fell asleep on the bench, nor would it be the last; he'd been taking catnaps since he was managing the Yankees in the 1950s. "He used to fall asleep about the third or fourth inning," recalled pitcher Clem Labine, "and [Don] Zimmer, who's an agitator, used to go right behind him and hit the wall and jump up and down as if somebody got a base hit. Sometimes we weren't even at bat."[2]

"One day," recalled catcher Joe Ginsberg, "it was about the seventh inning—he fell asleep. All of a sudden he heard the crack of the bat. He woke up and started applauding. We said, 'Casey, that's not us. That's the other team running around.' He said, 'That's all right. We'll get 'em next inning. We'll get 'em next inning.'"[3]

There were some people, the most vocal of whom was journalist Howard Cosell, who thought it was disgraceful that a major-league manager slept while his team lost more than 100 games a season.[4] "Casey Stengel is too old to manage," Jackie Robinson said. "He should quit. He's asleep on the bench."[5] Robinson had never liked Stengel, whose racial attitudes were typical of those born in the 19th century. Robinson was working for the Chock full o'Nuts coffee company, which prompted Stengel's retort that Robinson was "chock full o'nuts."[6]

Met fans didn't care if Stengel napped in the dugout, nor did his employers, because when he was awake, Casey was doing something none of the other 19 major-league managers could have accomplished. They knew when to order the hit-and-run and when to change pitchers, but Casey Stengel was perhaps the only human being capable of making one of the worst teams in baseball history more popular than the best team in baseball history—the Yankees, who were winning one American League pennant after another on the opposite bank of the Harlem River.

In 1962, playing in the decaying Polo Grounds, the Mets drew 922,530 fans,[7] better than four National League teams that finished above them in the standings. The Washington Senators, who finished last in the American League, drew 200,000 less in a brand-new stadium. In 1957, their last year in the Polo Grounds, the New York Giants' attendance had been just 653,923.

It was not just their fans who loved the Mets; the hapless expansion team received the most favorable press coverage of any last-place team in history, and the primary reason was Casey Stengel. When he managed the Yankees, Stengel began referring to the press corps as "my writers" and the reporters who covered New York baseball were his friends; he'd begun courting them as soon as he arrived in Brooklyn in 1912. When he joined the Mets, Casey leveraged his relationships and his charm to make the Mets the most-loved team in America, even though they were the worst team in America.

The Yankees won pennants while the Mets got all the love, and it was the Yankees' own fault. Stengel had worked for them and, despite winning 10 pennants and seven World Series in 12 years, the Yankees fired him after they lost the 1960 World Series.

There were a number of reasons why the Yankees wanted to be rid of their 70-year-old manager. First, they had anointed coach Ralph Houk as Stengel's successor and Houk was being courted by other teams. If Casey stayed, Houk might tire of waiting. Stengel had also alienated many of the young Yankee players, with whom he had little patience. Finally, Casey always prided himself on making unorthodox moves, but in the 1960 Series, every move he made seemed to turn out wrong.

Although the Yankees had reasons to dismiss Stengel, they chose to say they were not offering him a new contract because they had just established a mandatory retirement age of 65. They held a press conference to announce Casey's leaving; it was a fiasco. Yankee owner Dan Topping was no match for Stengel and Casey stole the show, making the Yankees appear mean, ungrateful, and unfair to senior citizens. "His writers" made sure the public knew Casey had been treated poorly, and threw a big bash for the deposed manager.

At the same time the Yankees asked Stengel to leave, they jettisoned longtime general manager George Weiss, who received a generous severance payment, with the caveat that he could not accept a job as general manager of another major-league club. When the Mets acquired a National League franchise the following year, they hired Weiss as the club's "President." The Yankees had taken enough lumps in the court of public opinion, and decided not to protest the obvious sham.

Weiss had hired Stengel to manage the Yankees in 1949, and when he became president of the Mets, there was only one person he wanted to lead the team. The two men had first become acquainted in the 1920s when Weiss owned the New Haven Eastern League franchise and Stengel managed Worcester in the same league. Still, many people were surprised when Weiss brought Stengel to the Yankees. Weiss was a serious baseball man running the best team in the major leagues while Stengel had failed as a National League manager and was known primarily for his comical antics and rambling syntax. Weiss knew better. He'd had long talks with Casey about inside baseball and respected his acumen.

When Weiss approached Stengel about managing the Mets, the latter was coy, initially rejecting the overtures. He said he was happy in retirement and didn't want to manage again. Leo Durocher, then a Dodger coach, desperately wanted the job, but Durocher would have been disastrous as manager of an expansion team; patience was not Leo's long suit.

Finally, majority owner Joan Payson called Casey directly and convinced him to take the job. It wasn't that hard, since Stengel had no interests in life other than baseball, and the longer he was away from the game, the more his celebrity would fade. He missed the limelight. The Mets upstaged the Yankees by announcing the hiring the day before the Yankees were to open the World Series against the Cincinnati Reds.

As soon as he was hired, Stengel threw himself into selling the Mets, commencing a public-relations blitz almost unprecedented in professional sports. Most teams tried to attract fans based upon the product they put on the field—their success, their stars. The Mets' sales pitch was Casey Stengel and Stengel was the man who delivered the pitch. The Mets had a float in the 1961 Macy's Thanksgiving Day parade, and New York Giant legend Monte Irvin, who was there, said later, "You could tell from the people in the street that day that the town was about to fall in love with the Mets, and Casey was going to lead them there."[8]

The Mets trained in St. Petersburg, which had been the Yankee training site for years. The Mets had the Yankees old general manager, their old manager, and their old training site. Casey arrived in St. Pete with more energy than might have been expected from a 71-year-old man. He'd had a year off and his batteries were re-charged. All spring, he could be found kibitzing with fans and reporters and constantly telling people to go see his Mets, repeating it almost as a mantra. Early in the exhibition season, Stengel referred to his club as "amazing" and the label stuck.

"[Stengel] created the only expansion team," wrote biographer Marty Appel, "ever to be considered 'lovable losers,' and he did it in a city that was known for accepting only winners. No expansion team that followed was able to mirror this formula."[9]

The fact that the Mets were fabulous at marketing was not due to George Weiss, who was typically described as "dour" or "efficient" rather than "madcap" or "creative." Weiss was no Bill Veeck,[10] yet he presided, albeit inadvertently, over one of the greatest public-relations coups in the history of Major League Baseball. "I'm grateful," he said in 1962 about his team's immense popularity, "but I don't understand it."[11]

No one expected the 1962 Mets to win the National League pennant, but neither did anyone expect them to lose 120 games. They had picked up a number of once-talented veterans like Gil Hodges, Roger Craig, Charley Neal, Frank Thomas, and Richie Ashburn, and most observers thought the Mets had a shot at 70 wins and possibly seventh or eighth place.

They never came close to 70 wins, but no matter how badly the Mets played, one might still expect that attendance would be fairly good; this was New York and old National League fans were excited about the opportunity to see their favorite Giants and Dodgers. National League fans had not flocked to Yankee Stadium, as Yankee attendance actually declined from 1957 to 1958. The Mets targeted those old NL fans and their team's colors featured Giant Orange and Dodger Blue.

During five days in late May and early June, the Giants and Dodgers made their first regular-season appearances in New York since leaving the area in 1957. The Dodgers came first, for a Memorial Day doubleheader that attracted 55,704 fans, the first time the Mets had drawn a crowd of more than 20,000. It was Major League Baseball's largest crowd of the year and the biggest gathering at the Polo Grounds since 1942. When the Giants played two days later, attendance was 43,742. In those five days, more than 197,000 fans watched a team that had been averaging just 10,390 per game to that point. The Mets spent $10,000 on newspaper ads thanking the fans for their patronage. For the season, the 18 games against the Giants and Dodgers accounted for about 40 percent of the Mets' total attendance.

Legendary New York writer Roger Angell made his first pilgrimage to the Polo Grounds the week the Giants and Dodgers came to town. About an hour into his first game, Angell concluded that "the crowds, rather than the baseball, might be the real news of the two series."[12] He was astonished by the manic enthusiasm of the young fans despite the fact that their team was losing 10–0 at one point and would eventually lose 13–6. Whenever a rally began, the "Let's Go Mets" chants thundered down from the stands, and sometimes the cry arose for no reason at all. The Mets lost all five games, running their losing streak to fifteen, but that hardly mattered.

Angell believed that Met fans were vastly different from Yankee fans. "This was a new recognition that perfection is admirable but a trifle inhuman," he wrote, "and that a stumbling kind of semi-success can be much more warming."[13] The Mets were a late-inning team, but their rallies usually turned a seemingly insurmountable 6–1 deficit into a 6–5 loss and often fizzled out with the tying or winning run on base. People could more readily identify with a team whose day was more like theirs, with trials, tribulations, and coming oh, so close, but usually falling short. Few people's lives were like the uninterrupted triumphs of the Yankees.

Met fans, who became known as the New Breed, tended to be younger and were known for their rabid and often irrational enthusiasm, as well as their habit of bringing clever banners to the ballpark. In most stadiums, including Yankee Stadium, banners were confiscated on the grounds that they obstructed the view of other fans. At first, Weiss prohibited banners (which Stengel always referred to as placards) but the Mets soon embraced the concept, instituting annual Banner Day contests in which the most original creations were given prizes.

When the Mets played the Yankees in the Mayor's Trophy Game in 1963,[14] Met fans brought their banners to Yankee Stadium, where they were seized by Yankee security guards. The game was an ongoing battle between Met fans and Stadium guards, and the fans won. Even more satisfying was a Met victory over the arrogant Yankees.

Met fans were a bit different, and so were the letters they wrote to their favorite team. Bill Adler and George Price published a book consisting of some of the unusual letters received by the team from their young fans. Several missives included advice on how to improve the team's play.

"Dear sirs: Do you think it will be possible to make one small change in the baseball rules? Now you have to get the other team out 27 times to win a game. It would be easier for our team [as it would have been for early Mets teams] if you could make it 25. The last two outs give us trouble. Frank W."

"Dear Casey: I wrote to the president. I asked for help for the Mets. I didn't hear yet. Love, Martin."

Note: Martin appeared to be fairly young, since every "s" was backwards.

"Dear team: It might be a good idea if you got the umpires Christmas presents and sent them a card for their birthday or took them out to dinner once in a while. It's not exactly a bribe but it wouldn't hurt to be nice…. Bruce K."

Andy H. wrote to his favorite player, second baseman Ron Hunt, the Mets first All-Star starter, to ask for six autographs. "I want six because you must have six Ron Hunt autographs to trade for one Mickey Mantle."

"Dear Al Jackson: I have seen you pitch and I think you would be a terrific first baseman. Johnny G."

Fans may have adopted the bumbling Mets, but baseball beat writers are a tougher sell. The New York press tends to be unforgiving, but they forgave the Mets everything. They adored them and perhaps the Met they most adored was Casey Stengel, who could seemingly do no wrong, no matter how many games his team lost.

The Mets had come along at the right time, during a period when a new generation of New York sportswriters was coming of age. Old timers like John Drebinger, Dan Daniel, and Arthur Daley, who wrote straightforward, unimaginative prose, were retired or declining and a new group of younger men who called themselves the "Chipmunks" was taking their place.

"The Met reporters," wrote George Vecsey (who was one of them), "were more visionary, more tolerant, some because they missed the Dodgers and Giants and would have been glad to cover a junior high school team, others because they were new to baseball and saw it from a fresh perspective."[15] They were also patient. "You don't spank a child," said columnist Dick Young, "until it reaches the age of reason. Usually, a child reaches the age of reason when it's seven."[16] That gave the Mets until 1968 to build a respectable team; it's exactly when Gil Hodges arrived on the scene and did just that. A year later, the Mets were World Champions and children no more.

For the first year, the press was remarkably kind. "Stengel must have made a deal with the writers," said former Met Rod Kanehl. "They made fun of the team collectively, but never got on any individual players."[17]

"The press would rather cover the Mets, who were in last place, than the Yankees, who were in first place," said pitcher Bob Miller. "Casey gave them ten stories a day."[18] In those days, there were morning and afternoon papers, and Stengel knew which reporters worked for which, when their deadlines were, and what type of material they were looking for. The morning papers reported the details of a night game, so Casey talked to them about the key plays, while he gave the reporters for the afternoon dailies color and background stories, since their readers already knew the basic facts.

"When we'd have a rainout," said pitcher Jay Hook, "the first thing he'd do is get the press in there and start regaling them with stories of the past. The writers really had to appreciate that. If you've got a dozen inches of column to fill every day, getting something like that to write about is terrific."[19] Across the river, Ralph Houk was cooperative with the writers, but he didn't create material and anticipate their needs like Casey Stengel.

Almost every evening, Stengel would hold court in the hotel bar, downing one drink after another while entertaining the writers with anecdotes from the old days. "Stengel rarely missed a drink when anyone was passing them out, and he had a reputation for holding his liquor better than any man in baseball," wrote sports writer Fred Lieb in his memoir *Baseball As I Have Known It*.[20] Casey would drink and talk well into the night and the next morning appear as spry as ever, while his companions, most of them much younger, could barely function.[21]

It doesn't take a genius to manage a major league team, or even to manage a team to a World Championship. Baseball is less dependent on strategy than football and basketball; success is more closely tied to the skill of the players. Stengel won with the Yankee stars and lost with the Met rejects. "You didn't have to be a great manager with either club," said former Yankee pitcher Ryne Duren. "One was going to win and the other was going to lose."[22] Former Met pitcher Al Jackson put it more bluntly. "You show me horseshit players," he said, "and I'll show you a horseshit manager."[23]

Part of Stengel's genius was his ability to understand his situation and the expectations. With the Yankees, winning was the important thing; wit and humor were secondary. When he first took over the Yankee club, Casey was more subdued than he had been when managing the ragtag Boston Braves and Brooklyn Dodgers in the '30s and '40s. With the Mets, he was the main act and what happened on the field was merely the material for his monologues. He went directly to center stage and let his personality flow.

Stengel was able to play different roles because, as eccentric as he could appear, he knew baseball better than almost anyone in the game. "As screwy as he sounded sometimes," said Met infielder Bobby Klaus, "he knew exactly what he was saying. He knew what he was doing."[24] "He could tell if a fastball was coming," wrote Marty Appel, "by how quickly the pitcher was chewing his tobacco, or by how wide the third baseman opened his eyes."[25]

When Klaus said, "As screwy as he sounded," he was referring to the famous Stenglese, the roundabout manner in which Stengel often spoke. "Stengelese was something he could turn on and off when he wanted to," said Jay Hook. "Casey was very quick-witted. He'd be talking about one subject and he'd be thinking ahead about the next thing he was going to talk about and then he'd jump to that subject. Then he'd remember that he didn't finish the last subject, so he'd jump back to that. There were two or three parallel thoughts going at the same time."[26]

"He'd hold a clubhouse meeting," said pitcher Larry Miller, "and talk for an hour and never make a point. He was the only guy I knew who could speak for an hour with no commas and no periods. It was just one continuous flow of words without ever, ever making a point."[27] But there usually *was* a point, and sometimes the point was to distract the listener from something Stengel didn't want to talk about.

Stengel, with help from veteran outfielder Richie Ashburn, helped the writers find heroes in unlikely places. Mets became popular not because of prodigious feats of skill, but because they were adopted as objects of affection by the press and fans. Yankee stars Mantle, Ford, and Maris won fame through their outstanding playing skill, while the most loved Mets were the mediocrities like Marv Throneberry, Rod Kanehl, and Choo Choo Coleman. Frank Thomas, who hit 34 home runs in 1962, was never as popular as Kanehl, who hit four.

The three Met heroes were an unlikely combination. The laconic Throneberry made errors, missed bases, struck out in key situations, and hit a few home runs. Kanehl was Casey's favorite. Nicknamed Hot Rod, he was a good-luck charm as a pinch-runner, a versatile jack-of-all-trades, and had a charismatic personality. Coleman became famous for having no personality whatsoever.

Reporters could have ripped Throneberry, and he was the one Met who was sometimes booed, but even the derision was good-natured. Marv was a bum, but he was

Casey Stengel dubbed the inaugural version of the Mets "amazin" in 1962. The name stuck; sportscasters often call the team "Amazins" in their reports. Stengel managed the Mets for three full seasons but left in late August 1965, when he was injured in a fall (National Baseball Hall of Fame and Museum, Cooperstown, N.Y.).

their bum. Who needed surly slugger Roger Maris when you had lovable, balding, bumbling Marv Throneberry?

In 1964, the Mets moved into spanking new Shea Stadium, a blue and orange marvel of modern construction, with plenty of parking and modern conveniences unheard of at the Polo Grounds. The old park had charm and tradition, but Shea had escalators and modern toilet facilities. The Mets weren't any better in 1964 than they were the previous two years, but they drew 1,733,000 fans to their new home, second in the majors only to the Los Angeles Dodgers and 400,000 more than the Yankees, who were winning their fifth straight pennant.

Moving to an antiseptic stadium in Queens didn't sanitize Met fans. The people who went to Shea in 1964 were basically the same people who'd gone to the Polo Grounds the previous two seasons. From the time they were organized, knowing they were eventually destined for Flushing Meadows, the Mets courted Long Island baseball fans. The banners that graced the Polo Grounds found their way to Shea, and so did the wild enthusiasm. The Polo Grounds was old and homey; Shea was new but just as homey.

The size of the Polo Grounds crowds and the exuberance of Met fans are legendary and most players, when interviewed, talk about playing in front of thirty or forty thousand people, but that only happened when the Dodgers and Giants came to town. In 1962, there were 29 crowds of less than 10,000, including a low of 1,481 who saw the Mets play the Colts on a chilly day in September. That changed in 1964. During the first year at Shea, there were only seven crowds of less than 10,000.

One of the benefits of the new stadium was that it was across the street from the World's Fair, which ran for two years on a schedule coincident with the baseball season. The fair opened April 22, 1964, just five days after the Mets played their first game at Shea, and closed its second and last season October 17, 1965, about two weeks after the final Met game. Fans could visit the Fair and then take in a Mets game which, as Casey would tell you, was even more amazing than the Fair's Small World exhibit, which was his personal favorite. Over two years, tens of millions of people attended the Fair, and many of them crossed the street to watch the Mets.[28]

The Yankees had a new manager for the 1964 season, and one of the major reasons was Casey Stengel. Although Ralph Houk won three pennants in his three years at the helm, attendance declined each year. In 1963, the pennant-winning Yankees drew 1,308,920, about 230,000 more than the Mets, who finished 48 games out of first.

One old adage says, "If you can't beat 'em, join 'em" and another, "Imitation is the sincerest form of flattery." The Yankees watched Stengel promoting the Mets and decided they needed someone like him. Houk was likeable, but he was a typical major-league manager. His interviews were almost always about what happened on the field and they weren't punctuated by *bon mots*. Other than his family, not many people came to Yankee Stadium because of Ralph Houk.

There were a few charismatic figures in Yankee uniforms, and perhaps the most loveable was Yogi Berra. Yogi was a 38-year-old player-coach in 1963 and his active career was winding down. Soon after the World Series, Yogi was named manager for 1964 and Houk ascended to the general manager's position to replace the retiring Roy Hamey.

Although Yogi had been mentioned as a possible manager (the Red Sox wanted him at one point) his appointment was a major surprise. Major-league managers were not expected to be great intellects, but Yogi's charm was his naïve simplicity. Many teammates, though they liked him, thought he wasn't very bright. When he first came to the major leagues, most people thought that, too. But Stengel always had a kind word about him. He was forever telling someone what a smart player Berra was in order to give the awkward youngster confidence.

If the Yankee plan was to match Yogi against Casey in a battle of wits, it was a contest that, had it been a prize fight, would have been stopped soon after the opening bell. Casey was an intelligent man playing the role of clown, while Berra was a relatively simple man whose "humor" was principally the creation of the media, particularly his old St. Louis buddy Joe Garagiola.

Yogi, like many first-year managers, had difficulty with basic strategy. He'd never managed in the minors and had to learn on the job, often with unfortunate consequences. Berra warmed up his relief pitchers so often that he wore them out without even using them. He never had the confidence of his players, many of whom went to Houk behind Yogi's back. Houk didn't discourage them and by the end of the season the Yankees had a morale problem. And they hadn't even gotten what they'd wanted, for Berra's press conferences were nothing like Stengel's. He was neither original nor spontaneous, and without Garagiola to help him, there wasn't a lot of humor.

Although the Yankees managed to win the pennant, they lost the World Series in seven games. Houk fired Berra and replaced him with Johnny Keane, who was a lot more like Ralph Houk than Casey Stengel. Stengel and the Mets had won yet another round; Yankee attendance was even lower in 1964 than it had been the previous year.

The Mets' 1965 spring training roster contained more aging celebrities than young prospects. Stengel was back for a fourth season. Berra had joined the club as a player-coach.[29] Future Hall of Famer Warren Spahn was a coach and starting pitcher. Former Olympic champion sprinter Jesse Owens was in camp trying to teach the Mets how to run faster. Although Stengel touted his fledgling players as "The Youth of America," Ron Hunt was the only homegrown young star, although powerful Ron Swoboda would join him that year.

The Met aura was still intact. But losing 100 games a season was starting to wear thin. Lovable losers have a shelf life, and the Mets were approaching their expiration date. Casey had been a cute, spry old man of 71 when he took the Met job, and he was about to turn 75. The Mets needed to think about the future, a future that would not include Casey Stengel.

Stengel's humor, which had been so entertaining in the early days, was now sometimes just mean, as it had been in his final years with the Yankees. It was one thing to make fun of the fading veterans on the 1962 expansion club, but it was not a good idea to poke fun at the youngsters the Mets were trying to develop. Critics pointed out that Casey was more loyal to "his writers" than he was to his players. In July 1965, with the Mets losing to the Braves, Casey brought in lefty reliever Larry Miller to pitch to slugger Hank Aaron, who tagged him for a three-run homer. When asked why he brought in a lefty to pitch to Aaron, Stengel replied, "You don't bring in the best surgeon when the patient is already dead."[30] Miller, who was struggling to stay in the major leagues, didn't think that was funny.[31]

Met President M. Donald Grant wanted Stengel to retire, but how to achieve that was a problem, for it seemed as though he was going to have to rip the uniform from Casey's back and end up as looking as sheepish as Dan Topping had in 1960. Fate, however, intervened on the side of Don Grant. In May, prior to an exhibition game at West Point, Casey fell and broke his wrist. He recovered quickly, but during an Old Timer's Day celebration at Toots Shor's restaurant at the end of July, Stengel fell again. This time it was a broken hip, the scourge of so many senior citizens. Casey could manage with a damaged wrist, but not with a slow-to-heal broken hip. Coach Wes Westrum became the Mets interim manager, and in early September, Stengel, recognizing he was physically incapable of continuing, announced his retirement.

Even in the matter of Casey's retirement, the Mets managed to make the Yankees look bad. While he left the Yankees with bitterness, Stengel departed from the Mets with a fondness that endured for the remainder of his life. He became a goodwill ambassador for the team, serving nominally as director of west coast scouting, but in reality simply being Casey Stengel and urging everyone to go see his amazing Mets.

The Mets retired Stengel's number 37 jersey right after he left the team, while the Yankees didn't do so until 1970. The Yankee ceremony was the first time Stengel had gone back to Yankee Stadium (except for the Mayor's Trophy Game) since 1960; he'd ignored every Old Timers' Day invitation. By 1970, Mike Burke had become president of the Yankees and understood what Stengel had done for the Mets; his main goal was to forge better connections with the fans, something the Yankees had always believed would come from winning pennants.

The Hall of Fame waived its five-year waiting period and inducted

Stengel in 1966. Although the Hall decided he should be portrayed in a Yankee cap, Casey topped off his induction speech by telling the audience to "keep coming to see the Mets play."[32] For the rest of his life, he signed autographs "Casey Stengel, Hall of Fame, NY Mets."[33]

Wes Westrum was as dull as Casey Stengel was fascinating. Under his leadership, the Mets nosed up to ninth place in 1966 before slipping back into the cellar in 1967. Worse than the tenth-place finish was a 400,000 drop in attendance, and it was clear the Mets needed to go in a different direction. They convinced the Washington Senators to release Gil Hodges from the final year of his contract to become the third manager of the Mets in 1968.

The Mets' miraculous World Series win was the great sports story of 1969. The team was more popular than ever, and Mets fans were as voluble and exuberant as they had been in 1962. But now they had something to be excited about. Casey Stengel had gotten Met fans excited when they had no reason to be, and he was probably the only man in baseball who could have done that.

In 2009, MLB Network named Stengel "Baseball's Greatest Character." Casey was clearly a character, but he knew what aspect of his character to emphasize at each stage of his career. As a player, he had birds flying out of his hat, but he was a good, reliable outfielder who knew where the line was and didn't cross it. When he managed the Yankees, he was supposed to win, and he did. With the Mets, he was a salesman wearing a manager's uniform, and it was in that role that Casey Stengel gave perhaps his finest performance.

NOTES

1. Joe Hicks, telephone interview with Bill Ryczek, June 3, 2001.
2. Clem Labine, telephone interview with Bill Ryczek, August 10, 2000.
3. Joe Ginsberg, telephone interview with Bill Ryczek, January 1, 2001.
4. Cosell had disliked Stengel since Casey, when managing the Yankees, made it difficult for Cosell to get access to Yankee players.
5. Maury Allen, *You Could Look It Up: The Life of Casey Stengel* (New York: Times Books, 1979) 249.
6. *Ibid.*, 250. Casey's views evolved somewhat as America changed. When he managed the Mets, he threatened to move the team to a different hotel if black pitcher Al Jackson wasn't allowed to use all hotel facilities on the same basis as the white players. Marty Appel, *Casey Stengel: Baseball's Greatest Character* (New York: Doubleday, 2017), 302.
7. Attendance figures are from baseball-almanac.com.
8. Marty Appel, *Casey Stengel: Baseball's Greatest Character*, 286.
9. *Ibid.*, 289.
10. Although Veeck and Stengel had a shared gift for promotion, Veeck initially didn't think much of Casey. When Veeck was overseas during World War II, he was distraught to find that his partners had engaged Casey to manage their Milwaukee club. *Ibid.*, 134. Later, after Stengel piloted the club to the 1944 American Association championship, Veeck admitted he had been wrong.
11. William J. Ryczek, *The Amazin' Mets: 1962–1969* (Jefferson, NC: McFarland and Company, 2008), 38.

12. Roger Angell, *The Summer Game* (New York: Penguin Books, 1972; Penguin Books, 1990) 36. Citations are to the 1990 edition. The book's title page explains, "The material in this book, with exception of the introduction, first appeared in *The New Yorker*, some of it in different form."

13. *Ibid.*, 41.

14. The Mayor's Trophy Game had been inaugurated in 1946 and, until the National League abandoned New York in 1957, featured the Yankees, Dodgers, and Giants. It was revived in 1963, and the Mets and Yankees continued the series through 1983, after which it was dropped.

15. George Vecsey, *Joy in Mudville: Being a Complete Account of the Unparalleled History of the New York Mets from Their Most Perturbed Beginnings to Their Amazing Rise to Glory and Renown* (New York: The McCall Publishing Company, 1970), 47.

16. *Ibid.*, 48.

17. Rod Kanehl, telephone interview with Bill Ryczek, March 2004.

18. Bob Miller, telephone interview with Bill Ryczek, September 5, 2001. This was Robert G. Miller, the left hander on the 1962 Mets, not Robert L. Miller, the right-hander who was also on that Met team and had a long major-league career.

19. Jay Hook, telephone interview with Bill Ryczek, September 2001.

20. Fred Lieb, *Baseball as I Have Known It* (New York: Coward, McCann & Geoghegan, 1977), 250.

21. Stengel was also a fairly heavy smoker and it was in defiance of all medical logic that he lived to the age of 85.

22. Ryne Duren, telephone interview with Bill Ryczek, February 27, 2002.

23. Al Jackson, telephone interview with Bill Ryczek, January 31, 2004.

24. Bobby Klaus, telephone interview with Bill Ryczek, July 15, 2002.

25. Marty Appel, *Casey Stengel: Baseball's Greatest Character*, 143.

26. Jay Hook, telephone interview with Bill Ryczek.

27. Larry Miller, telephone interview with Bill Ryczek, September 24, 2002.

28. The New York City Department of Parks & Recreation states the attendance as 51,666,300. "Flushing Meadows Corona Park: World's Fair Playground," https://www.nycgov parks.org/parks/flushing-meadows-corona-park/highlights/12712.

Actual attendance at the Fair is difficult to ascertain. Some who have studied the Fair believe it to be much lower and that reported attendance figures were inflated.

29. Berra wasn't eager to play, and took part in only four games before retiring for good.

30. William J. Ryczek, *The Amazin' Mets: 1962–1969*, 126.

31. Larry Miller, telephone interview with writer, September 24, 2002.

32. Maury Allen, *You Could Look It Up: The Life of Casey Stengel*, 268.

33. *Ibid.*, 269.

The Concerts
at Shea Stadium

Derek Stadler, Elizabeth Jardine
and Alexandra Rojas

On July 18, 2008, musician Billy Joel was the last in a long list of artists who performed at Shea Stadium.[1] Former home to the New York Mets baseball franchise, William A. Shea Municipal Stadium (its formal name) hosted nonsporting events during its 44-year history, mostly musical concerts.

Shea Stadium was the first large stadium of its kind to host a rock-and-roll music concert when the English group The Beatles performed in 1965. Largest in terms of attendance at the time, the concert lasted 35 minutes and was barely heard by the nearly 55,600 screaming and fainting fans over the stadium's public address system and primitive amplifiers.[2] Over the years, concerts at Shea Stadium became more elaborate. By 2008, concerts had matured to include tributes on large video screens. While technology definitely improved, obstacles unlike any other venue of its kind plagued Shea. With its proximity to LaGuardia Airport, aircraft noise disturbed both concerts and sporting events. Shea also had poor sightlines.[3] However, baseball and music played on. Shea Stadium welcomed artists including Grand Funk Railroad, The Rolling Stones, the Clash, The Who, the Police, Elton John, Bruce Springsteen, Simon & Garfunkel, and the Staples Singers. In 2008, VH1 named Shea Stadium "the most hallowed venue in rock music."[4]

For all this, Shea Stadium attained a revered place in musical history. John Lennon once remarked to Sid Bernstein, the promoter who brought The Beatles to the United States, "You know, Sid, that concert in 1965 at Shea Stadium.... I saw the top of the mountain on that unforgettable night."[5]

Stadium Beginnings

The first proposal to build a stadium in New York City's Borough of Queens was in November 1940 when the Chamber of Commerce of the Rockaways petitioned the City to build a sports and entertainment venue near the former World's Fair exposition, held during the years 1939 and 1940 in Flushing Meadows Park, a former ash dump made famous in F. Scott Fitzgerald's *The Great Gatsby*. In the 1930s, master-builder Robert Moses had converted the ash site to a park for the exposition.[6] A controversial figure in New York City for 50 years, Moses was involved in the planning and construction of several infrastructure projects, including parkways, expressways, and bridges. Moses led construction of Shea Stadium and the 1964–1965 World's Fair in Flushing Meadows Park.[7]

The second proposal to construct a sports venue in Queens began in the 1950s. At the time, New York City was home to three teams: Yankees, Giants, and Dodgers. Walter O'Malley, principal owner of the Dodgers, rejected Robert Moses's proposal of a new stadium in Flushing Meadows. Moses, the Chairman of the Triborough Bridge and Tunnel Authority, had the civic power to utilize land for a public purpose but refused O'Malley's argument that a baseball stadium qualified. O'Malley moved the Dodgers to Los Angeles; New York Giants owner Horace Stoneham found a new home in San Francisco.

Following the departure of the two ball teams, New York City Mayor Robert Wagner asked local attorney William A. Shea to spearhead a project to bring back National League baseball. First, Shea tried to persuade an existing franchise to move to New York. Then, he and Branch Rickey headed the Continental League to bring another team of major-league caliber to New York; Denver and Toronto were also on the list of potential cities. The CL disbanded in 1960, resulting in Major League Baseball getting four expansion teams: Los Angeles Angels, Washington Senators, New York Mets, Houston Colt .45s.[8]

For the new National League team, the City planned to erect a ballpark in Flushing Meadows Park. Tentatively named Flushing Meadows Municipal Stadium, the facility's groundbreaking ceremony was on October 28, 1961, with Robert Moses and Mayor Wagner both in attendance.[9] For Moses, the stadium was another project in a long list of "public works on a scale unrivaled by any other public official in American history."[10] According to Robert Caro, author of *The Power Broker: Robert Moses and the Fall of New York*, Moses had the stadium designed to look like Rome's Colosseum.[11] A dedication ceremony took place on April 16, 1964. The Mets played their first game in the new, $26-million stadium the following day. The year prior, the New York City Council voted to name the venue William A. Shea Municipal Stadium, in honor of his work to bring National League baseball back to New York City.[12]

The World's Fair, which used the venue for special events, hailed Shea Stadium as "the ultimate in modern sports arenas."[13] The Stadium was the latest in comfort and convenience and of the most modern design for sporting arenas. It could hold 55,000 spectators for baseball games. For football games, ten thousand seats located in two arc-shaped stands on the lower level were moved on tracks to provide better sideline viewing and an additional five-thousand bleacher seats were set up at the venue's open end. The stadium lacked columns, enabling all patrons to enjoy an unobstructed view of the field.[14]

The First Concert

A common misconception is that The Beatles' appearance at Shea Stadium was the first rock-and-roll concert held in a large, outdoor American sports stadium.[15] In truth, between 1956 and 1957, Elvis Presley performed concerts at the Cotton Bowl in Dallas, Memorial Stadium in Spokane, Sick's Stadium in Seattle, Multnomah Stadium in Portland, and Honolulu Stadium. The Beatles also played at four open-air sports stadiums on their 1964 North American tour. In fact, The Beatles drew similar attendance in 1964 to Elvis's concerts in the 1950s, roughly between 12,000–18,000 fans at each performance.[16]

The idea of a rock-and-roll music concert at Shea Stadium came from music promoter, agent, and manager Sid Bernstein, who is most famous for bringing The Beatles to the United States in 1964.[17] After hearing of their success in Europe, Bernstein offered Beatles manager Brian Epstein $6,500 for two performances at New York City's Carnegie Hall. Epstein and The Beatles accepted. During the same U.S. visit, CBS variety show host Ed Sullivan booked The Beatles to perform in February 1964.[18]

In late 1964, Bernstein came up with the idea of booking The Beatles at a large venue. He called Shea Stadium management and presented the idea. Management claimed they never had a concert before and reminded Bernstein that the Stadium had over 55,000 thousand seats. Bernstein said he could fill them. In the end, management said they would provide the venue, ushers, lights, and scoreboard, but Bernstein would need to get a stage, insurance, and select a date when the Mets were on the road. Bernstein agreed to pay management $25,000 for hosting the concert on Sunday, August 15, 1965, with a start time of 8:00 in the evening. Initially, management wanted $50,000, but Bernstein balked and claimed he would consider an alternative.[19]

With the venue secured, Bernstein called Epstein and presented the idea.

Epstein's concern was whether they could fill the stadium. Bernstein assured him that they could and offered Epstein the amount of $10 for each unsold ticket. He also guaranteed that The Beatles would gross $300,000 and be able to clear $150,000 for one night's work. After consideration, Epstein accepted the offer and requested a $50,000 deposit. Bernstein raised deposit money by selling tickets in advance. Epstein did not want advance promotions or advertisements, so Bernstein sold tickets by word of mouth.[20]

With The Beatles scheduled, Bernstein focused on the logistics of the show. He asked radio personality Murray the K to be the master of ceremonies and Ed Sullivan to introduce The Beatles. For opening acts, Bernstein booked King Curtis and his band, Brenda Holloway, Cannibal and the Headhunters, Sounds Incorporated, and dancers to warm up the crowd. To construct the stage, Bernstein hired engineer Chip Munk, who created lights and sets for most of the major rock and roll acts of the day. Bernstein envisaged the stage to be near second base so that all those in attendance could see The Beatles. The initial projected cost of the stage was $10,000. However, this skyrocketed to $25,000 prior to the show. Munk erected the stage the day before the concert.[21]

Bernstein's overriding concern was security. Triple barricades protected the area between the seats and the field, making it difficult for attendees to rush the stage. In addition to ushers and security men patrolling the aisles and corridors, moonlighting cops acted as a buffer between the barricades and the stadium security. Bernstein also hired 40 karate black belts. Not only did they give an exhibition before the concert, they were the final barrier to anyone trying to rush the stage. Lastly, a full contingent of New York City police officers and mounted police waited outside the stadium, if needed. Above all, however, Bernstein alerted security not to use excessive force against attendees if it could be avoided, no matter how they might be provoked.[22]

Initially, Bernstein planned for The Beatles to ride in a limousine from Manhattan's Warwick Hotel to a Wall Street heliport where they would fly "directly into Shea." However, the mayor's office objected to this claiming it was too dangerous. In the end, the helicopter landed at the nearby World's Fair exposition where they boarded a Wells Fargo armored car that took them to the Stadium. For The Beatles' exit after the show, a vehicle pulled up to the stage and drove them back to the World's Fair.[23]

Rock-and-roll historians consider The Beatles' 1965 performance at Shea Stadium "the single most important concert in the history of rock-and-roll."[24] It proved that rock and roll groups could fill a large venue and set a precedent for all groups that followed. After the show, concertgoers emptied out slowly, "as when one departs from a loved one or an object of admiration."[25] In his autobiography, Bernstein claimed The Beatles were in awe when he

Shea Stadium was more than a home for the Mets. Beginning with The Beatles in 1965, it became a desired New York venue for rock-and-roll performers (National Baseball Hall of Fame and Museum, Cooperstown, NY).

met them in the dressing room at Shea Stadium, no doubt, taking in the moment of what would be the climax to date of their live performances. He also commented that during the show, Epstein was more concerned about The Beatles' safety and did not take in the moment, focusing instead on how to get The Beatles out of the Stadium.[26]

Legacy of The Beatles at Shea Stadium

In a 1971 conversation with Beatle John Lennon, Bernstein claimed Lennon said to him "you know, Sid, that concert in 1965 at Shea Stadium.... I saw the top of the mountain on that unforgettable night."[27] Indeed, Shea Stadium was an apex for both The Beatles and Epstein. They proved that a British group could not only make it in the United States, but also break records set by Elvis Presley.[28] The Shea concert had the largest audience to date at 55,600, largest overall take, and largest fee for a band.[29] The Beatles also set a standard. Most bands that followed would play in large stadiums, with Shea Stadium as the ultimate edifice, or "top of the mountain."[30]

The Beatles' 1966 North American tour was their last. They returned to Shea Stadium on August 23. Bernstein called upon audio genius Bill Hanley for an improved sound system over the 100-watt Vox amplifiers and stadium public address system used for the 1965 show. Luckily, Shea Stadium management saved the 1965 stage so it could be used again.[31]

In his autobiography, Bernstein noted that the 1966 show drew a lot of screaming fans, but what happened in 1965 was "a once-in-a-lifetime experience [and] could not be duplicated."[32] While historians claim there were about 10,000 empty seats, Bernstein stated in reality there were only two thousand unsold tickets. Bernstein suggested that because Epstein primarily booked the Beatles in stadiums throughout the Northeast, it was overexposure in a small geographic area leading to Shea Stadium not being sold out. However, upon shaking Epstein's hand at the end of the concert, Bernstein felt the Beatles touring days were over.[33]

Indeed, The Beatles were on "top of the mountain" at the 1965 Shea Stadium concert. From this point forward, their career as live performers and a touring band petered out. The audience was no longer coming to hear music. As John Lennon said, "Shea Stadium was a freak show [where] you couldn't hear any music."[34] Concertgoers came to see the Beatles as popular music icons in a display and not necessarily for their music. Six days after the second Shea Stadium concert, they played their last live performance to a paying audience at San Francisco's Candlestick Park.[35]

Subsequent Shows

Sid Bernstein booked other acts at Shea Stadium following the Beatles. After organizing a peace concert at Madison Square Garden, he scheduled a follow-up, 12-hour "festival for peace"[36] at the request of Peter Yarrow of the folk group Peter, Paul and Mary. Held on August 6, 1970, acts included Richie Havens, Miles Davis, The Staple Singers, Paul Simon, Janis Joplin, Steppenwolf, Creedence Clearwater Revival, the cast of *Hair*, Peter Yarrow, and The Rascals. The lower stands at Shea were built on rails, underpinned by springs so that they could be moved for football games—the jumping concertgoers rocked the stadium to the point where management almost halted the concert.

Another Shea Stadium concert arranged by Bernstein was Grand Funk Railroad on July 9, 1971.[37] In less than 72 hours, all 55,000 tickets were sold. Ticket prices ranged from $4 to $6.[38] The band Humble Pie opened for Grand Funk Railroad.

One of the more interesting events in the early days of Shea Stadium concerts happened in 1966. The first concert in a five-week series of programs featuring rock-and-roll, jazz, and television artists was a "Batman Concert" in the afternoon and evening of June 25. The event featured Adam West, star of the 1960s *Batman* television show, and Frank Gorshin, who portrayed The Riddler. Several rock-and-roll acts also performed at the event.[39]

Top of the Mountain

Elton John played at Shea Stadium on August 21–22, 1992. Known for his eccentric costume and stage antics when he became a household name in the early 1970s, John performed at several stadium concerts. By the 1990s, he had toned down the glitz and glitter, turning attention to humanitarian causes such as AIDS research.[40]

On October 3–4, 2003, Bruce Springsteen and the E Street Band rolled into Shea Stadium to put a wrap on The Rising tour, which started one year earlier and consisted of 120 dates. Springsteen concerts are legendary for their length and energy level; as to be expected, Bruce and company did not disappoint. The Boss gives himself to his audience with every fiber of his being. The tour contained some controversy over the anti–police brutality anthem "American Skin (41 Shots)," a song that references a police-brutality incident that happened in New York.[41]

Another act who remained on top of the mountain following their Shea Stadium concert is Simon and Garfunkel. The legendary 1960s folk-music duo broke up in 1970 but reunited for many live performances in the succeeding years. One early reunion was a free concert in New York City's Central Park in 1981, which sparked a world tour. Two years later, on August 6, 1983, Simon and Garfunkel performed at Shea Stadium. In the 1990s, and continuing into the 21st century, the duo reunited on a few occasions, including their induction into the Rock and Roll Hall of Fame.[42]

The Rolling Stones, who were in the audience for the Beatles' first Shea performance but left because of the poor sound and uncontrolled audience,[43] adopted "tactics that allowed them to regularly perform in massive stadiums while producing an illusion of intimacy."[44] On six sell-out nights in October 1989, The Rolling Stones played Shea Stadium on their groundbreaking Steel Wheels tour. Prior to this, the Stones had not gone on the road since 1982. During the 1980s, relations between band members Mick Jagger and Keith Richards had become strained—Richards felt that Jagger's ego was out of control as he began to treat his bandmates as hired help. When the Stones signed a record deal in 1983, Jagger also signed a contract to record three solo albums, reportedly without telling the band.[45] However, in an interview,

Jagger claimed he had spoken to the band about doing solo work and heard no criticism.[46] The following year, relations between Jagger and Richards broke down while planning a tour to support the album *Dirty Work*. Consequently, the tour never happened. Jagger had delayed committing to it, instead announcing his plan to tour and promote his second solo album. The future of the band looked grim.[47]

In the end, Jagger's solo career never took off and the pull of The Rolling Stones as a band was too strong to resist. Jagger and Richards patched things up enough to complete the *Steel Wheels* album and go on tour.[48] Steel Wheels is an example of how The Rolling Stones either invented or perfected much of what is common today in the rock and pop music concert business. The tour unified promotion instead of using regional marketing. The Stones innovated the income stream with add-ons including VIP seating; a wider variety of merchandise; and various pay-per-view, television, and film productions of the concerts.[49] The tour used what may have been the most ambitious stage set for a rock concert at the time—it had to be torn down and reassembled about three dozen times in half as many weeks.[50] Tickets for the Shea Stadium concerts sold out within hours. Two concert dates were later added to the original four scheduled, courtesy of the Mets falling out of the pennant race in the National League East and allowing more open dates for Shea Stadium.[51] Jagger reportedly used manager Davey Johnson's office as a suite. The Stones' road crew removed all of the furniture and redecorated the office with "drapes, leather chairs, plants, and video games."[52]

In the 1980s, The Rolling Stones went from almost disbanding to the top of the mountain. They continue to stay there as each tour sets money-making records. Artistically, they set standards for the modern stadium concert. When concerts began to use video screens so that every fan could see performers up close, the Stones learned how to make the screens part of their performance in order to maintain a connection with the audience.[53] In a 1985 interview, Jagger—then 41 years of age—said that he could not see The Rolling Stones existing by the time band members turned 50.[54] How wrong he was. The Rolling Stones are still popular. Jagger, after undergoing successful heart valve surgery early in 2019,[55] is still rolling with Richards and the rest of The Rolling Stones. But the Covid-19 pandemic ended plans for a 2020 tour.[56]

The Who played at Shea Stadium on October 12–13, 1982. But strained relationships among band members, Pete Townshend's drinking, and Roger Daltrey's unhappiness with drummer Keith Moon's replacement, Kenney Jones, cast a dark cloud over what was reported as The Who's farewell tour. Band members arrived separately, and each had their own dressing room.[57] Binky Philips, musician and music industry entrepreneur, in the audience at Shea, saw the tension between Daltrey and Townshend.[58] The concert was filmed, but not released until 2015 as "Live at Shea Stadium 1982." The Who was overshadowed by opening acts The Clash and David Johansen.[59] At this time, Johansen was a few years away from his Hot Hot Hot persona of Buster Poindexter and the New York Dolls, a band whose importance and influence has only increased with time.[60]

The Who broke up after the tour, with both Daltrey[61] and Townshend claiming responsibility for the disbanding. Around 1999, the band members made peace with their legacy and each other, going on tours with renewed energy, enjoyment, and appreciation for what they had stood for and went on to celebrate their bond of more than 50 years—Daltrey, Townshend, and John Entwhistle were childhood friends.[62]

When British New Wave trio The Police played at Shea on August 18, 1983, they were at the top of their game. The *Synchronicity* album was Billboard's number one album for four months against Michael Jackson's *Thriller* and other tough competition. The biggest hit from the album "Every Breath You Take" was number one for eight straight weeks.[63] Media channel MTV sponsored and heavily promoted the Synchronicity tour,[64] which sold out arenas and stadiums in the U.S. and abroad.[65]

In hindsight, guitarist Andy Summers claims he understands why The Beatles broke up as he saw The Police heading the same way. By this time, the business aspect of show business—lawyers, record companies, fans, press—surrounded the musicians.[66] The noise combined with the "fragile democracy" of the band enabled the "dictatorship" of lead singer and songwriter Sting. While each band member had also experienced success with individual projects, Summers claimed that Sting's priority was to perform as a solo act.[67] Internal tension resulted in band members traveling separately from show to show, each having their own dressing room. Interaction was limited to sound checks and performances.[68]

The Shea concert became the turning point. Tickets for the concert had sold out in hours.[69] So momentous was the event that Summers used the day of the concert as a frame for his memoirs. He saw the end coming as Sting had already begun to express that the band had reached the apex.[70] Towards the end of the concert, Sting "thank[ed] The Beatles for lending them their stadium."[71] He felt this was "as good as it gets"[72] and would even come to refer to that night as Everest.[73] Six months later, at the end of the tour, the group disbanded and the members went their separate ways.[74] They were done climbing mountains. Almost 20 years later, the band did come together for a very successful, worldwide reunion tour. Sting said he enjoyed it but was reminded of why he had left the "forced democracy" of the band.[75]

Conclusion

It was a sad day when Shea Stadium was demolished in 2009. It was an innovation offering unobstructed viewing and movable seats for different events, unlike its predecessors. When you heard someone say, "Shea is rocking," it was a statement of truth, not opinion. To close out the history of concerts at Shea, Mets management wanted Paul McCartney to perform the last show. According to his friend Billy Joel, McCartney did not think he could top The Beatles performance from 1965. However, Joel convinced management that he was the perfect artist to play the final concert—he was from Long Island and lived only 20 miles away. He also persuaded management to let him perform during the baseball season—something not done since Elton John and Eric Clapton in 1991—and sell most tickets for less than $100 so that fans could afford the show. From The Beatles to Billy was how the shows were marketed—as rock music history.[76]

Joel's concert was originally set for July 16, but demand led to the addition of a second night on July 18.[77] At the July 18 concert, Joel wore the Wells Fargo badge worn by Ringo Starr at the first Beatles concert.[78] Guests for the final show included Garth Brooks, Roger Daltrey, and Steven Tyler.[79] When Joel was backed by a chorus of New York City first responders, the audience was reminded of 9/11 and Mike Piazza's inspirational home run against the Atlanta Braves in baseball's return to New York after that tragedy.

However, the surprise of the evening was the appearance of Paul McCartney, who flew to New York for the occasion. With a police escort, McCartney went from JFK Airport to Shea in an astounding 11 minutes.[80] The same person who had driven The Beatles onto the field back in '65 drove McCartney out to the stage this time in a golf cart.[81] McCartney sang "I Saw Her Standing There" complete with trademark head shake, and Joel stepped aside to let the former Beatle, who had inaugurated large stadium concerts all those years ago, sing the final encore, "Let It Be."[82] Joel considers the 2008 concerts at Shea something special among the hundreds of concerts that he has performed over the years.[83] Perhaps this was the top of his mountain. Joel has received the highest honors awarded to a performer in this country, both the Kennedy Center Honors as well as the Gershwin Prize for Popular Song. In 2014, Madison Square Garden took the unprecedented step of booking him for a "residency." Joel plays a concert a month and will continue for as long he feels he wants to.[84] One year after the last show, Joel continued tradition and made a guest appearance when McCartney performed the first-ever concert at the Mets' new home, Citi Field.[85]

NOTES

1. Jon Pareles, "With Friends, Billy Joel Gives Shea Its Own Last Waltz," *New York Times*, July 17, 2008: B1.

2. Dave Schwensen, *The Beatles at Shea Stadium: The Story Behind Their Greatest Concert* (Cleveland: North Shore Publishing, 2013), 181; Mark Lewisohn, *The Complete Beatles Chronicle* (New York: Harmony Books, 1992), 199.

3. Peter Watrous, "Masses Converge Across Generations on Two Pop Icons: The Generations Converge on 2 Legendary Pop Stars," *New York Times*, August 23, 1992: C11.

4. Michael O'Keeffe, "Shea Trippers: The Beatles Punch Ticket to Ride for Stadium Rock," *Daily News* (New York), September 21, 2008: 35.

5. Sid Bernstein as told to Arthur Aaron, "The Top of the Mountain," introduction to *It's Sid Bernstein Calling: The Amazing Story of the Promoter Who Made Entertainment History* (Middle Village, NY: Jonathan David Publishers, Inc., 2002), xvi.

6. Jason D. Antos, *Shea Stadium*, Images of Baseball (Charleston, SC: Arcadia Publishing, 2007), 7.

7. Owen D. Gutfreund, "Moses, Robert," in *Encyclopedia of Urban Studies*, vol. 1, ed. Ray Hutchison (Thousand Oaks, CA: SAGE Reference, 2010), 525.

8. Antos, 7.

9. *Ibid.*, 8. For more on Robert Moses, the Continental League, and the genesis of Shea Stadium, see Michael Shapiro, *Bottom of the Ninth: Branch Rickey, Casey Stengel, and the Daring Scheme to Save Baseball from Itself* (New York: Times Books/Henry Holt and Company, 2009).

10. Gutfreund, "Moses, Robert," 521

11. Robert A. Caro, *The Power Broker: Robert Moses and the Fall of New York* (New York: Knopf, 1974), 829, 1113.

12. Antos, *Shea Stadium*, 9.

13. Editors of Time-Life Books, *Official Guide New York World's Fair 1964/1965* (New York: Time Incorporated, 1964), 247.

14. Editors of Time-Life Books, *1965 Official Guide New York World's Fair* (New York: Time Incorporated, 1965), 235.

15. Jeffrey Roessner, "From 'Mach Schau' to Mock Show: The Beatles, Shea Stadium and Rock Spectacle," in *The Arena Concert: Music, Media and Mass Entertainment*, eds. Robert Edgar, Kristy Fairclough-Isaacs, Benjamin Halligan, Nicola Spellman, eds. (New York, NY: Bloomsbury Academic, 2015), 18.

16. Peter Guralnick and Ernst Jorgensen, *Elvis Day by Day: The Definitive Record of His Life and Music* (New York: Ballantine Books, 1999), 86, 109, 110.

17. Elli Wohlgelernter, "Bernstein, Sid," in *Encyclopaedia Judaica*, 2nd ed., vol. 3, ed. Fred Skolnik (Editor in Chief) and Michael Berenbaum (Executive Editor) (Farmington Hills, MI: Macmillan Reference USA, 2007), 484.

18. Bernstein, 119, 127, 153, 156.

19. *Ibid.*, 165–166.

20. *Ibid.*, 167–174.

21. *Ibid.*, 169–170, 181–182, 184.

22. *Ibid.*, 180–182, 184.

23. *Ibid.*, 180–181. "The boys would then hop in and speed out of the stadium to the waiting helicopter for the short flight back to Manhattan. The security people, the Mayor's Office and I felt that once we got them through those outfield gates, we would be home free."

24. *Ibid.*, 340.

25. *Ibid.*, 190.

26. *Ibid.*, 186, 188–189.

27. *Ibid.*, xvi.

28. Roessner, "From 'Mach Schau' to Mock Show: The Beatles, Shea Stadium and Rock Spectacle," in *The Arena Concert: Music, Media and Mass Entertainment*, 19.

29. Lewisohn, *The Complete Beatles Chronicle*, 199.

30. Roessner, 15.

31. Bernstein, 199–200, 204; Robert Kronenburg, "From Shed to Venue: The Arena Concert Event Space," in *The Arena Concert: Music, Media and Mass Entertainment*, eds. Robert Edgar, Kristy Fairclough-Isaacs, Benjamin Halligan, Nicola Spellman, eds. (New York, NY: Bloomsbury Academic, 2015), 75

32. *Ibid.*, 204.

33. *Ibid.*, 200, 202, 205.

34. Andrew Solt and Sam Egan, *Imagine: John Lennon*, produced and directed by Andrew Solt and David L. Wolper (Burbank, CA: Warner Home Video, 1988, videocassette [VHS]), 106 min.

35. Roessner, 16.

36. John Darnton, "20,000 Youths Attend Rock 'Festival for Peace' Here," *New York Times*, August 7, 1970: 26.

37. Bernstein, 236–237; Mike Jahn, "Grand Funk Railroad Presents Heavy Rock in Concert at Shea," *New York Times*, July 10, 1971: 13.

38. Paul Sexton, "Grand Funk Outdo the Beatles at Shea Stadium," uDiscover Music, accessed June 5, 2019, http://mentalfloss.com/article/31470/night-beatles-rocked-shea-stadium.

39. "Five Jazz and Pop Shows to Rock Shea This Summer," *New York Times*, May 21, 1966: 18; David Krell, "Batman, Baseball, and 1966," *The Sports Post*, www.thesportspost.com, June 25, 2016 (site discontinued), republished on Prime Sports Net, accessed November 23, 2019, https://primesportsnet.com/baseball-history-batman-shea-1966/.

40. "Elton John," in *Encyclopedia of World Biography* (Detroit: Gale Virtual Reference Library, vol. 18, 2nd ed. 2004), 212–214; Watrous, "Masses Converge Across Generations on Two Pop Icons."

41. David Swanson, "Springsteen's Big Finish: Tour Ends with Dylan Cameo and Police Drama," *Rolling Stone*, accessed November 27, 2019, https://www.rollingstone.com/music/music-news/springsteens-big-finish-246523/, November 13, 2003.

42. Kembrew McLeod, "Simon and Garfunkel," in *St. James Encyclopedia of Popular Culture*, ed. Thomas Riggs (Detroit: Gale Virtual Reference Library, St. James Press, 2nd edition, vol. 4, 2013), 553; Stephen Holden, "Folk-Pop: A Stadium Full of Simon and Garfunkel," *New York Times*, August 2, 1983: C11.

43. Schwensen, 135.

44. Mark Duffett, "Beyond Beatlemania: The Shea Stadium Concert as Discursive Construct," in *The Arena Concert: Music, Media and Mass Entertainment*, eds. Robert Edgar, Kristy Fairclough-Isaacs, Benjamin Halligan, Nicola Spellman, eds. (New York, NY: Bloomsbury Academic, 2015), 23–24.

45. Keith Richards, *Life* (New York: Little, Brown and Company, 2010), 453–462.

46. "Mick Jagger," interview by Christopher Connelly, 1985, *The Rolling Stone Interviews: The 1980s*, The Editors of Rolling Stone, ed. Sid Holt (New York: St. Martin's Press/Rolling Stone Press, 1989), 75–77.

47. Richards, 463–478.

48. *Ibid.*, 482–511.

49. Ray Waddell, "Ladies & Gentlemen, the Rolling Stones," *Billboard* 124, no. 41 (November 17, 2012), Business Source Complete.

50. Patricia Leigh Brown, "A City Built for Rock 'n' Roll," *New York Times*, October 5, 1989: C1.

51. "The Rolling Stones Add Fifth Concert at Shea," *New York Times*, September 28, 1989: C22.

52. "Sports World Specials: Baseball; Rock-'n'-Roll Managing," *New York Times*, October 23, 1989: C2.

53. Jon Stewart, "'Hello Cleveland...!' The View from the Stage," in *The Arena Concert: Music, Media and Mass Entertainment*, eds. Robert Edgar, Kristy Fairclough-Isaacs, Benjamin Halligan, Nicola Spellman (New York, NY: Bloomsbury Academic, 2015), 135.

54. Jagger, 77.

55. "Ronnie Wood Calls Mick Jagger a 'Medical Marvel' After Heart Surgery Recovery," *UWIRE*, June 24, 2019, Academic OneFile.

56. "Live," The Rolling Stones, accessed July 7, 2019, https://www.rollingstones.com/live/.

57. Wes Orshoski, "The Battle of Shea Stadium," *Relix*, November 2008, 59.

58. Kenney Jones, "Kenney Jones, Drummer of Small Faces, Faces with Rod Stewart

and the Who, Looks Back (and Forward)," interview by Binky Philips, January 17, 2014, updated March 19, 2014, *Huffington Post* (U.S.), in *The Who on the Who: Interviews and Encounters*, ed. Sean Egan (Chicago: Chicago Review Press, 2017), Hoopla.

59. Orshoski, 85.

60. "Hard Rock Music Time Machine—1982: The Who's 'Farewell Tour'—Shea Stadium, NY," Hard Rock Daddy, accessed November 12, 2019, https://hardrockdaddy.com/2013/10/30/hard-rock-music-time-machine-1982-the-whos-farewell-tour-shea-stadium-ny/, October 30, 2013.

61. "Look Who's Talking!," interview of Pete Townshend and Roger Daltrey by Adrian Deevoy, *The Mail on Sunday/Event* (UK), October 26, 2014, republished in *The Who on the Who: Interviews an Encounters*, ed. Sean Egan (Chicago: Chicago Review Press, 2017), 380–389.

62. Simon Garfield, "Generation Terrorists," *Observer Music Monthly* (UK), September 2006, republished in *The Who on the Who: Interviews and Encounters*, ed. Sean Egan (Chicago: Chicago Review Press, 2017), 345–358.

63. Andy Summers, *One Train Later: A Memoir* (New York: Thomas Dunne Books, 2006), 3.

64. Aaron J. West, *Sting and the Police: Walking in Their Footsteps* (Lanham, MD: Rowman & Littlefield, 2015), 37, 69. For more on the marketing of The Police, see Chapter 4, "Selling the Police and Sting to the World," 57–79.

65. Ibid.

66. Summers, 4. "From this elevation, with its weird brew of light and claustrophobia, you see why the Beatles finally blew apart."

67. Ibid., 336.

68. Christopher Gable, *The Words and Music of Sting* (Westport, CT: Praeger, 2009), 20.

69. Summers, 337.

70. Ibid., 4.

71. Jon Pareles, "Rock: Police Perform for 70,000 at Shea Stadium," *New York Times*, August 20, 1983: 9.

72. West, 37.

73. *The Last Play at Shea*, directed by Paul Crowder (2010; [United States]: Virgil Films and Entertainment, 2014), Hoopla.

74. West, 38.

75. Stephen Rodrick, "Sting's Rock & Roll Salvation," *Rolling Stone*, December 15, 2016, 48, MasterFILE Complete.

76. Fred Schruers, *Billy Joel: The Definitive Biography* (New York: Crown Archetype, 2014), 280–281.

77. Ibid., 282.

78. "Concert Review: Billy Joel 'The Last Play at Shea'—Friday 7/18/08," *Centerfieldmaz* (blog), accessed November 12, 2019, http://www.centerfieldmaz.com/2008/07/this-was-epic-concert-of-biblical.html, July 18, 2008.

79. Ben Sisario, "An Act Not to Be Followed: A Beatle Returns to Shea," *New York Times*, July 19, 2008: B2.

80. Schruers, 286–288.

81. *The Last Play at Shea*.

82. Schruers, 288.

83. Joe Neumaier, "The Piano Man's Home Run," *Daily News* (New York), October 21, 2010: 35.

84. Schruers, 347–348.

85. Ibid., 334.

Sky King of Queens

*The Iconography of Dave Kingman
in New York*

CHARLIE VASCELLARO

Among the most enigmatic and captivating players to wear a New York Mets uniform, an argument can be made that one David Arthur Kingman is the most quintessential Met of them all. During his two stints with the team spanning six seasons, Kingman was catapulted to cult-hero status by a significant portion of the team's fan base.

My interest in Dave Kingman began with him belting balls over the wall for the Mets when I was 11 years old in 1975. There is one dream-like moment—I retrieved one of the home-run ball that he hit during an awesome three-home run barrage as a member of the visiting Chicago Cubs at Shea Stadium in 1979.

The man they called "Sky King" cast a large and looming presence over Shea Stadium and the Flushing Faithful. He was and remains an object of fascination for a group of Mets fans that witnessed his prodigious long-ball blasts and mercurial propensities with the middling Mets teams of the mid–to late 1970s. It isn't just Mets fans; Kingman captured the hearts and minds of baseball fans coast-to-coast from his earliest days in the minor leagues.

A huge New York City Subway Mets promotional poster featuring "The King of Swing" autographed, mounted, and handsomely framed are among the types of items available. "I followed all the teams he played for. Wish he'd have played in Detroit. He would have been huge playing in Tiger Stadium. And we have the water for his boating," said Robert Koppel, creator of the Dave Kingman Facebook page.

What Kingman Symbolizes and Means to Mets Fans and My Personal Odyssey

Kingman's franchise-record 36 home runs for the 1975 Mets provided a lone source of power for an offensively anemic ball club, reminiscent of Frank Thomas's 34 home runs for the fledgling franchise in 1962.

It was all brand new for Mets fans that were not used to winning ball games with home runs. First baseman John Milner led the Mets with 23 home runs in 1973 and 20 in 1974. At the time of Kingman's arrival, 12-year veteran outfielder Cleon Jones was the Mets all-time leader with 93 home runs.

Kingman's brought instantaneous excitement. With one swing, Sky King could provide the margin of victory or get the Mets back in the game.

I was among this new group of young Mets fans enthralled by the possibility presented with each of Kingman's at bats. We were mesmerized by his long loping swing and the arch and trajectory of the balls that he launched into the flight paths of incoming jets landing at LaGuardia Airport. At least they seemed to be that high.

I was 11 years old when Sky King landed in Queens at the start of the 1975 season, in the throes of my budding romance with baseball, still recovering from my first broken-heart suffered at the Mets' loss of the 1973 World Series to the Oakland A's, and, caught up in the kind of hopelessly romantic delirium known to inflict young baseball fans of a certain age, clinging to the belief that this same team could return and win the Series. My childhood fascination with Kingman manifested itself in the form of writing about him incessantly in my high-school and college years and later in life as a professional journalist. His home runs didn't just clear the fence. They cleared buildings and neighborhoods. They are the stuff of myths and folklore, and that is his greatest contribution to the game. Home runs are what people go to the ballpark to see.

I'm not sure if they called him Kong in San Francisco but it was a perfect nickname in New York, where the 6'6" former Giant stood out like the Empire State Building in the city's skyline. During his first two-and-a-half-year stint with the Mets, he was the team's number one marquee attraction. He quickly became an object of fascination for the New York sports media outlets as well.

When Kingman was embroiled in contentious contract negotiations with the Mets during the off-season of 1977, *Daily News* reporter Jack Lang explained his value and Mets fans obsession with him: "No one, not even Tom Terrific, puts people in the seats the way Sky King does. On days when Seaver is advertised to pitch, there is no appreciable increase in attendance. But when Kingman is on one of his home run hot streaks, he brings the fans out. Every father wants little junior to see the mighty Kong connect."[1]

Breaking In with the Giants

Kingman knocked a grand slam for his first major-league home run, off Pittsburgh's Dave Giusti on July 31, 1971. He was called up to the Giants the previous day, after hitting 29 home runs with 99 RBI in 105 games and 392 at-bats for the team's AAA Pacific Coast League affiliate in Phoenix, Arizona.

On August 2, he knocked a pair of two-run dingers in the second game of a double-header versus the Pirates, filling in at first base and the cleanup spot in the batting order for future Hall of Famer Willie McCovey, who rested after homering in the first game.

Kingman finished the 1971 season with six home runs, 24 RBI, and a .278 batting average in 115 at-bats spanning 41 games. He finished with a flurry, hitting the game-winning, NL West division-clinching home run with Willie Mays on base in the final game of the regular season. And thus, the legend of Sky King was born.

Coming on the heels of a strong spring training performance at the same Phoenix Municipal Stadium where he tore up the Pacific Coast League in 1971, Kingman earned a spot as the Giants Opening Day third baseman in 1972, but was moved to first base after just four games; McCovey suffered a broken arm in a collision at the bag. Kingman went back to third base upon McCovey's return and also split time in left field. He had 20 home runs at the season's half-way point. Kingman took mighty swaths that resulted in his 6'6" frame being twisted into a corkscrew like Reggie Jackson.

Kingman finished the 1972 season with 29 home runs, including a towering blast hit off Mets lefty Jerry Koosman on August 25, at Shea Stadium, originally estimated to have traveled 460-feet before landing next to the Giants' team bus in the parking lot. The tape-measure shot was later exaggerated to have flown 500-feet on his bio page in the Mets' 1975 yearbook but either way, the big blast was a harbinger that put Kingman on the Mets radar.

The Mets were willing to trade Koosman straight up for Kingman in 1973, but the deal was nixed when the Giants turned down the offer and asked for 1972 NL Rookie of the Year pitcher Jon Matlack instead.

Giants' catcher Dave Rader finished second in the voting. Mets first baseman John Milner, who hit 17 home runs with 38 RBI and a .238 batting average, finished third. Apparently, with the inclusion of time served in 1971, Kingman had exceeded Rookie of the Year eligibility. But he finished 24th in NL MVP voting anyway, in front of three Mets: Tug McGraw, Seaver, and Rusty Staub.

Kingman hit 24 home runs in limited action with just 305 at bats in 1973, many of the tape-measure variety. The back of his 1974 Topps baseball card contains a cartoon drawing of a ball bouncing off the top of a bus above a sentence reading: "Dave homered into Shea Stadium parking lot in 1973," which may be in reference to the 1971 shot off Koosman or another similar blast. Over his 16-year career Shea Stadium proved to be his favorite launching pad.

With 18 home runs, 55 RBI, and a .223 batting average in 1974, Kingman slumped his way through the worst season of his career, committing 12 errors in 59 chances at third base.

Sky King Lands in New York

The Mets paid cash-strapped Giants owner Horace Stoneham $150,000 to bring Kingman to New York and signed him to a three-year, $300,000 contract. He split time between first base, left field and third base.

I was a 10-year-old fan growing up on Long Island when Kingman arrived. Right out of the spring training gate, he immediately captured the imagination of the Mets collective fan base with reports of titanic home runs testified to by the likes of Yogi Berra and Mickey Mantle. Yogi labeled Kingman's 500-foot shot off New York Yankees hurler Jim "Catfish" Hunter, "the longest shot I've ever seen." The Mick reiterated what Yogi said, claiming nobody had hit one further, at least not one that he had seen.

Mets fans gravitated to Kingman for the fleeting flashes of glory he provided with his prodigious long-ball blasts. I was a *Newsday* paperboy back then with an afternoon route. A neatly tied-up stack of papers would be waiting at the end of the driveway to my house when I got home from school around 3:00 p.m. each day. There were about 50 houses on my route covering a couple of square miles in the winding and woodsy suburb of Setauket/Stony Brook, Long Island. Before embarking on my bicycle, I read the stories concerning the Mets and baseball. If I talked to any of my subscribers along the way, I could tell them what reporters like Joe Gergen or Steve Jacobson had to say about the Mets that day.

I accumulated points that could be converted into tickets to Mets games at Shea Stadium by signing up new subscribers to *Newsday* and other prizes, including the famous poster of Farrah Fawcett-Majors and posters of Charlie's other Angels. My points total reached the level of Master Carrier status, signified for all-the-world to see on my *Newsday Master Carrier* sweatshirt.

My father occasionally acquired box-seat tickets belonging to Blitzer, a plumbing supply company, for being such a valuable client. The company's name was engraved on a nameplate on the front corner seat of the four-seat box, right next to Mets owner Joan W. Payson's box. My father was not a big baseball fan, so oftentimes he would pass the tickets along to my mother's brothers, who would take me to the games. Sometimes my friends and I would take the Long Island Railroad from Stony Brook Station, transferring at Huntington and hopping on the number 7 subway train at Woodside.

On the days and nights when I was lucky enough to go to a game at Shea, I'd be whoopin' it up with the rest of Mets' faithful in eager anticipation for every one of Kingman's at-bats.

During his first few seasons with the Mets, Kingman established himself as the greatest home-run hitter in the teams' relatively brief history. His 1975 tally and franchise record of 36 home runs was good enough for second place in the National League, just behind Mike Schmidt of Philadelphia.

Kingman's long-ball exploits instantly developed a cult following, becoming an attraction for a mediocre Mets team that finished 82–80 in third place for the NL East, behind Philadelphia and Pittsburgh.

Sky King burst from the starting blocks again in 1976, knocking 17 home runs before the end of May.

With 30 home runs at the All-Star break, Kingman was on a tremendous pace and speculation focused on both Hack Wilson's National League single-season, home-run record of 56 and Roger Maris's Major League Baseball mark of 61. He became the seventh Met elected to start the All-Star Game and reached 32 home runs by July 18 before making an awkward diving attempt to catch a knuckling line drive off the bat of Phil Niekro, resulting in torn ligaments in his left thumb. The injury interrupted the most productive season of his career to date.

He knocked five more home runs after returning to the lineup on August 27, finishing with 37, one behind Mike Schmidt for the NL for the second consecutive season; the Mets finished third in the NL East, also for the second year in a row.

Kingman was a focal point of the New York sports media as he remained engaged in hostile ongoing contract negotiations with the Mets conducted largely on the pages of the city's dailies. Entering the final year of his three-year deal with the Mets, he sought a contract extension that would have made him one of the highest paid players in the major leagues and perhaps the highest paid player on the Mets, seeking upwards of Seaver's $700,000 three-year deal. Both players remained embroiled in hostile contract negotiations largely conducted in the newspapers until they were cast out of town together in what came to be known as the "Midnight Massacre" on June 15.

Kingman was sent to the San Diego Padres for future Mets manager Bobby Valentine and a relatively anonymous pitcher named Paul Siebert, who would win a total of three games in his five-year career, two of them for the '77 Mets.

Seaver became the newest cog in Cincinnati's Big Red machine in exchange for pitcher Pat Zachry, infielder Doug Flynn, and outfielders Dan Norman and Steve Henderson.

Mets fans were almost as dismayed about losing Kingman as they were about losing Seaver. Three different Mets, John Stearns, John Milner,

Dave Kingman's mighty swings resulted in 442 career home runs. More than one-third of them happened when Kingman wore a Mets uniform (National Baseball Hall of Fame and Museum, Cooperstown, N.Y.).

and Henderson finished in a three-way tie to lead the team with 12 home runs.

The Mets floundered through the remainder of the season finishing 64–98, deep in the basement, 37 games back of the NL East division-leading Philadelphia.

Kingman hit nine home runs in 58 games with the Mets in 1977 and 11 home runs in 56 games with San Diego. The California Angels selected him off waivers on September 6. He hit two home runs in 10 games for the Angels before being traded to the New York Yankees for Randy Stein and cash. He knocked four home runs in 24 at bats for the Yankees, becoming the first player to hit home runs as a member of four different teams in all four of the major league divisions in the same season. Kingman was granted free agency on November 6 and signed a three-year contract with the Chicago Cubs for $875,000.

Kingman Blows to the Windy City but Baseball Blooms in the Desert

It was a tough time to be a Mets fan and the 1978 season began without much hope. In the middle of the season, this time I was traded. Almost a year to the date that Kingman was dealt to San Diego, my family packed up and moved from Setauket, Long Island, to Fountain Hills, Arizona, at the height of my teenage baseball fandom in June of 1978.

Meanwhile, Kingman was off to a great start with the Cubs, knocking three home runs in one game against the Dodgers on May 14, 1978. KLAC radio reporter ignited a curse-filled monologue by Dodgers manager Tommy Lasorda after the game.

OLDEN: What's your opinion of Kingman's performance?

LASORDA: What's my opinion of Kingman's performance? What the fuck do you think is my opinion of it? I think it was fucking horseshit. Put that in, I don't fuckin, opinion of his performance? Jesus Christ, he beat us with three fuckin' home runs. What the fuck do you mean, "What is my opinion of his perform-ance?" How could you ask me that question like that? What is my opinion of his performance? Jesus Christ, he hit three home runs. Jesus Christ. I'm fuck-ing pissed off to lose a fucking game. And you ask me my opinion of his per-formance. Jesus Christ. I mean that's a tough question to ask me, isn't it? What is my opinion of his performance?

OLDEN: Yes it is, I ask it and you gave me an answer.

LASORDA: Well, I didn't give you a good answer because I'm mad.

OLDEN: It wasn't a good question.

LASORDA: That's a tough question to ask me right now: "What is my opinion of his performance?" I mean you want me to tell you what my opinion of his per-formance is?

OLDEN: You just did.
LASORDA: That's right. Jesus Christ. The guy hits three home runs against us. Shit.
   I don't mean to get pissed off or anything like that, but you know, you asked
   me my opinion. I mean put on a hell of a show. He hit three home runs. He
   drove in what seven runs?
OLDEN: Eight.
LASORDA: Eight runs. Well, what the hell more can you say about him? I didn't
   mean to get mad or anything like that but god damn, you asked me my opinion of his performance.[2]

It didn't take long for me to catch up with Kingman, or more accurately, to have him catch up with me. In the spring of 1979, I made the serendipitous discovery of Cactus League spring training baseball in Arizona through the window of a school bus on the way to my new junior high school. From my seat I spied the Chicago Cubs' HoHoKam Park training facility in Mesa, Arizona, which was about two blocks away from Kino Junior. High. Needless to say, I didn't go to school that day—Kingman and I were together in the same ballpark again.

I chased him all around the ballpark, peeling off paparazzi shots on my Kodak Instamatic camera. Then, I took the film to the Photomat's one-hour, developing drive-through booths and brought them back to the ballpark for him to sign the next day.

In the summer, my parents would send me back to New York to visit with friends and family. Of course, visits to Shea Stadium were a regular part of my itinerary. On June 28, 1979, together with a pair of old pals, I rode the Long Island Railroad to Shea Stadium to see Kingman and the Cubs play the Mets. With the sole intention of catching a Kingman home run ball, we purchased $1.50 general admission tickets and chose to sit almost by ourselves in the left-field mezzanine section.

The cops and ushers working the lonely section laughed when I explained to them why I had chosen such seats; we could have sat anywhere in the ballpark. But when Kong knocked three home runs that day and the second one was retrieved by me, I had the last laugh. Somehow after the game I was able to talk myself past the players' entrance into the ballpark and just as quickly, Kingman emerged from the visiting clubhouse. A couple of smaller kids followed me as I approached Kingman, who seemed to be in a hurry to leave.

"Mr. Kingman," I said, "this is the second home run you hit today, would you sign it for me?" Without answering me directly he simply said, "just one" to our small group, grabbed the ball from my hand, signed it and handed it back to me.

Two years later I was assigned by my 11th grade English teacher Ms. Tower to write about a significant day in my life. At that time, I couldn't think of a more significant day than the one at Shea when I got the home run ball. It's still way up on the list. I wrote a blow-by-blow narrative account of the day, "Kingman's Shot," which received a perfect score. Ms. Tower even wrote the word "Great" on top of the paper. Here's an excerpt:

> We had purchased the dollar-fifty grand stand seats, and every time Kingman came to bat, we would stand ready, in hopes that he would hit us a shot. During his second at-bat of the game, my dream was to be fulfilled. As he hit the ball, my eyes followed it. As it appeared I could sense the people all around me charging for the ball. I leaped over a few seats and grabbed Kingman's shot on a bounce. As I held the ball in my clutches, I wished the moment would last forever.

Sky King led the National League in 1979 with a career-high 48 home runs, on pace to threaten Roger Maris' then single-season record of 61, before being sidelined by a late-season injury that cost him the last 17 games of the season and continued to nag him the following year. He hit 18 home runs in 81 games in 1980 and after two-and-a-half seasons Kingman, had overstayed his welcome in Chicago.

He was traded by the Cubs back to the Mets prior to the 1981 season for outfielder Steve Henderson and plodded through an injury-riddled 1981, hitting 22 home runs in 100 games with a .221 batting average.

Kingman's three final seasons with the Mets solidified his status as one of the team's all-time icons. He hit a league-leading 37 home runs for the last-place club in 1982 while batting .204—the lowest average ever posted by a player to lead his league in home runs and/or by a first baseman with enough plate appearances to eligible for the batting title.

Although his time in New York was often marked by squabbles with management, reporters, and teammates, the fans loved him mostly because he was the only one providing the team with any offense even while his batting average hovered just above and below the Mendoza line.

Postscript

Kingman spent the last three years of his 16-year career with the Oakland A's, finally getting to be the DH he was born to be and enjoying the three most productive seasons he ever strung together. He hit 35 home runs with 118 RBI and a .268 batting average in 1984.

But his time in Oakland was also marked by, in this writer's opinion, a particularly disturbing incident involving his belief that female reporters should not be allowed in the clubhouse. After refusing to speak with or even be in the company of *Sacramento Bee* reporter Susan Fornoff for the first three months of the 1986 season, Kingman had a wrapped package delivered to Fornoff in the Kansas City Royals press box; it contained a live rat with a tag that read "My name is Sue" tied around one of its feet. Kingman got fined $3,500. The A's released him at the conclusion of the season.

Kingman's home-run output in Oakland was consistent: 35 in 1984; 30 in 1985; 35 in 1986.When he was unceremoniously released by the A's after the 1986 season, it was later deemed that he was victim of collusion by major-league owners and awarded a $829,849.54 settlement. Kingman made an aborted attempt at a comeback in 1987, playing about a month for the San Francisco Giants' AAA club in Phoenix.

Of course, I was there for the first and last games of his abbreviated six-week stint. In his first game, Kingman provided the fireworks for the firebirds on July 11. I was standing on line for a hot dog and a beer when I heard the crack of the bat and picked up the ball's flight as it soared high in the night sky over the left-field wall out onto Van Buren Street towards the Papago Buttes.

Kingman would hit one more home run during the next four weeks, deciding to throw in the towel after his final month in the minors. I received the news that it would be Kingman's last game while listening to the radio in my truck on the morning of August 4 and figured I ought to be there. I brought the home run ball from 1979 with me. I had foolishly brushed clear nail polish over Kingman's signature, which was now cracking and turning yellow. I figured that I would ask him to re-sign it. I also brought a copy of my original hand-written 11th grade English paper to give to my boyhood hero.

It was a rainy night and Kingman was not in the starting line-up. He wasn't even in the dugout. There was a situation early in the game when the Phoenix pitcher had already given up a bunch runs and was due to bat with the bases loaded and two outs. I thought it was the ideal time for Kingman to pinch hit. He was standing at the end of the tunnel, where the players entered the field from the clubhouse behind a belt-high chain-link fence looking out over the field. I was sure he was thinking that he should be batting.

I still think he was trying to convey that message with his body language in the way that he was standing there in full sight of everyone. There were periodic rain delays throughout the rest of the night and Kingman would occasionally emerge from the tunnel but he did not play or even get an at bat in this his final game. It was close to midnight when the game was completed and I was among the very few fans that chose to stick it out. I waited by the players' exit in the parking lot. It seemed like 24 of the 25-man roster had left before Kingman finally came up the stairs. He was carrying a large Oakland A's duffle bag on his shoulder, which I imagine contained the contents of his locker and all of his big-league memories. When I approached him, I think I caught him a bit off guard. I don't think he expected anyone to still be there.

"Hey Dave, can you sign this ball for me? It's one of three you hit against the Mets on July 28, 1979. You signed it for me then but it's kind of fading." He looked a bit incredulous and slightly perturbed, but I also thought I saw the beginning of a smile. I don't think he had planned on putting the big bag down until he got to his car, but he did and he signed the ball again for me. I asked if he wouldn't mind writing the date on the ball as well but he said I could do that myself and started to walk away.

"Wait!" I said, "This is an essay I wrote in high school a couple of years ago about the day I got the ball. Look!" I exclaimed. "It's great!" Pointing to where Ms. Tower had left her mark, I asked, "Can you sign it too?"

He autographed the essay as well.

"Wait!" I pleaded, one more time. "I made a copy for you. Maybe you can read it later."

He folded it up and stuck it in his back pocket. I figured there was a 50/50 chance he'd actually read it.

A couple of years ago, I caught up with Kingman at one of the afore-mentioned autograph tables during a spring training game at Hohokam Park in Mesa. I introduced myself just as I did before and mentioned the home run ball from 1979, and some of the writing I had done on him since. He didn't acknowledge having any memory of our previous meetings, which I thought was kind of peculiar. I thought for sure he must have remembered that last night of his career in Phoenix or that he may have seen or read the *Baseball Weekly* piece or any of our other encounters.

After seeing Kingman on the first day that I was in Arizona for the 2018 Cactus League season this past spring, I caught up with him again, sitting at the autograph table at Scottsdale Stadium on his last day in town. I told him I just wanted to say hello and goodbye and mentioned a presentation I would be making about him and the influence he had on my career at the 50th Anniversary of the New York Mets Conference at Hofstra University.

Dave Kingman bashed 442 home runs, struck out more than 1,800 times, and played for seven teams in his 16 MLB seasons. But he is an object of peculiar fascination to Mets fans, occupying a high-in-the-sky corner of the team's mythic universe and stirring the imagination with thoughts of long, arcing home runs and mighty, breeze-stirring strikeouts.

NOTES

1. Jack Lang, "Mets Wonder: Will David Demand Goliath-Size Pact," *Sporting News*, January 22, 1977, 38.

2. "Kingman's Performance" (lasorda answers questions), You Tube, accessed November 10, 2019, https://www.youtube.com/watch?v=LIwrYH6Urbs, May 14, 1978.

Bibliography

Adler, Bill, and George Price. *Love Letters to the Mets.* New York: Simon & Schuster, 1965.

Allen, Maury. *You Could Look It Up, the Life of Casey Stengel,* New York: Times Books, 1979.

Anderson, Will. *The Breweries of Brooklyn: An Informal History of a Great Industry in a Great City.* New York: self-published, 1976.

Angell, Roger. *The Summer Game.* New York: The Viking Press, 1972.

Appel, Marty. *Casey Stengel: Baseball's Greatest Character.* New York: Doubleday, 2017.

Bernstein, Sid. *It's Sid Bernstein Calling: The Amazing Story of the Promoter Who Made Entertainment History.* Middle Village, NY: Jonathan David Publishers, Inc., 2002.

Branon, Dave. *Safe at Home 2: More Winning Players Talk About Baseball and Their Faith.* Chicago: Moody Press, 1997.

Carter, Gary, and John Hough, Jr. *A Dream Season.* San Diego: Harcourt, Brace, Jovanovich, 1987.

Cashen, J. Frank. *Winning in Both Leagues: Reflections from Baseball's Front Office.* Lincoln: University of Nebraska Press, 2014.

Crowder, Paul, director. *The Last Play at Shea.* 2010; [United States]: Virgil Films and Entertainment, 2014.

D, Chuck. *Chuck D Presents This Day in Rap and Hip-Hop History.* New York: Black Dog & Leventhal, 2017.

Darling, Ron, and Daniel Paisner. *The Complete Game: Reflections on Baseball, Pitching, and Life on the Mound.* New York: Alfred A. Knopf, 2009.

De Longeville, Thibault, director. *Just for Kicks.* Image Entertainment, 2005.

DeMotte, Charles. *Baseball and American Society: How a Game Reflects the American Experience.* San Diego: Cognella, Inc., 2014.

Ewoodzie, Joseph C. *Break Beats in the Bronx: Rediscovering Hip-Hop's Early Years.* Chapel Hill: University of North Carolina Press, 2017.

Gable, Christopher. *The Words and Music of Sting.* Westport, CT: Praeger, 2009.

Gasteier, Matthew. *Illmatic.* London: Bloomsbury Academic, 2009.

Gooden, Dwight, and Ellis Henican. *Doc: A Memoir.* Boston: New Harvest Houghton Mifflin, 2013.

Guralnick, Peter, and Ernst Jorgensen. *Elvis Day by Day.* New York: Ballantine Books, 1999.

Hernandez, Keith, and Mike Bryan. *If at First....* New York: Penguin Books, 1987.

Johnson, Davey, and Peter Golenbock. *Bats.* New York: G.P. Putnam's Sons, 1986.

Landis, John, director. *Coming to America.* Paramount Pictures, 1988.

Lang, Jack, and Peter Simon. *The New York Mets: Twenty-five Years of Baseball Magic.* New York: Henry Holt and Company, 1986.

Lee, Spike, director, *School Daze,* Columbia Pictures, 1988.

Lewisohn, Mark. *The Complete Beatles Chronicle.* New York: Harmony Books, 1992.

Markusen, Bruce. *Tales from the Mets Dugout.* Champaign, IL: Sports Publishing LLC, 2005.

McGirt, Ellen. "raceAhead: A New Nielsen Report Puts Black Buying Power at $1.2 Trillion."

Fortune, February 28, 2018, fortune.com/2018/02/28/raceahead-nielsen-report-black-buying-power/.

Mitchell, Jerry. *New York: The Amazing Mets*. New York: Grosset and Dunlap, 1964.

New York Mets. *New York Mets 1977 Yearbook*.

New York Mets. *New York Mets 1980 Media Guide*.

New York Mets. *New York Mets 1980 Yearbook*.

New York Mets. *New York Mets 1983 Yearbook*.

Patterson, James T. *Restless Giant: The United States from Watergate to Bush V. Gore*. New York: Oxford University Press, 2005.

Pearlman, Jeff. *The Bad Guys Won: A Season of Brawling, Boozing, Bimbo-Chasing, and Championship Baseball with Straw, Doc, Mookie, Nails, the Kid, and the Rest of the 1986 Mets, the Rowdiest Team to Put on a New York Uniform, and Maybe the Best*. New York: Harper-Collins, 2004.

Richards, Keith. *Life*. New York: Little, Brown and Company, 2010.

Ryczek, William J. *The Amazin' Mets 1962–1969*, Jefferson, NC: McFarland, 2008.

Schruers, Fred. *Billy Joel: The Definitive Biography*. New York: Crown Archetype, 2014.

Schwensen, Dave. *The Beatles at Shea Stadium: The Story Behind Their Greatest Concert*. Cleveland: North Shore Publishing, 2013.

Siegel, Barry, ed. *The Sporting News Official 1984 Baseball Register*. St. Louis: The Sporting News, 1984.

Staub, Rusty, and Phil Pepe. *Few and Chosen: Defining Mets Greatness Across the Eras*. Chicago: Triumph Books, 2009.

Strawberry, Darryl, and John Strausbaugh. *Straw: Finding My Way*. New York: Ecco, 2009.

Summers, Andy. *One Train Later: A Memoir*. New York: Thomas Dunne Books, 2006.

Time-Life Books Editors. *1965 Official Guide New York World's Fair*. New York: Time Incorporated, 1965.

Time-Life Books Editors. *Official Guide New York World's Fair 1964/1965*. New York: Time Incorporated, 1964.

Topel, Brett. *Miracle Moments in New York Mets History: The Turning Points, the Memorable Games, the Incredible Records*. New York: Sports Publishing, 2018.

Vecsey, George. *Joy in Mudville: Being a Complete Account of the Unparalleled History of the New York Mets from Their Most Perturbed Beginnings to Their Amazing Rise to Glory and Renown*. New York: McCall Publishing Company, 1970.

West, Aaron J. *Sting and the Police: Walking in Their Footsteps*. Lanham, MD: Rowman & Littlefield, 2015.

Wilson, Mookie, and Erik Sherman. *Mookie: Life, Baseball, and the '86 Mets*. New York: Berkley Books, 2014.

Wood, Simon. *The Ultimate Sneaker Book*. New York: Taschen, 2018.

About the Contributors

Debra Schmidt **Bach** is the Curator of Decorative Arts at the New-York Historical Society. She has curated numerous popular and social history exhibitions, including the 2012 *Beer Here: Brewing New York's History*. She has contributed widely to exhibition and collection catalogues, and written articles on an extensive range of design and social history topics.

Scott **Doughtie** is an enforcement supervisor at the U.S. Equal Employment Opportunity Commission in San Francisco. He is a lifelong Mets fan.

Rob **Edelman** passed away in 2019. He often contributed to *Base Ball: A Journal of the Game* and *Baseball Research Journal*. He also teamed with his wife, Audrey Kupferberg, to co-write biographies of Walter Matthau and Angela Lansbury, in addition to a dual biography of William Frawley and Vivian Vance, who played Fred and Ethel Mertz in *I Love Lucy*. He was a longtime lecturer at University at Albany (SUNY).

Donna L. **Halper** is a professor of media studies at Lesley University in Massachusetts. A former broadcaster, she is the author of six books and many articles, including "Written Out of History: Women Baseball Writers, 1905–1945" in *The Cooperstown Symposium on Baseball and American Culture, 2017–2018* and "Broadcasting Red Sox Baseball: How the Arrival of Radio Impacted the Team and the Fans" in *Baseball Research Journal* (Fall 2017).

Leslie **Heaphy** is a professor at Kent State University, regular speaker at Society for American Baseball Research conferences, expert in the history of the Negro Leagues, and writer of "Joan Whitney Payson: A Pioneer for the New York Mets" in *The National Pastime* (2017). She contributed an article about the ownership history of the New York Mets for SABR's Team Ownership Histories Project.

Paul **Hensler** is the author of *Bob Steele on the Radio*, *The New Boys of Summer*, and *The American League in Transition (1965–1975)*. He contributed the essay "Cheers, Reggie! Everybody Knows Your Name!" for *The New York Yankees in Popular Culture*. He is a frequent contributor to *NINE: A Journal of Baseball History and Culture*, various SABR publications, as well as the Cooperstown Symposium on Baseball and American Culture.

Elizabeth **Jardine** is an associate professor and the Metadata Librarian at LaGuardia Community College in Long Island City, Queens. Her scholarship includes the case study "The Library Leading: Knowledge Management Supporting Community College Institutional Strategy" in *New Review of Academic Librarianship*.

Douglas **Jordan** is a business professor at Sonoma State University in Northern California and a lifelong Mets fan. His writing includes the article "Baseball Championship Windows: How Long Are They?" in *Baseball Research Journal* (Spring 2018).

Jemayne Lavar **King** is a professor at Johnson C. Smith University in Charlotte, North Carolina. His areas of academic research are the music, sports, and media influences on the African American consumer. He is the author of *Sole Food: Digestible Sneaker Culture* and is a longtime Mets fan.

David **Krell** is the author of *Our Bums: The Brooklyn Dodgers in History, Memory and Popular Culture*—Honorable Mention for the Society for American Baseball Research Ron Gabriel Award highlighting Brooklyn Dodgers scholarship—and the editor of *The New York Yankees in Popular Culture*. He is a regular speaker at SABR conferences, Cooperstown Symposium on Baseball and American Culture, and Mid-Atlantic Nostalgia Convention.

Bill **Lamb** has written more than 130 biographies for SABR's Baseball Biography Project, including one on John B. Day, the founder of the 19th century New York Mets. He contributed an article about the New York Giants ownership history for SABR's Team Ownership Histories Project. For his commitment to baseball history research, SABR awarded him with the Bob Davids Award in 2019.

Martin **Lessner** is a corporate lawyer at the firm Young Conaway Stargatt & Taylor in Wilmington, Delaware. An avid Phillies fan, he favors the Phillie Phanatic as the standard for mascots. He contributed the essay "That Damn Yankees Cap" to *The New York Yankees in Popular Culture*.

David M. **Pegram** is an English professor at Paradise Valley Community College in Phoenix, Arizona, where he serves as co-chair of the annual NINE Baseball Conference. His other publications include "Baseball and Graphic Novels: An Effective Approach to Teaching Literature" in *Developing Contemporary Literacies through Sports* and "The Hero with Mad Skills: James Bond and the World of Extreme Sports" in *The International Journal of James Bond Studies*.

Richard **Pioreck** passed away in 2020. He wrote for *Memories & Dreams* and *MLB Insider*. His ballpark experiences included attending Opening Day at Shea Stadium since 1976 and watching games at more than 30 past and present major-league ballparks, including the first and last Montreal Expos games at Shea Stadium, as well as the last game at Shea, and the first game at Citi Field. He taught creative writing and literature at Hofstra University.

Alexandra **Rojas** is the Head of Reference and Public Services at LaGuardia Community College. Her scholarship includes co-presenting "Being Seen: Moving Beyond the Library to Mix, Connect, and Promote" at the 2017 program *Developing*

Credit—Bearing Information Literacy Courses for the Greater New York Metropolitan Chapter of the Association of College & Research Libraries.

Matt **Rothenberg** is a freelance writer from Ossining, New York. He was the manager of the Giamatti Research Center at the National Baseball Hall of Fame and Museum from 2014 to 2019. He also contributed the essay "E-61*" to *The New York Yankees in Popular Culture.*

William J. **Ryczek** is the author of *The Amazin' Mets: 1962–1969* and several books about 19th century baseball history. He recounted the genesis of the Mets' fellow Shea Stadium occupant in *Crash of the Titans: The Early Years of the New York Jets and the AFL.* He was the keynote speaker at SABR's Frederick Ivor-Campbell 19th Century Conference.

Derek **Stadler** is the Web Services Librarian at LaGuardia Community College. His research topics include the history of Long Island, William Randolph Hearst's involvement in politics, and the expansion of Greater New York in the late 19th and early 20th centuries.

Charlie **Vascellaro** is a frequent speaker on the academic baseball conference circuit and the author of a biography about Hank Aaron. His articles have appeared in *The Washington Post, The Baltimore Sun, Los Angeles Times, Chicago Tribune, Arizona Republic,* MLB.com *ESPN W, La Vida Baseball, Spitball,* and the *Museum of the Native American.* He is a longtime Mets fan and presented at Hofstra University's New York Mets 50th Anniversary Conference in 2012.

Index

Numbers in **bold italics** indicate pages with illustrations

227

Index